I0214539

ARCHITECTURE AND CHILDREN

ARCHITECTURE AND CHILDREN

GUIDE FOR TEACHERS

ANNE TAYLOR, PHD, ARTS EDUCATOR

GEORGE VLASTOS, ARCHITECT

ALISON MARSHALL, PHD ARTS EDUCATOR

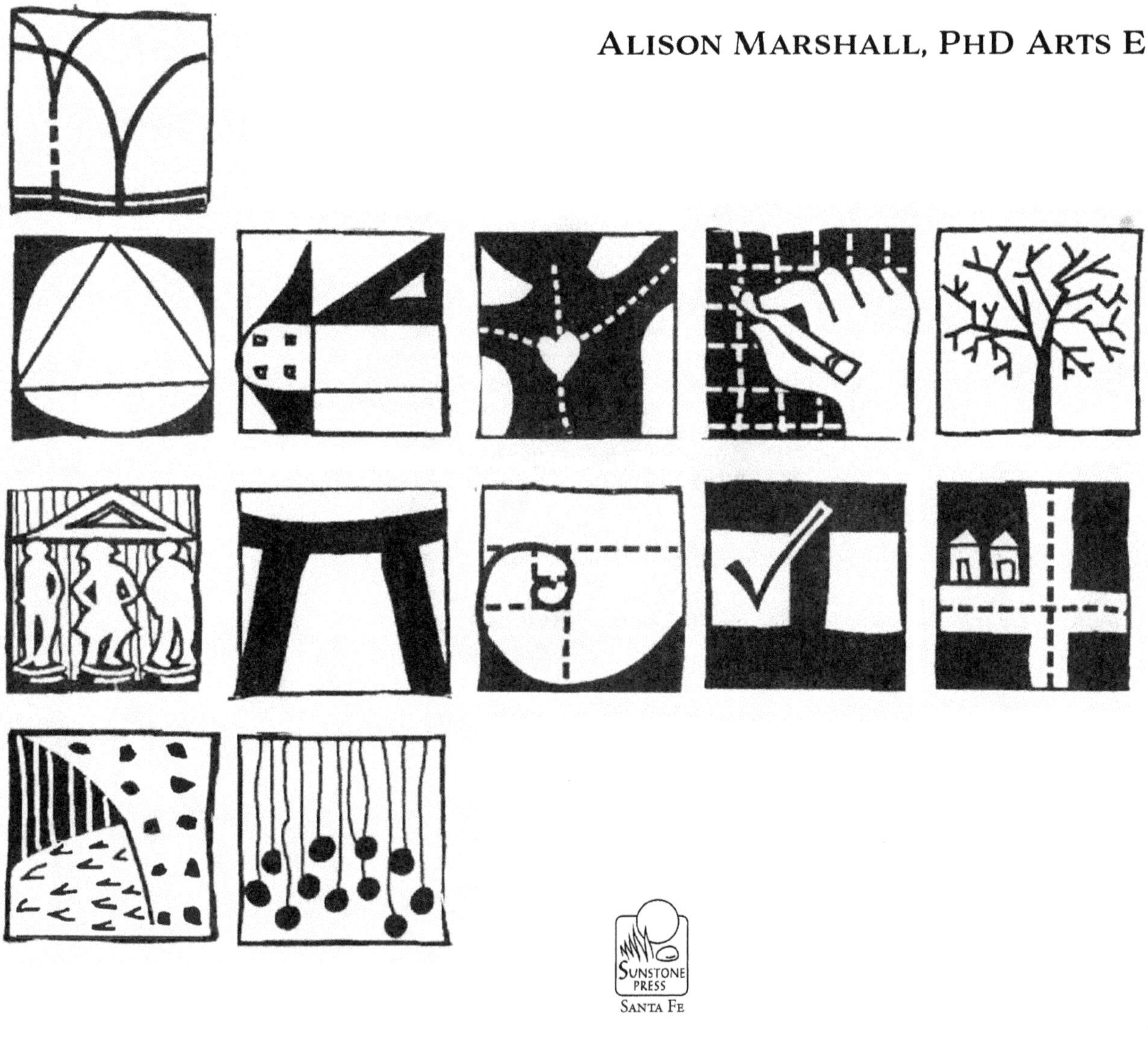

SANTA FE

Disclaimer

This book contains drawings of figures engaging in various physical acts mimicking the structure of architectural principles. These illustrations are for artistic and informational purposes only and are not intended to be instructional or suggestive of actions that should be attempted, imitated, or replicated in any way.

The author and publisher make no representations or warranties, express or implied, regarding the safety, accuracy, or appropriateness of any depicted actions. Any attempt to perform, recreate, or engage in activities similar to those shown in this book is done at the reader's own risk. The author and publisher assume no responsibility for any injuries, damages, or legal consequences resulting from such actions.

By using this book, you agree that the author and publisher shall not be held liable for any direct, indirect, incidental, consequential, or other damages arising from the interpretation or application of the content within.

Sunstone books may be purchased for educational, business, or sales promotional use.
For information please write: Special Markets Department, Sunstone Press,
P.O. Box 2321, Santa Fe, New Mexico 87504-2321.
Printed on acid-free paper
∞

Library of Congress Cataloging-in-Publication Data

Title: Architecture and Children: Guide for Teachers
Description: Santa Fe : Sunstone Press, [2024] | Includes bibliographical references and index. | Summary: "A Guidebook for teaching Integrated Design Education through the architectural, natural, and cultural environment for students P/K-12 "-- Provided by publisher.
Identifiers: LCCN 2024038449 | ISBN 9781632936684 (paperback)
Subjects: LCSH: Architecture--Study and teaching (Primary) | Architecture--Study and teaching--Activity programs. | LCGFT: Lesson plans.
Classification: LCC NA2000 .A693 2024 | DDC 720--dc23/eng/20240820
LC record available at https://lccn.loc.gov/2024038449

WWW.SUNSTONEPRESS.COM
SUNSTONE PRESS / POST OFFICE BOX 2321 / SANTA FE, NM 87504-2321 /USA
(505) 988-4418

CONTENTS

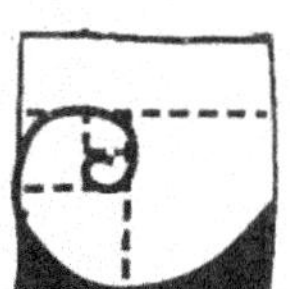
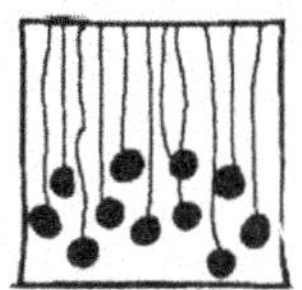
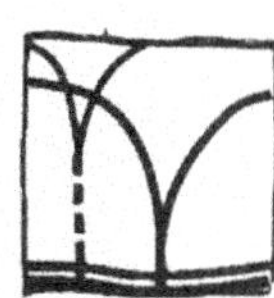

Foreword // 9

Acknowledgments // 11

Introduction // 13

Interdisciplinary Curriculum and Instruction Model // 15

How to Use this Curriculum // 17

Setting Up an Architectural Center // 18

Visual Vocabulary // 19

The Basics of Visual Communication

Positive Form Negative Space // 23

Concepts of Form and Space

Plans and Perspectives // 25

Development of a Design for a Space

Structure in Architecture // 29

An Introduction to Structural Engineering

Entryways // 33

Social and Cultural Communication Through Entryway Design

You Are Architecture // 37

Physiology Lesson

Colors and Textures // 41

Making and Articulating Reasons for Choices in Design

Design in Nature // 45

Relationships Between Nature and Design

Form in Architectural History // 49

Geometry and Great Buildings in the History of Architecture

Bridges // 53

Problem Solving Techniques Used in Design and Model Building

Super Wall Graphics // 57

Scale Measurement, Color, Design and Painting Techniques

Preferences // 61

Statistical Analysis Used to Design a New Classroom

Landscape // 65

Teamwork Used in Site Analysis and Design of a New Playground

City Planning // 69

Walking Tour and Development of a Model for Urban Design

Appendix // 73

Portfolio Assessment // 115

Relationship of Architecture and Children Themes to Science, Math and Technology Learning Goals // 119

Books and Other Resources on Architecture // 121

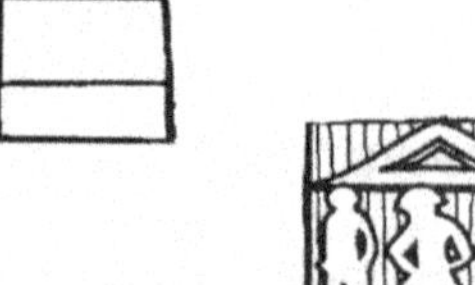

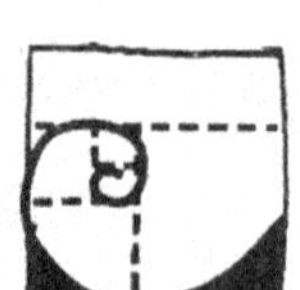
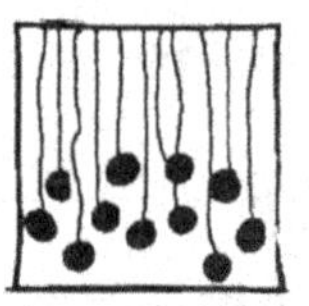

FOREWORD

The Architecture and Children curriculum is part of a larger project that has been fifty years in the making. It stemmed from a beach walk and shell gathering with children and has grown to encompass the design of learning environments, architectural programming for schools, lecture presentations, book and article authorship, design of a museum exhibition, a teacher training program and research. Anne Taylor began the project with a curiosity about the aesthetic choices children make in the environment, in this case, on the beach while collecting shells. Her initial work has gone on to include the invaluable skill and graphic insight of architect George Vlastos. The program has been significantly aided by additional architects internationally, who have taken the Architecture and Children workshop.

The program uses the order in the universe as a window to study the world and the ideas, laws and principles that govern it—the physics of structure, design in nature and similarities between body systems and building systems. The curriculum integrates content and specific skills, and is most significantly concerned with the integration of academic and artistic disciplines and the interdependency of all things on the planet. While teaching about architecture, the program is largely interested in the process of learning through visual thinking, problem solving, creative thought, group interaction and team building, presentation and communication skills.

The Architecture and Children curriculum is a tool that encourages children's confidence to develop and communicate their own ideas. Though children may repeat the design process many times, a blank sheet of paper or model building material becomes a palette for their self-expression which grows in complexity to higher levels of visual communication as the student matures. The curriculum borrows from the Architectural Design Studio by which architects are trained. Through years of use in elementary and secondary classrooms, students have excelled. Those who are challenged in the classroom, also have excelled by becoming more interested in education through applied learning.

We now invite you to use the curriculum and teachers' guide and to involve your students in an exciting new integrated program that promises to help students not only look thoroughly at their environment, but to see it and have an equitable stake in it.

Alison Marshall, PhD
Arts Educator

ACKNOWLEDGMENTS

The new *Architecture and Children Teachers Guide* has been facilitated by many contributors from writers to funders to careful revisions of early text from the first edition of the Teachers Guide (published in 1991). We would like to acknowledge the following people and organizations:

Sunstone Press, our publisher in Santa Fe, New Mexico
James Smith, editor of the new second edition of the *Architecture and Children Teachers Guide*
Carl Condit, Director of Operations, Sunstone Press
Alison Marshall, PhD, Writer, Dancer, Arts Educator
George Vlastos, Architect, Architectural Educator, SZI Board Member
Catalina Salinas, Architect, SZI Board Member
Anne Taylor, PhD, President of School Zone Institute
Jennifer Fenstermacher, Administrator

A component of the development of this document was supported by Publiclaw100-297, the Dwight D. Eisenhower Mathematics and Science Education Act, and funds from the U.S. Department of Education administered by the Office of the Washington State Superintendent of Public Instruction.

Albuquerque Private Funders to School Zone Institute for the new edition:
The American Institute of Architects, Albuquerque Chapter
The New Mexico Architectural Foundation
The University of New Mexico School of Architecture + Planning
Meredith Taylor, Illustrator

The people in Seattle, Washington should be acknowledged for the original project for teaching, writing and funding of the first teachers guide, making it possible for the second edition from School Zone Institute.

Thanks especially goes to SAFECO Insurance Company and the Norman Archibald Charitable Foundation in Seattle for supporting the first edition.

The second edition of Architecture and Children is supported by School Zone Institute and private donors in New Mexico.

INTRODUCTION

The content included in the Architecture and Children program, first developed and used fifty years ago, continues to be relevant today as learners consider, represent, and share their thinking about design and structure in built, natural, and cultural environments. It has been translated into Japanese and Spanish and used in various locations and settings. The ideas addressed in this curriculum framework are essential for developing visual thinking and design literacy. This curriculum is a guide to active building block learning experiences that help learners identify and apply varied approaches to design as they observe and make drawings and models themselves. It shows how to connect ideas across disciplines, considering the purpose of what, why, and how natural and built forms and objects are designed and made.

The Architecture and Children framework puts inquiry at the center of learning. Questions woven through each design experience are written to help learners develop and assess their understanding of the curriculum topics, employing questions to prompt reflection and assessment about thinking and making. What do you imagine will happen when...? What did you see that makes you think that…? How else might you show...? What do you see when...? Questions provide opportunities for learners to visit and revisit their understandings.

Each design problem presents a goal identifying what learners should understand by the end of the particular learning experience. Then, it outlines the experiences learners will have to develop their understanding. The reflection or assessment included in each lesson asks learners how they know they understand the lesson topic and what they want to explore further. The design ideas they create and then share with others during a follow up verbal presentation and critique become their evidence of understanding. The curriculum uses the scientific method in design to solve problems.

The Architecture and Children Guidebook outlines experiential lessons for educators, teaching artists, parents, and architects to use in school, after-school, and community-based settings. It is helpful as a form of professional development for educators and facilitators presenting design-based learning experiences. This curriculum supplements STEAM (science, technology, engineering, arts/architecture, mathematics) programs. The concepts in the curriculum can be explored through physical movement (such as changing one's physical position in the negative surrounding space) and linked to digital technology that allows the sharing of ideas and information, including text, visuals, and resources that facilitate the creation, storage, and management of data. The interactive design experiences presented in the Guidebook are connected across disciplines using throughlines such as perspective, design conventions, parts to whole, positive form and negative space, and balance in composition.

Sir Winston Churchill is quoted as saying, "We shape our buildings; thereafter, they shape us." As we explore and choose to use aspects of design, whether in a written composition, algebraic equation, or arrangement of color in a room, design is for and about us. This active learning program is for all learners because we all create and navigate built, natural, and cultural environments. The program emphasizes visual thinking while learners also explore ideas through movement and communicate with others about what they have created. Equity is built into the program because any student has ideas, and creates and uniquely expresses those ideas. This curriculum guidebook helps learners observe and use design intentionally and will help provide a building block for lifelong learning.

Alison Marshall, PhD

Arts Educator

Interdisciplinary Curriculum and Instruction Model©

What is learned

CONCEPTS represent the knowledge to be learned.
The curriculum model on which the teaching of Architecture and Children is based is **INTERDISCIPLINARY**. It is an integrated curriculum that uses **CONCEPTS** from subject matter disciplines now already taught in the schools. This base of knowledge is viewed as universal, representing the **ORDER IN THE UNIVERSE** and is taught, not within disparate or separate disciplines, but across disciplines. One concept may be related to another concept. One discipline may be related to another discipline through a common concept. One example is **BALANCE**.
CONCEPTS ARE UNIVERSAL.

How knowledge is acquired

Knowledge or **SKILL** acquisition is progressive and uses a learning sequence that includes sensory perception, observation, language and labeling, scientific, intuitive creative problem-solving and valuing. A design studio format for individual and cooperative learning is recommended.
SKILLS ARE UNIVERSAL.

Context for learning

The **CONTEXT** for learning concepts across disciplines will vary from place to place depending on life zone, geographic area and culture. In this way the concepts and skills can be used in a site-specific way. This program uses the **CONTEXT** of the local environment to teach basic **CONCEPTS** and **SKILLS**.
CONTEXT IS SITE-SPECIFIC.

School Zone method of integration moves across disciplines

Subject matter disciplines of math, life science, physical sciences, social studies, art, music, dance and movement, and philosophy are comprised of **CONCEPTS**. A concept is an idea representing the meaning of a universal term associated with certain characteristic attributes. Concepts can be very concrete or they can be representative of abstract ideas. For instance, in the various disciplines noted in the accompanying diagram, a concept can have a similar or related meanings in concrete or abstract form.

e.g. the **CONCEPT** of **BALANCE**

Subject Matter Discipline	Meaning of concept
Math	The concept of **balance** in math relates to one to one correspondence, or scale and weight, or symmetry and asymmetry.
Life Sciences	In life sciences, we may study ecological **balance**. It relates to equilibrium of systems; also chemical **balance**.

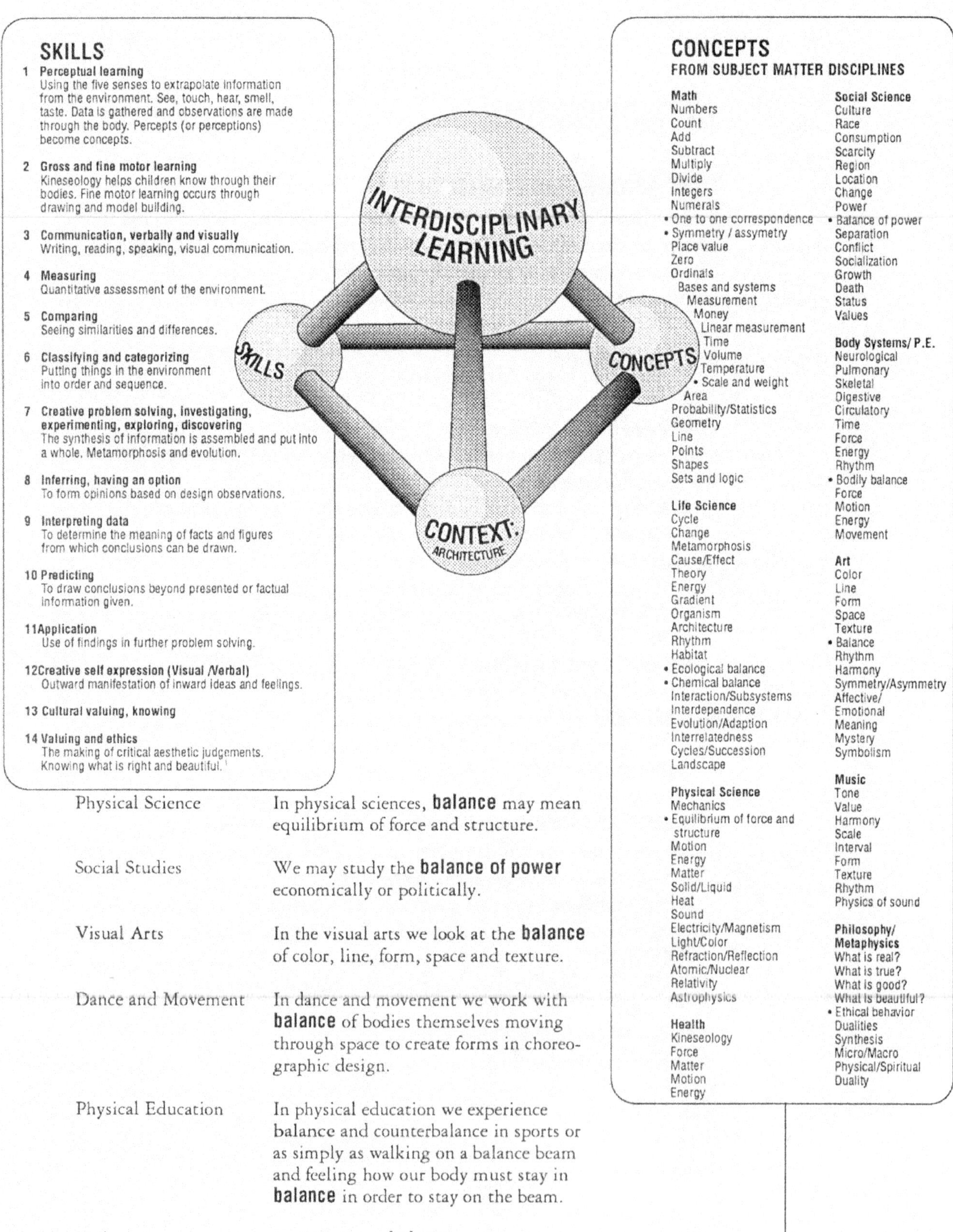

Physical Science	In physical sciences, **balance** may mean equilibrium of force and structure.
Social Studies	We may study the **balance of power** economically or politically.
Visual Arts	In the visual arts we look at the **balance** of color, line, form, space and texture.
Dance and Movement	In dance and movement we work with **balance** of bodies themselves moving through space to create forms in choreographic design.
Physical Education	In physical education we experience balance and counterbalance in sports or as simply as walking on a balance beam and feeling how our body must stay in **balance** in order to stay on the beam.
Philosophy	In philosophy, **balance** means ethical behavior, a more abstract concept, but related to the basic concept of **balance**.

Anne Taylor and Alison Marshall

How to use this curriculum

The Architecture and Children curriculum is an interdisciplinary curriculum created by educator, Anne Taylor, Ph.D., architect, George Vlastos and others. The basic curriculum is graphically presented in the following order:

GOAL Statement of what students will be able to do by the end of the lesson
ASSIGNMENT Statement of the student production which is brought together by the learning activities in the lesson
MATERIALS Those items needed for task completion
SKILLS AND CONCEPTS Teaching processes and subject areas used in the lesson
SETTING Educational locale
ARCHITECTURAL VOCABULARY Items and concepts from the discipline of architecture which are essential to each activity
PRESENTATION Introductory activities
CLIENT A hypothetical client who presents a challenge to the students
ARCHITECTURAL PROGRAM Requirements for the projects
EVALUATION Summative activity which provides a vehicle for assessment
RELATED ACTIVITIES Learning activities which may or may not appear on the poster but which directly contribute to building the disciplinary and architectural skills represented in the lesson
APPENDIX Information that goes beyond the lessons but is keyed to one or more parts of the curriculum and is presented on masters for photocopying
BIBLIOGRAPHY Lists of books that pertain to the curriculum
RESOURCES List of national organizations which can provide assistance

Open-ended creative problem solving

Many activities in this curriculum are open-ended problems which are intended to invite many unique student responses. Clues offered to start teachers and stu-dents toward an answer are not intended to restrict the responses but rather to increase the fluency and creativity of students' solutions by helping them overcome difficult problems.

Anne Taylor PhD

SETTING UP AN ARCHITECTURAL CENTER

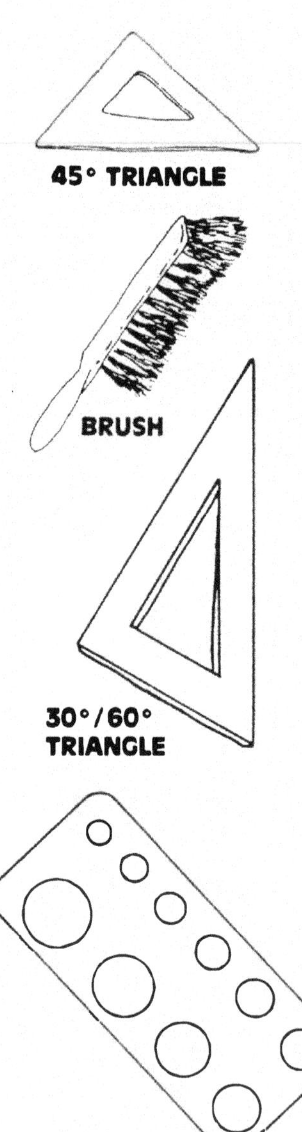

One of the best ways to teach concepts using architectural processes is through the creation of a design center in the classroom. Many architectural experiences in the classroom will be group learning experiences with children at their desks or in small groups. However, it is a good idea to have an architectural center in the classroom for individual work and to emphasize the importance of having a well organized place to work. If possible, set aside a zone in your classroom and furnish it with work tables, drawing tools and display space.

A low drafting table on which the students can use a T-square along one side, with another table or shelf unit for storing supplies and tools, are basic furnishings for an architectural design center. A vertical display area to exhibit children's drawings and pictures of great architecture should be available adjacent to the work center. You can use a regular bulletin board for this or install tackable panels, such as celotex or firtex from your local lumber yard. Cover the panels with fabric or paint them white and install them in an easily accessible place.

The following drawing tools should be provided for the architectural center and should always be available for the students to use: Flair pens, sharp #2 pencils, crayola markers, pink erasers, 30°/60° and 45° triangles, circle template, french curve, drafting tape, "fox tail" brush to clean the table, ruler, grid paper, 12" x 18" white drawing paper, a roll of architect's tracing paper, compass, white glue, scissors, clip boards and building blocks. Proper storage of tools is important. A good plan is to hang the larger tools with S-hooks on pegboard and draw an outline around every tool when it is hanging in place, so that students can easily tell where it goes and see what is missing.

VISUAL VOCABULARY

GOAL

To help students to observe, think and express ideas visually.

ARCHITECTURAL VOCABULARY

Schematic drawing A visual way to present an idea of something such as space or shape; areas of activity; or patterns of movement, sound, light

Diagram A linear representation of something

Bubble diagram "Bubble" outlines which represent spatial relationships

Contour line drawing A drawing of the edge or outline of a shape

Negative space The space outside an object in a drawing

Positive form An object depicted in a drawing

Geometric forms Two dimensional (flat) and three dimensional (solid) forms

PRESENTATION

Line drawings express both what an object is and what it does. The following exercises provide drawing practice and prepare students to make diagramatic and schematic drawings.

1. Hand contour drawing

The hand contour drawing exercises review the concept already known by children that a contour line expresses the idea of what an object is. Subsequent exercises will show more ideas that lines can express. Have the students carefully trace around their hand with a felt tip marker. Explain that contour means "outline." The line they drew around their hand is the contour. Explain that the hand is the "positive" part of the drawing. The space around it is the "negative space."

2. The "no peeking" hand contour drawing

This is a five-minute timed drawing exercise. Tell the students to tape down on their table or desk two diagonal corners of the sheet of paper with their hand contour drawing. They should place their marker on the starting point of their previous drawing and keep it on the paper until the drawing is finished. Then they turn their heads and hold out the hand they traced. Tell them not to peek. Tell them that they are to draw very slowly. Ask them to imagine that their marker is a ladybug tracing around the edge of each finger. Use a timer to give them 60 seconds to draw each finger; call out the time every ten seconds. Tell students to wait if they complete their drawing of a finger before 60 seconds. This exercise is a lot of fun. It is one that is used to help artists draw more freely. Encourage the students to try drawing their friends and family this way.

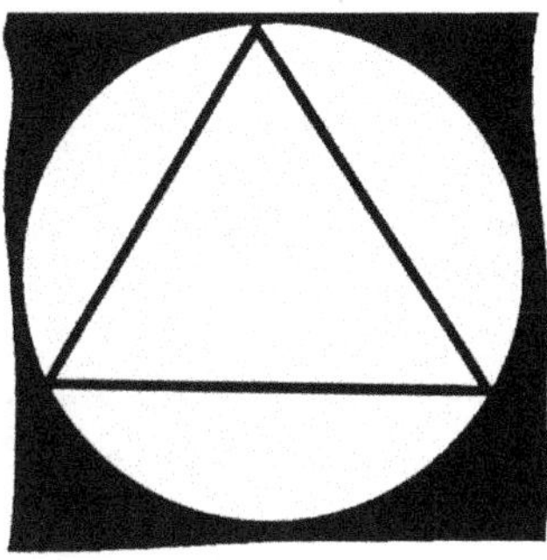

ASSIGNMENT

Students will make a series of contour and schematic drawings to be displayed.

MATERIALS

Drawing paper
Two colored markers for each student
Masking tape
Balloon
Sound maker
Non-mechanical toy: Slinky
Bubble liquid and wand

SKILLS AND CONCEPTS

Math
Geometry
Science
Art
Creative problem solving
Observation skill
Visual communication
Spatial relationships

SETTING

Classroom

Visual stories

These stories introduce the concept that a simple line can show what an object does.

1. The balloon explosion story

Blow up a balloon and pop it in front of the class. Then have students draw a "visual story" of the explosion. They should try not to draw a balloon, just the explosion.

2. The stamping foot story

Walk across the room and stamp your foot three times. Have the students draw a "visual story" of the movement and sound of the stamping foot. Tell them not to draw the leg, the foot or the shoe, just draw the movement and sound.

client

An artist asks the class to present a show of Visual Stories based on drawings of time, movement, change and sound. The artist wants the student architects to discover that everyone has a special way of expressing what they see through their drawings. The Visual Stories will be called THE LIFE OF A BUBBLE, THE GREAT BALLOON RACE, THE TOY DIAGRAM and THE SOUND GRAPHIC.

architectural program

Students will prepare a 12" x 18" sheet of paper for their drawings by folding it into four sections. The sections should be labeled THE LIFE OF A BUBBLE, THE GREAT BALLOON RACE, THE TOY DIAGRAM and THE SOUND GRAPHIC.

1. The life of a bubble

Explain to the students that you are about to blow several large bubbles. Ask them to watch closely. Advise them that after observing the fourth or fifth bubble, they should begin drawing the birth, life and death of a bubble in the section labeled THE LIFE OF A BUBBLE. By the end of the tenth bubble all of the students should have completed the first drawing exercise.

2. The great balloon race

Blow up three different colored balloons and hold them together with one hand so that when released, the balloons start their "race" from one starting point. Have the students watch all three balloons as they fly around the room and then have them draw the way each balloon flies through the air. This is a retrospective movement drawing showing how each balloon flew through space. Label this drawing THE GREAT BALLOON RACE.

3. The toy diagram

Find a toy that does not operate with a mechanism (no wind up or battery toy). For example, choose a Slinky. Show the class how the toy works. Ask them to illustrate in graphic form their knowledge of how it works. Encourage them to use arrows to show how it moves and write notes to explain concepts such as gravity, motion and direction, up, down, coiling, retracting, springing. Tell the students that you will work the Slinky ten times. Count out the number of times as you work it. At the end of the tenth time, the drawing exercise should be completed. (Other possible toys: balloon powered race car, Mexican cup-string-and-ball toy, tumbling jack and ladder). They should label this drawing THE TOY DIAGRAM.

4. The sound graphic

Find a simple musical instrument which makes a sound that moves from one pitch to another (kazoo, jew's harp, a slide whistle). Demonstrate the sound made by the musical instrument. Repeat several times in exactly the same rhythm or manner. Have the students draw a graphic representation of what they have just heard. Tell them to imagine that they are creating a sign that will be placed on a door to warn people that this sound is in the room. The students should create the sound graphic with visual images only. They should not use words. This drawing is labeled THE SOUND GRAPHIC.

Learning to identify geometric forms around us

Help the students become more observant of basic geometric shapes by sending them on a walking tour or a scavenger hunt to look for geometric shapes in the neighborhood or around the school. Have them draw these basic two-dimensional shapes across the top of a sheet of paper: square, circle, half circle, triangle and rectangle. Show them the geometric solids that relate to these shapes. Then go

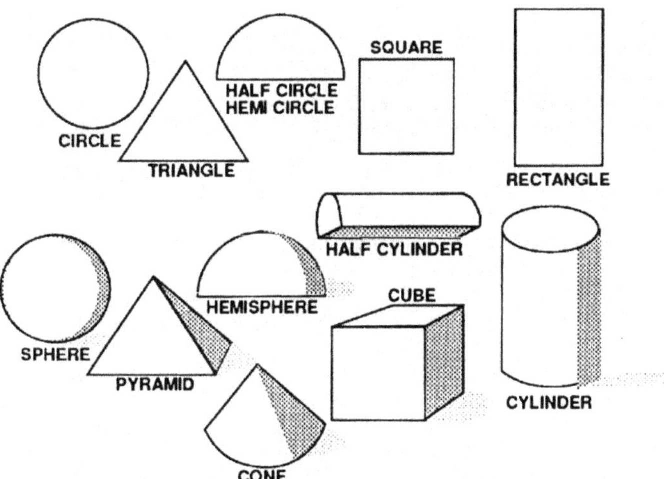

Show students these simple steps to draw a cube and a cylinder

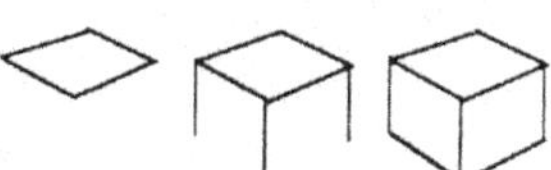

Draw a diamond.
Draw lines down from three corners.
Draw lines to connect the corners.

Draw an ellipse.
Draw lines down the sides.
Connect the lines with a curved line.

out for a walk around the school with the students and compile a list of examples of each type of geometric shape they find. On the walls of a building one sees such shapes as squares, rectangles, circles, and triangles. In considering the entire building one sees cubes, boxes, cylinders, spheres and hemispheres, cones, pyramids and tetrahedrons. Ask the students to think of and draw examples of the use of these shapes in other buildings. You may give them a photocopy of the appendix pages 74-76, Historical Structures / Famous Buildings, to find examples of geometric shapes.

evaluation

When the students have finished drawing their visual stories of the life of a bubble, the great balloon race, the toy diagram and the sound graphic, the drawings should be displayed on a wall in a public space in the school. Make sure that each drawing touches the next drawing so they cover the display wall like wall paper. Show the students how to mount the drawings by masking tape loops placed on the back of the drawing. Evaluate these drawings from the standpoint of how well they express the concepts of time, movement, change and sound through the use of schematic drawing. Encourage students to do more drawings in a similar fashion. Try to facilitate the ideas of schematic drawing and visual thinking. This exercise should show students that drawings can illustrate concepts and that people can express the same concept in different ways.

RESOURCES AND BIBLIOGRAPHY

Appendix:

Historical Structures / Famous Buildings (p. 74)
Visual Vocabulary (p. 77)
Visual Verbal Journal (p. 78)
Hand Lettering (p.79)
Arrows and Multiple Views (p. 86)
Visual Notetaking (p. 104)
How to Develop a Walking Tour (p. 107)
Visual Survey Form (p. 119)

D'Alelio, Jane. I Know that Building! Washington, D.C.: The Preservation Press, 1989.

Isaacson, Philip. Round Buildings, Square Buildings, and Buildings That Wiggle Like a Fish. New York: Knopf Books, 1988.

Pevsner, Fleming and Honour. A Dictionary of Architecture. Woodstock, New York: The Overlook Press, 1976.

Young, Caroline, and Colin King. Castles, Pyramids and Palaces, London: Osborne Publishing, Ltd., 1989.

POSITIVE FORM NEGATIVE SPACE
Concepts of Form and Space

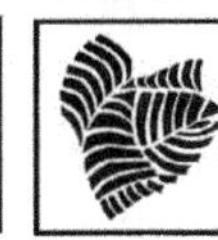

GOAL

To understand how positive form (shapes or objects) and negative space (empty areas) work together in a composition and in the real world.

VOCABULARY

Positive Form: a shape or object

Negative Space: the empty space around a positive form

Geometric Shapes: what characterizes a square, rectangle, circle, and triangle

Fractions: parts of a whole

ASSIGNMENT

Students will make designs by cutting black paper shapes and arranging them on white paper backgrounds to illustrate principles of positive form and negative space. First, look around the classroom and point out shapes/solids and the spaces that surround them (wall/windows; hand/spaces between fingers, tables and chairs/empty spaces between legs/rungs). Outside (tree/sky; chain link fence/spaces between wires). Identify geometric shapes.

MATERIALS

7-inch black paper shapes: squares, circles and triangles

12" x 18" white paper

Scissors

Glue

Rulers and Pencils as needed

GEOMETRIC SHAPES

What characterizes a square, rectangle, circle, triangle. Fractions: parts of the whole.

ARCHITECTURAL STUDENTS PROJECT FOR A CLIENT

A theater owner wants to create a dramatic set design or backdrop for a dance performance. The designs must form a wall of black and white art that illustrates concepts of positive form and negative space as well as principles of geometry.

ARCHITECTURAL PRCESS

Students select a 7-inch black paper shape to use in their designs. They cut the shape to mount on the white paper. As each cut is made, the black piece is glued to the white paper reassembling the original shape, but with space in between each black piece. White paper should show between each black piece (the negative space). You can slant your work, move it around sideways to form any composition.

EVALUATION

Set up the theater wall of finished designs. Each designer describes his/her thought process for making the design. Is it symmetrical? What mathematical shapes do you see? What part is positive form and what part is negative space?

INSERT ILLUSTRATION

Positive form, Negative space with black and white paper cuts.

The forms shown in the frames are examples of positive form (black paper) and negative space (white paper) with parallel cuts in the black form now glued to the while paper.

RESOURCES AND BIBLIOGRAPHY

Edwards, Betty, *Drawing on the Right Side of the Brain.* Los Angeles: J.P. Tarcher, Inc., 1979.

Ching, D.K. Francis. *A Visual Dictionary of Architecture.* New York: Wiley and Sons, 1995.

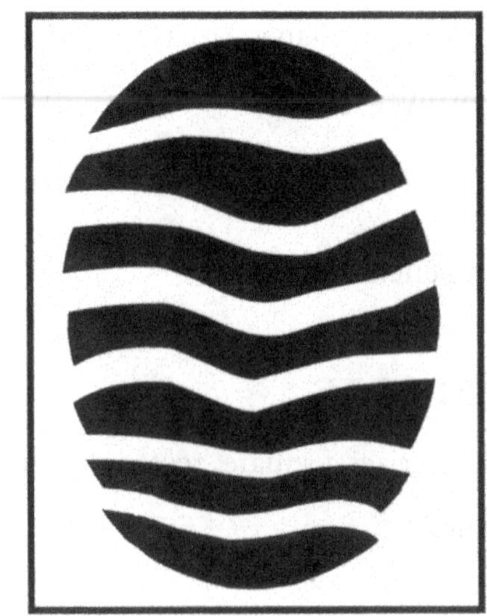

PLANS AND PERSPECTIVES

GOAL

To help students develop visual and spatial thinking skills and techniques.

ARCHITECTURAL VOCABULARY

Bubble diagram Closed curved forms or bubbles which represent spaces and spatial relationships

Elevation drawing A drawing of the front view of an object such as a house front.

Horizon line In perspective drawing, an imaginary line at eye level

Model A three-dimensional representation of an object

Plan view A view of a site or building from above

Perspective drawing Drawing that shows depth by means of lines that converge; a technique of depicting volumes and spatial relationships on a flat surface.

Vanishing point In perspective drawing, a point toward which a series of parallel lines seem to converge

Section drawing A flat two-dimensional representation of the inside of a building showing the internal parts (sometimes called an X-ray drawing in children's art.)

PRESENTATION

Peanut analysis

The purpose of this exercise is to introduce the students to elevation and section drawings by drawing a simple, familiar object in an architectural way. Give every student a sheet of paper and one peanut with its shell intact. Have them fold the paper into three sections and write the title, PEANUT ANALYSIS at the top of the page. In the top space, ask the class to draw two ELEVATION drawings of their peanut, a side elevation and an end elevation. In the middle area of the paper students should draw two IMAGINARY SECTION views of what their peanut would look like if they could take a surgical laser saw and cut it in half in two directions, through the middle and lengthwise. In the bottom section of their paper, have the students draw what they really see when they carefully crack open their peanut shell and draw a REAL SECTION drawing of the peanut. After they have made the "real section drawing" of their peanut, the students may eat their peanuts. Note: To encourage quick, fluid drawing, time each drawing exercise for three minutes. Call out the time remaining every thirty seconds. Each drawing should be labeled.

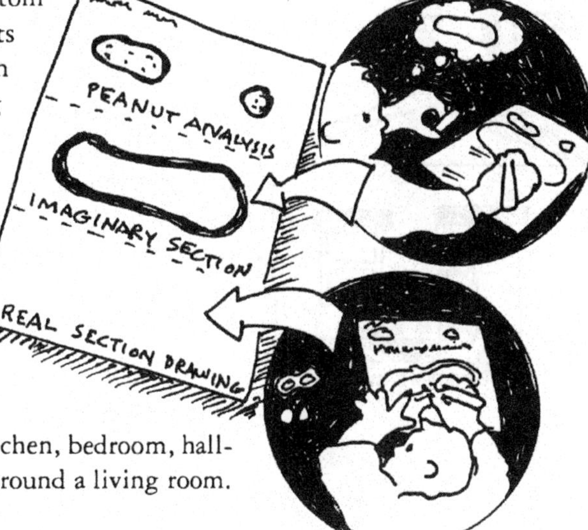

client

Your client, a mouse, needs a house. It should have a kitchen, bedroom, hallway, bathroom and a cheese storage room, all arranged around a living room.

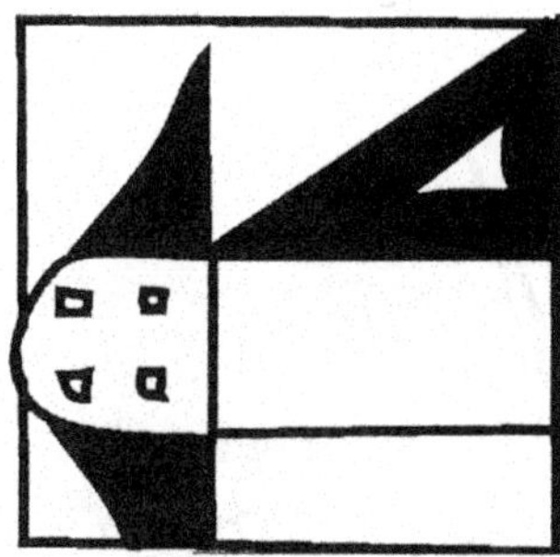

ASSIGNMENT

The students will develop architectural plans and a model for a mouse house.

MATERIALS

Black medium felt tip pen
White glue, tape
Drawing Paper
Tracing Paper
Cardboard
Scissors, X-Acto knife

SKILLS AND CONCEPTS

Math
Geometry
Art
Using tools
Visual/verbal communication
Recognizing 2D and 3D
Measuring
Using ratio and scale
Problem solving
Measurement
Habitat study

SETTING

Classroom

architectural program

The students will use schematic drawings to develop a design, starting with a bubble diagram, proceeding to a floor plan, elevation, perspective and model.

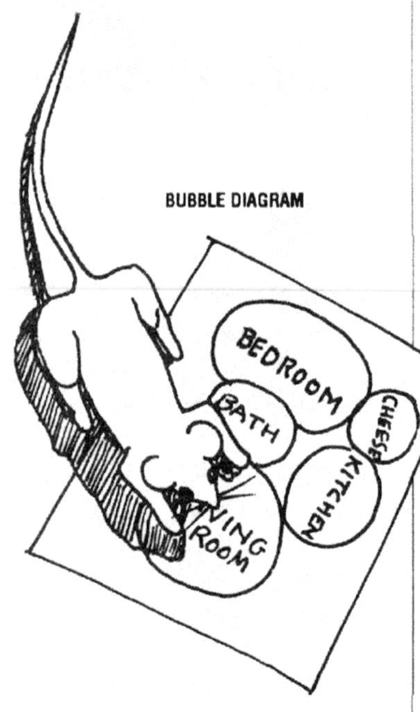

BUBBLE DIAGRAM

Schematic Drawings

1. Bubble diagram

Have the students draw a bubble to represent each space needed by the mouse: a kitchen, cheese storage room, bedroom, bathroom, and living room. Each bubble represents a space and has a label. Have them arrange the bubbles in various ways until they find their best arrangement. They can use architect's tracing paper, called "flimsy" to trace and keep a record of their trial arrangements. Tracings enable them to keep ideas. Then they can compare the various arrangements and choose the best one.

2. Floor Plan

A plan view converts the bubble diagram to a form which begins to resemble a building. Explain to younger students that a floor plan is a view of a room or house which is seen as if the roof has been removed and someone is above the building looking straight down on the rooms. It is a bird's-eye view. Give older students a copy of the appendix page, Drawing A Floor Plan. Have the students look at the features of the plan view of this poster in order to see how architects draw walls, doors, door swings, and windows. Translate the bubble diagram for the mouse house into a floor plan.

3. Elevation drawing

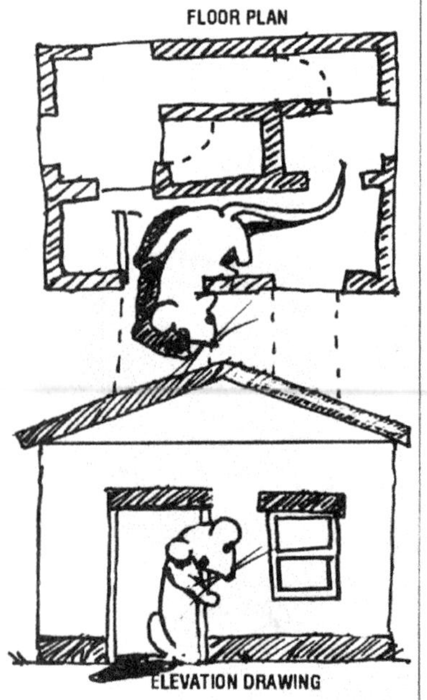
FLOOR PLAN

ELEVATION DRAWING

Elevation drawings are two dimensional drawings that show the outside walls of a building. Have the students draw a front elevation of their mouse house design. The front elevation would be the side of the house which contains the front door. Show the students how the front elevation is drawn by tracing lines up from the corners of the floor plan. Explain that elevation drawings are based on the infor-mation found in the floor plans. The students should use an architect's scale to determine the height of the walls, roof, doors, and where windows are placed. Elevation drawings also show the pattern or texture on the walls. Ask them to imagine that they have X-ray vision and draw the walls and other parts of the inside of the house that they can see with X-ray vision behind the elevation drawing they have made.

4. Perspective drawing (for older students)

Explain to the class that while elevation and section drawings look flat and diagramatic, a perspective sketch will enable them to draw a house that is three dimensional looking, more like a photograph. On the chalkboard demonstrate these step-by-step instructions for perspective drawing:

(Step 1) For perspective drawing, start with the horizon line and two vanishing points. On the chalkboard draw a horizon line and vanishing points, A and B.

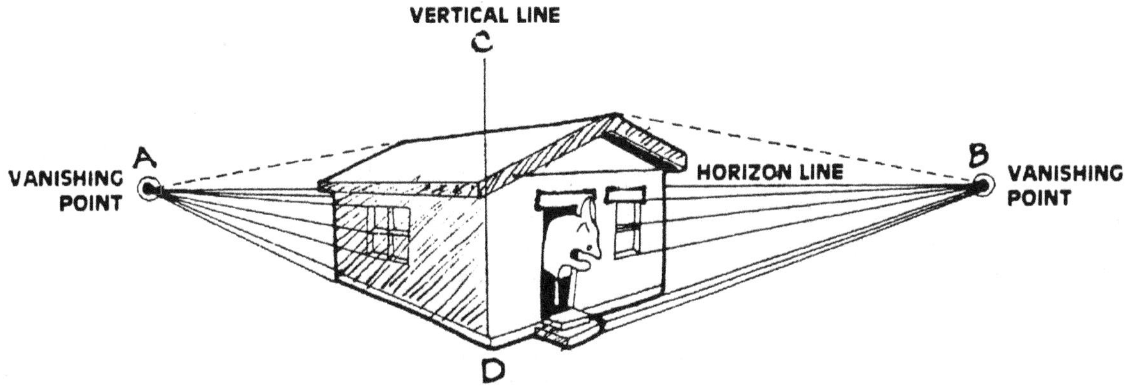

(Step 2) In the middle of the horizon line, draw a vertical line, C, which crosses the horizon line. This represents the corner of the building.
(Step 3) Draw lines from D, the bottom corner of the building, up to the vanishing points.
(Step 4) Draw lines from E, the top corner of the roof, down to the vanishing points. Now two side of the building can be seen.
Have the students draw in the details following the rule (indicated in steps 3 and 4) of having the lines go toward the vanishing points. This includes the lines of the siding, bricks, and other details.

Optional advanced drawing exercise: Oblique Perspective

This is a special drawing used by architects to help them see how a building looks and feels inside. To make an oblique perspective drawing, the student will need the floor plan and a sheet of tracing paper. Show the student how to tip the floor plan toward him/her at a 45° angle. Then the tracing paper is laid over the plan and vertical pencil lines are drawn from all the corners within the plan. In this way the walls are drawn as they would rise up from the floor plan. Once the pencil drawing is complete, have the students go over the lines with a felt tip marker to complete the oblique plan drawing.

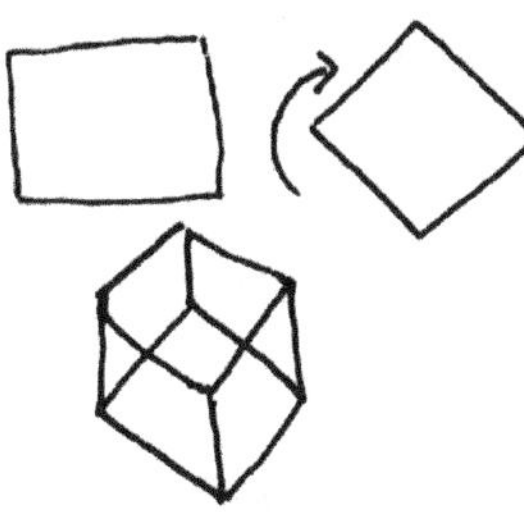

Model construction

There are several ways of constructing a model. The floor plan and elevation drawings are used as patterns for making models. Young students could simply decorate a shoe box with elevation drawings of their house. Another simple way to make a model is to have the student draw each side of the house next to another on a long piece of tagboard. Score the corners with a butter knife and fold them to form the walls. Older students can use the detailed instructions for materials, making patterns and constructing models on appendix page 105, "Model Building."

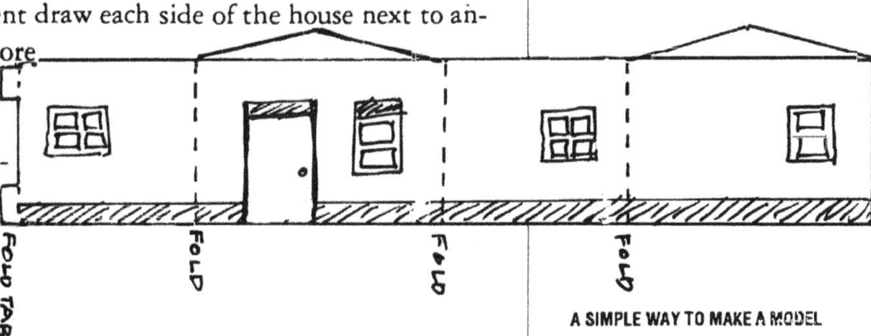

A SIMPLE WAY TO MAKE A MODEL

evaluation

Give each student time to present his or her mouse house plan and model to the class. Ask each student how the use of the bubble diagram and plan view helped him or her to achieve a creative design for the mouse house. Evaluate their progress in visual thinking and visual communication through schematic drawing.

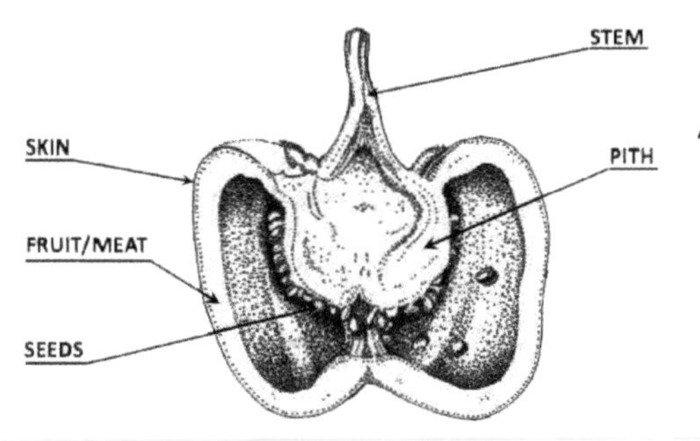

The drawing techniques used in these activities will be used again and again in the exercises that follow on the other pages. The students will get more practice as they continue with the other sequences. Remind them, this is as much a way of thinking as a way of drawing. Positive reinforcement for visual thinking and creative problem solving is very important in the early stages of this new way of learning.

SECTION VIEW OF A GREEN PEPPER

Section of a House

BUBBLE DIAGRAM OF A FAST FOOD VEGETARIAN RESTAURANT

RELATED ACTIVITIES

Designing a Fast Food Vegetarian Restaurant

This gives students an opportunity to work with organic forms that are more like bubble diagrams. The client is an entrepreneur who has just come into your town. He wants the students to design a fast food vegetarian restaurant. The students should begin by making drawings of the outside of a green pepper and an orange, then cut them and make section drawings of them. The purpose of this is to start thinking about the internal organization of two different organic forms and to become more experimental as they organize the interior space for the many functions of a restaurant. In developing the architectural program, have the students brainstorm ideas about the spaces needed (eating and preparation areas, delivery space storage, restrooms, parking, etc.—spaces only, not equipment.) They should make a bubble shape of each space, label it, cut it out, and experiment with arrangement of the spaces, rearranging the diagram as often as they like and changing the size, shape, spatial relationships, number of bubbles. Have them use tracing paper to trace the different arrangements that they try. Then they should draw a plan view possibly using a combination of geometric shapes and organic, curved shapes. The four steps of the final drawing can placed on one large sheet of drawing paper folded into four sections. Section 1 should have the bubble diagram. Section 2 should have the plan view. Section 3 should show an elevation. Section 4 should show a perspective drawing. This drawing should be colored.

RESOURCES AND BIBLIOGRAPHY

Appendix:
Visual Vocabulary (p. 77)
Visual Verbal Journal (p. 78)
Drawing a Floor Plan (p. 81)
Perspective (p. 83)
People (p. 84)
Arrows and Multiple Views (p. 86)
Model Building (p. 105)

Andrews, J.J.C. The Well Built Elephant and Other Roadside Attractions. New York: Congdon & Weed, Inc. 1984.
Ching, Frank. Architectural Graphics. New York: Van Nostrand, 1985.
laseau, Paul. Graphic Thinking for Architects and Designers. New York: Van Nostrand, 1980.
McCauly, David. Unbuilding. Boston: Houghton Mifflin Co., 1973.
Ratensky, Alexander. Drawing and Modelmaking: A Manual for Students of Architecture and Design. Whitney Library of Design, 1983.
Weiss, Harvey. Model Buildings and How to Make Them. New York: Thomas Crowell, 1979.

STRUCTURE IN ARCHITECTURE

GOAL

To help students understand, use and be able to explain elementary structural principles.

ARCHITECTURAL VOCABULARY

Arch A curved structure built so that the parts support each other

Asymmetrical Not equally balanced; off center

Balanced Distributed evenly

Greek capital "orders"

Doric - Like a boxy cushion

Beam Horizontal structural part supported by columns; lintel

Cantilever A beam supported at one end and appearing to be unsupported at the other end

Column Vertical beams (posts) used to support the horizontal beam (lintel)

Column capital styles A column has a base, shaft and capital; the capital is the top; three Greek styles called "orders"are often seen in architecture

Ionic - With scrolls

Flying buttress An arch with a supporting column which accepts some of the weight of the roof; characteristic feature of Gothic architecture

Load The weight supported by a structure

Structure A construction made by combining related parts

Symmetrical Designed with parts that are the same on each side

Corinthian - With rows of leaves

Tension Force stretching or pulling apart

Compression Force pressing on a body

Tetrahedron Triangular solid with four faces and six edges

Thrust Push or force exerted by a structure

Truss Two dimensional (planar) support system of characterized by use of triangular supports

Space frame Three dimensional equivalent of a truss

Polyhedron A many-sided geometric form

ASSIGNMENT

Students will build a model space frame structure.

MATERIALS

Toothpicks and modeling clay or mini-marshmallows
White glue
Cardboard and mat board
Construction paper
Toilet paper tubes
Scissors
Popsicle sticks

SKILLS AND CONCEPTS

Math
Science
Social Studies
Art
Physical Education
Planning, problem solving
Communication skills
Geometric construction
Proportion, ratio and scale
Cause and effect
Environmental impact

SETTING

Classroom
Playground

PRESENTATION

"Be a structure" activities

In these activities students will learn how structures are shaped and how they "feel" by acting them out.

Post and beam Load books on three different types of "beams" made with arms and hands: (1) hands touching, (2) hands interlocking, and (3) hands and arms interlocking. Which hand position works best? Why?

Arch Two students interlock hands while facing each other. They move their feet as far back as possible. They feel compression in their hands and tension in their feet.

Dome

Compression ring Six students stand in a circle, placing arms around one another's waists. Keeping feet together in a comfortable position, all lean back to feel the compression.

Tension ring Students form circle and face the same direction. Each student places elbows on his/her own waist and hands on the waist of the student in front of him/her. At the same time, all sit on the lap of the person behind them. Sit as long as you can.

Tension ring

Truss Trusses are based on triangles. Students should grasp each other's arms, spread legs apart until they touch their partner's feet, and form a straight line.

Truss

Dome One student holds a basketball and five others form a circle at arm's length around the basketball holder, place their hands on the basketball, spread their feet and touch their neighbor's feet and lean toward the basketball to form a dome.

Barrel vault

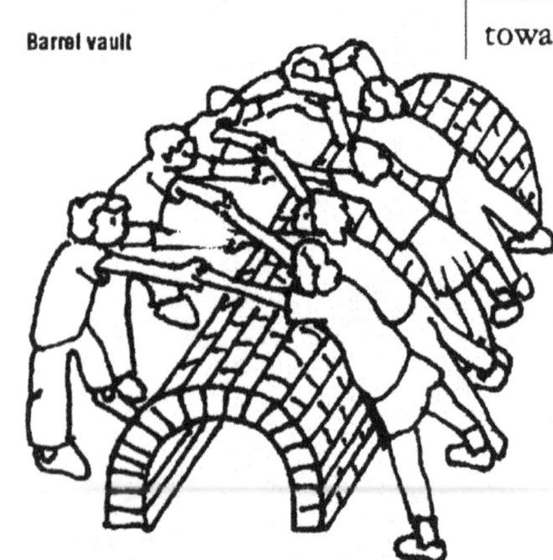

Barrel vault Eight students form a barrel vault by interlocking hands of student opposite them and next to them in pairs of four. (See sketch.)

Flying buttress Eight students form an arch with two flying buttresses and footings as shown in sketch. Two students stand by to give needed support, if necessary.

Flying buttress

Test the strength of triangles

Triangles make the strongest structures for their weight. Make a bridge from a piece of paper. Fold an 8 1/2 x 11" sheet of paper into 1/2" accordian folds. Lay it between two stacks of books and support an empty milk carton on it. Add water to the milk carton in increments to measure the safe load of your bridge.

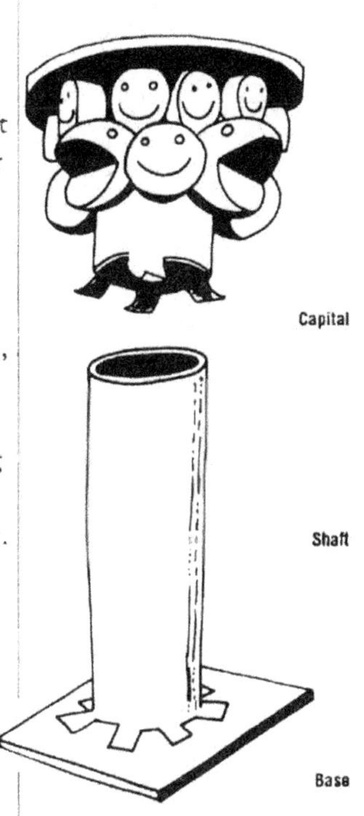

Design an ornamental column

Show the students that a column has a capital, shaft and base ("head, body and feet"). Have them draw a column and design its capital, thinking about animals, plants or toys to decorate it. Have them make a model of their column, using a toilet paper tube to support the shaft and a square of cardboard for a base. Have them surround the tube with colored paper and connect it to the base by cutting and folding tabs at the bottom and gluing the tabs to the base. For paper sculpture ideas, distribute copies of appendix page 96. Display and ask about all work.

client

The mayor has requested designs by young people for new picnic shelters that will be built in several parks in your city.

architectural program

The picnic shelters must use a space frame structure for their roofs. Each shelter will have four picnic tables, and the space frame will rest on at least four columns.

Introducing space frames

Explain that the most important element of a space frame is the triangle. The triangle is the strongest form used in architecture. Polyhedra of different kinds are used in space frames. The three points of a triangle support each other. Four triangles together make a tetrahedron, a kind of pyramid with four faces and six edges. Five triangles together make a regular pyramid with five faces and eight edges. This is the kind the students will use. Space frames are a light, strong, economical and versatile structural form. Space frames withstand the forces of tension and compression without bending or warping. A simple model of the pyramid that is the building block of a space frame can be made connecting eight toothpicks with five mini-marshmallows or gumdrops, as illustrated. Space frames can be used to cover large areas with a few columns because they are light and spread roof's weight evenly through the whole system.

space frame pyramid

Space frame

Grid pattern and plan view of picnic shelter

Organize the classroom into teams of two. Give each team 24 toothpicks (or cut straws) and have them lay out a grid of squares. The grid's edge can take various shapes that the students create. After designing the grid pattern, they should draw a plan based on the grid and include four or more columns and four picnic tables. They should try different arrangements of columns and picnic tables.

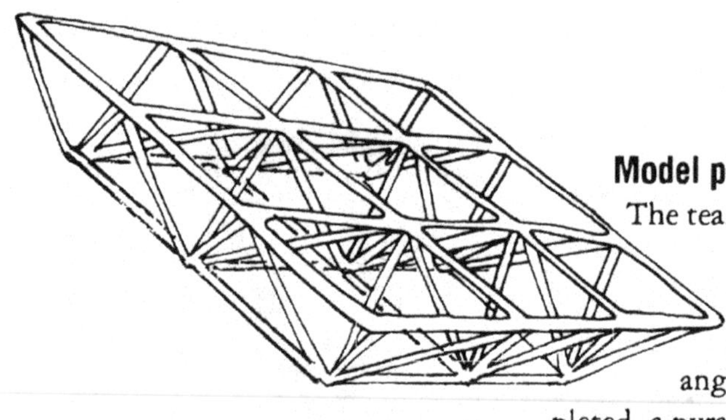

Space frame roof

Model picnic shelter

The teams should build their grids using modeling clay, mini-marshmallows or gumdrops to attach the toothpicks to each other. (Or if students wish to use hollow coffee stirring straws, they can attach them with paper clips cut in half and bent to a 90• angle and slipped into into straw ends.) Once the grid is completed, a pyramid should be assembled over each square. When all the pyramids are assembled, they should be connected at the top of each pyramid to every other pyramid point so that a second grid is formed at the top of the pyramids. This will complete the space frame roof. A base is made for the model and the four columns should be firmly attached to it, in the arrangement worked out in the plan. Students should then make four picnic tables and attach them to the base. People cut out and placed in the shelter will give a sense of its scale.

evaluation

Have the class imagine that they are attending a public meeting called by the mayor to review the design proposals. The class should act the part of active and interested members of the community who attend the meeting and look at each design in turn, asking questions of the team that designed it. Let the students know that the "public" expects accountability in the spending of its tax dollars and is also interested in having the finest picnic shelters in its parks. The "public" asks questions that relate to the specific requirements of the project, such as "What kind of a roof is that? Why did you use that design for the roof? Will you tell me about the columns and furniture." The design teams in turn should answer the "public's" questions and convince them of the good points about space frames and their design in particular.

Lower half of picnic shelter model

RESOURCES AND BIBLIOGRAPHY

Appendix:
Hand Lettering (p. 79)
People (p. 84)
Understanding the Forces of Structure (p. 87)
Physics of Structure Exercise (p. 94)
Design a Column Capital (p. 95)
Paper Structures for Architectural Models (p. 96)
Paper Patterns for Geometric Forms (p. 97)

Cesarini and Ventura. Grand Constructions. New York: G.P. Putnam's Sons, 1983.
Ericksen and Wintermute. Students, Structures, Spaces: Activities in the Built Environment. Menlo Park, CA: Addison-Wesley Publishing Company, 1983.
Gordon, J.E. Structure or Why Things Don't Fall Down. New York: DaCapo Press, 1978.
Hilton and Pendersen. Build Your Own Polyhedra. Menlo Park, CA: Addison-Wesley, 1988.
Lewis, Alun. Super Structures. New York: Viking Press, 1980.
McGregor, Anne and Scott. Domes: A Project Book. New York: Lothrop, Lee and Shepard Books. 1981.
Prenis, John,, ed. The Dome Builder's Handbook. Philadelphia: Running Press, 1978.
Salvadori and Tempel. Architecture and Engineering: An Illustrated Teacher's Manual on Why Buildings Stand Up. New York Academy of Sciences, 1983.
Wilson, Forrest. What It Feels Like to Be a Building. Washington, D.C.: The Preservation Press, 1988.
Zubrowski, Bernie. Messing Around With Drinking Straw Construction: A Children's Museum Activity Book. Boston: Little Brown and Company, 1981.

ENTRYWAYS

GOAL

To help students understand the significance of an enrtyway, both architecturally and symbolically, and to express their understanding in an architectural project.

ARCHITECTURAL VOCABULARY

Entryway Entry passage or opening; a way to enter a building
Passageway A space connecting one area with another
Mapping Drawing the features of an area of the surface of the earth
Measurement Size ascertained by measuring
Transition Movement, passage or change from one position to another
Vestibule An entrance before a doorway

PRESENTATION

Meaning and function of an entryway

Ask the students to focus on the act of entering their school. When entering the school, the environment outside is left behind and there is another environment inside. You feel different inside. A doorway is a transition point for coming and going. A door and entryway give a message. They can reflect what is going on inside the building and welcome the people who come in.

GATE OF TOSHOGO SHRIINE, TOCHIGI, JAPAN

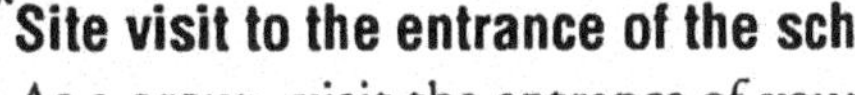

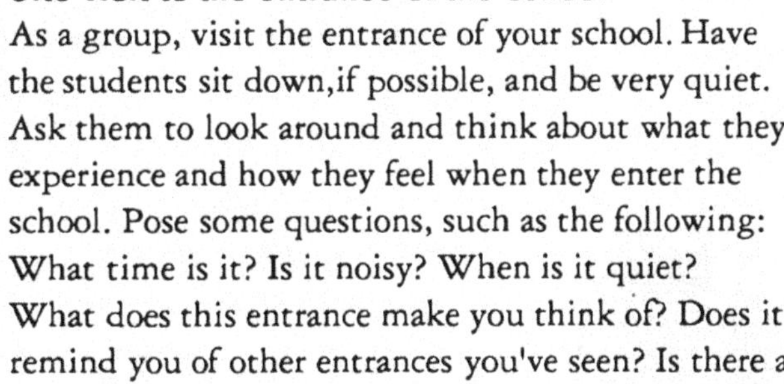

Site visit to the entrance of the school

As a group, visit the entrance of your school. Have the students sit down,if possible, and be very quiet. Ask them to look around and think about what they experience and how they feel when they enter the school. Pose some questions, such as the following: What time is it? Is it noisy? When is it quiet? What does this entrance make you think of? Does it remind you of other entrances you've seen? Is there a passageway? What is it like? Is there a vestibule? What is it like? Have students measure the width and length of the entryway. Give the students a survey form on which to record their likes and dislikes about the school's entrance area. It should include aspects of design such as size, color, materials, doors, windows, landscaping. Leave space for additional observations and comments. Ask the students to work quietly and keep their answers to themselves until the class returns to the classroom and makes a tally of students' likes and dislikes.

Tally student likes and dislikes

When the students have completed the survey of likes and dislikes and returned to the classroom, have them make a talley. Count the total number of like and dislike votes received by each item on the survey. By subtracting the "dislikes" from the "likes" the class can get the tally for each item. Rank the items from high to low.

ASSIGNMENT

The students will analyze the school entryway and create their own design for a new entryway for the school.

MATERIALS

Clipboards
Drawing paper
Markers
Measuring tape
Model building supplies

SKILLS AND CONCEPTS

Math
Social Studies
Measurement
Site analysis
Visual survey
Data collection
Data analysis
Summarizing data
Visual communication
Teamwork
Observation
Scale
Model making
Symbols
Use of color

SETTING

Classroom
School
Neighborhood

PORTION OF A LIKE AND DISLIKE TALLY

SUBJECT	LIKE	DON'T LIKE	TALLY
COLOR	+1[illegible]	-6	12
SIZE	[illegible]	-6	12
HEIGHT	+17	-7	10
DO[illegible]	+16	-8	8
[illegible]DOWS	+15	-9	6
[illegible]TIBULE	+15	-8	6
TEXTURE	+14	-10	4

Data analysis

Use the questions below to discuss each important feature of the entrance area Save notes from this discussion and review them during the evaluation process.

- What did you notice or observe? (Consider size, color, furniture, landscaping, signs, decoration, hinges, door stops, fire bar, etc.)
- How would you describe that feature?
- Does the entrance work well?
- Is it clean and well maintained?
- What messages does it give to people who enter the school? How does it make you feel?
- How would you like to improve or change the entryway?

Symbols that describe your place

On the chalkboard or a large tablet, write questions such as the following:

- What would you like to show someone from another country about your school?
- How would you describe your town or the school neighborhood?
- What characteristics could be included in the new entrance area that would reflect the feelings you have about your area?
- Is there an industry or livelihood that could be incorporated into the design?
- What cultural elements are prominent within the community that could be reflected in the entry design?
- Should the entrance make a modern statement or a traditional statement?
- Should the entry mural show plants and animals that are abundant in the area?
- What colors would be appropriate?
- Can you think of anything else to put in the design that would help visitors from another country understand what your area is like?

client

A delegation of people from another country is coming to your school for a visit. The principal has asked you to redesign the entryway of your school in order to express some good things about the spirit of the school and of the community.

architectural program

Entryway design requirements

There are four requirements for your new design for the entryway:

1. Passageway The entry will have a passageway as a transition from the outside to the inside. It should make people feel welcome to your school.

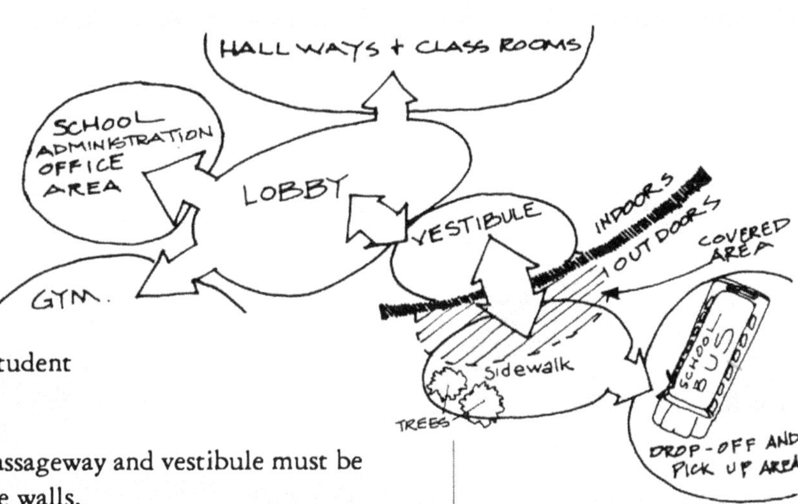

BUBBLE DIAGRAM OF A SCHOOL ENTRY

2. Vestibule and lobby
The passageway leads to a vestibule and lobby on the inside. These areas should let people know something about the students who inhabit the school. It could, for example, include a student art gallery or student murals.

3. Color and graphic symbols The entrance passageway and vestibule must be colorful. They may include graphics on the walls.

4. Furniture There should be benches inside and outside of the entryway for both students and visitors to use.

Design process

Bubble diagram

Bubble diagrams are one technique architects use to start developing their ideas into designs that are built. Have the students draw "bubbles" to represent the bus and car passenger loading zone, sidewalk area, passageway, vestibule, lobby, office, classroom and other activity complexes connected to the entry area. They can cut out their "bubbles" and move them around into different arrangements until they have a solution that they like.

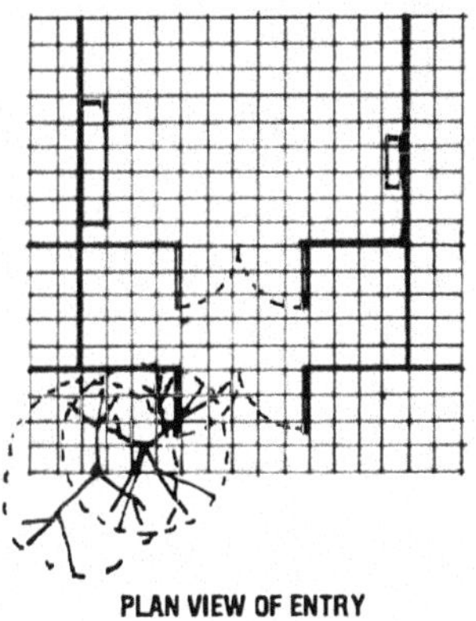

PLAN VIEW OF ENTRY

Floor plan

The next step is to draw the major outlines of a floor plan, showing the walls and other major structural elements. If the students are advanced, they should use an architects scale and give the walls and posts proper thickness. Major built-in elements, such as doors and windows, are drawn next. Finally details, such as fixtures and furniture, are drawn.

Elevation

The final drawing is an elevation of the entrance area. This drawing should be colored and include the graphic symbols the student has chosen to express some ideas about the school and community. The graphic symbols can be shown in detail in separate sketches arranged around the drawing of the elevation. People should be drawn in the elevation drawing to give a sense of the scale.

ENTRY ELEVATION

Optional activity: Model

With the floor plan and elevation drawings as patterns, the students may build a scale model of their designs for the entrance area as an optional activity. This is a good activity for cooperative learning. Detailed instructions for model building are found in the appendix on page 105. The students should use people in the model to give it a sense of scale. There is no need to build a model of the whole school, though they should think of a way to show how the lobby relates to the halls and doorways that are inside the building.

evaluation

Students present their plan and elevation drawings and explain them. They should tell and be evaluated on the ways in which their design meets the requirements of the architectural program: (1) passageway, (2) vestibule and lobby, (3) color and graphic symbols, and (4) furniture. They should explain what they wish to communicate about the school and its students. Use some of the questions previously used in data analysis discussion to focus this discussion on the ways that each design expresses the meaning and function of an entrance area.

Related activities

- On a walking tour, pick the four most pleasing or interesting entrance areas in your neighborhood or city. While looking at them, invite comments and discussion on why they are pleasing or interesting. Photograph them.
- Build a model of the entryway the class likes best.
- Study pictures of entryways from other cultures. What are the architectural determinants? (Climate? Materials? Customs? Religious practice? Special reasons for these entryways?)
- Draw the entrance area of your home as it is. Then draw a design of how you would like to change it.
- Design and build an entrance to the mouse house.
- Design a new entryway to your classroom.

RESOURCES AND BIBLIOGRAPHY

Appendix:

Hand Lettering (p. 79)
Using an Architect's Scale (p. 80)
Drawing a Floor Plan (p. 81)
People (p. 84)
Paper Structures for Architectural Models (p. 96)
Paper Patterns for Geometric Forms (p. 97)
Model Making (p. 105)
How to Develop a Walking Tour (p. 107)
Visual Survey Form (p. 119)

Allied Arts of Seattle. Lydia S. Aldredge, Ed. Impressions of Imagination: Terra Cotta Seattle, 1986.
Blumenson, John J. Identifying American Architecture: A Pictorial Guide to Styles and Terms. New York: W.W. Norton & Co., 1981.
Clinton, Susan. I Can Be an Architect, Chicago: Children's Press, 1986.

YOU ARE ARCHITECTURE

GOAL

To help students understand similarities between body and building systems.

ARCHITECTURAL VOCABULARY

Membrane Covering of the body or its internal parts; covering of an object
Mechanical systems Systems with machinery (examples: forced-air furnace, faucet, drain and sewer system, elevator, automatic garage door opener)
Electrical system System which distributes electricity
Machine A structure consisting of a framework and various fixed and moving parts for doing some kind of work
Structural system A group of parts that support a building
Aesthetics Philosophical principles of art and design
Balance Harmonious visual or physical arrangement of forms
Architectural determinants Factors of style, culture or imagination which influence a design
System Combination of interrelated parts forming a functional whole

PRESENTATION

Corresponding body parts and building parts

Conduct a class discussion about the similarities between body parts and systems and building parts and systems using the examples below:

Skin A person's body has a skin. A building has an outside covering too. What are the similarities and differences of these two coverings?
Circulation system A person's body has a heart to circulate blood through the body. A building has a heating system. How does a heating system distribute heat through a building?
Respiratory system A person's body has lungs to breathe. A building has windows and ventilation. Some buildings have windows that are fixed in a closed position. How do you think a building like this delivers fresh air to different parts of a building?
Nervous system A person's body has nerves to control the functions of different parts of the body. A building has electical wires. What do the electrical wires do?
Digestive system A person's body has a digestion and waste disposal system. A building has a plumbing and sewage system. How is the plumbing system similar to your digestive system?
Structural system A person's body has a skeleton to hold it up. A building

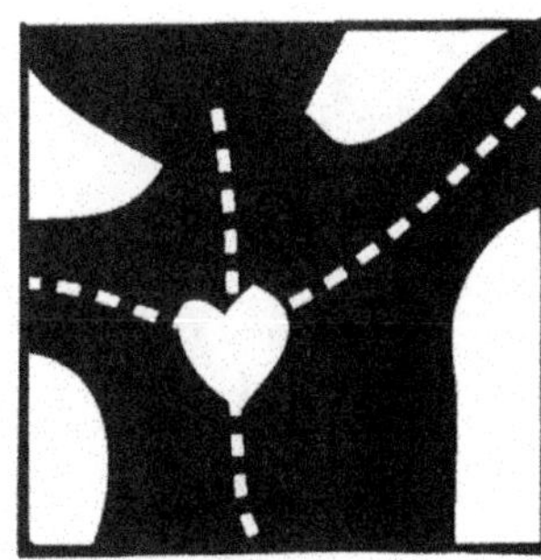

ASSIGNMENT

Students will make two types of illustrations showing corrresponding architectural systems and body systems.

MATERIALS

Pointed colored markers
Scissors
Blank index cards or
12 x 18 drawing paper
8 1/2 x 11 index weight paper
Stapler or tape

SKILLS AND CONCEPTS

Life science
Math
Ratio
Measuring
Proportion
Scaling
Observing
Organic relationships

SETTING

Classroom
School
Home
Studio

A work from *The City* by artist Jimmy Grashow

has a framework to hold it up. If a skeleton is on the inside it is called an endoskeleton. If it is on the outside it is called an exoskeleton. What is your school's framework made of?

Muscular system A person's body has a system of muscles. Many buildings have mechanical devices that lift and push things. What mechanical devices do you have at your school?

EIFFEL TOWER
PARIS, FRANCE
DESIGNED BY
GUSTAV EIFFEL

Compare characteristics in structures to body parts

Here are some examples:

Thin shelled construction
Thin curved concrete is self bracing and rigid; it is exceptionally strong for its weight

Cranium
Protects the brain; strong and light like an eggshell, giving maximum protection with minimum weight

Tower
Held together by guy lines

Spine
Held together by muscles and ligaments

Crane
Provides access to out-of-the-way places

Elbow
Smoothly operated hinge

Space frame
Stress bearing beam is removed; result is light and open

Pelvis
Arches take the weight of the torso when you are seated

Curved beams
Used on under side of floor where stress occurs

Femur
The longest, strongest bone; adjusts according to stress, something which buildings cannot do

Write a list of building parts and systems on the chalkboard and invite students to come up to the board and write in the corresponding bodily systems in a parallel list.

Building parts:	**Body parts:**
Membrane	(Skin)
Mechanical systems	(Muscular system)
Heating cooling	(Circulatory system)
Ventilation	(Respiratory system)
Sewage system	(Waste elimination)
Energy consumption	(Digestive system)
Electrical system	(Nervous system)
Machines	(Skeletal system)
Structural system	(Exoskeleton)
Load bearing walls	(Endoskeleton)
Post and beam structure	(Feet)
Foundation	(Style, imagination, culture)
Architectural style	

Tour a building

Arrange a tour of the school (or another building) electrical, mechanical and plumbing systems. Have the students complete an energy and plumbing survey investigating the energy and plumbing systems. (Use the Energy and Plumbing Survey Form found in the appendix, pg. 102.)

Ergonomics

Ergonomics is the study of the proportions of the human body and how these relate to the scale and shape of objects. It is also the study of movements. It is used by designers of everything from space shuttles to spoons. It is definitely used in designing classroom furniture. Give students five minutes to make a list of examples of ergonomically designed objects they can find at school, at home, or elsewhere.

An early study of human proportions was made by the ancient Roman architect and theorist Vitruvius. He made a diagram showing a human "reaching" into a circle and a square. The 20th century Swiss French architect and theorist, Le Corbusier, developed an architectural system based on mathematical proportions. His diagram is called the modular man. The symbol of a person in a wheelchair reminds us to think of the scale and proportions required by people confined to wheelchairs.

VITRUVIUS' DIAGRAM

LE CORBUSIER'S MODULAR MAN

Have students take measurements of each other's proportions: distance from floor to horizontally outstretched hand, from floor to knee, distance from floor to chair seat to, arm length, etc.). Then have them measure items in the classroom (e.g. height of pencil sharpener, most comfortable range for shelves, coat hooks, light switches, height of chair seats, height of writing desks, height of keyboard desk, etc.). Have them make these measurements using both the metric system and the English system.

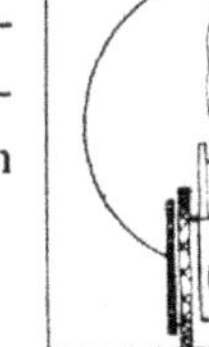

WHEELCHAIR USER DIAGRAM

client

A biology teacher and an architect have both observed similarities between body systems and building systems. They are commissioning you, as student architects, to illustrate these similarities for a new textbook.

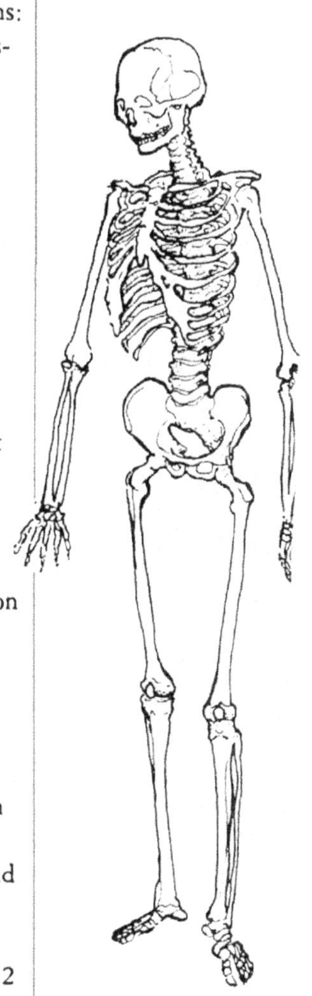

architectural program

Two types of illustrations are requested for this textbook. The first illustration is a set of diagrams of body systems and a corresponding set of diagrams of building systems. The second is a paper doll figure with architectural parts..

Body and building systems diagrams

Have the students fold a piece of drawing paper in half. One side should be labeled BODY and the other side should be labeled BUILDING. Have them draw parallel rows of 6 boxes on each side of the fold, for a total of 12 boxes. Instruct them to draw systems of the body in each box on the BODY side and draw corresponding systems of a building in the parallel boxes on the BUILDING side. They should connect the corresponding systems with dotted lines. Another method for this would be to give the students sets of 12 index cards for their drawings. The finished drawings could then be mounted on a piece of tag board or poster board and dotted lines (or yarn, etc.) applied between the related drawings.

Paper doll with architectural features

The second illustration is a cut out human shape with building parts drawn on it instead of the regular body parts. A pattern for the human shape can be photocopied on index weight paper or the students can trace around the patterns themselves. The students should cut out the shapes, illustrate both the front and back sides with building parts, and make the figure stand on the base by taping or stapling the tabs under the feet to the base.

evaluation

All the student illustrations should be displayed. Discussion of the work should focus on the following: Does the illustration communicate information clearly? Is the information correct? Did the student use clear colors and lines so that the information can be seen easily? Is the illustration well organized? Will this illustration help a user of the new texbook to understand the human body? Will the illustration encourage the user of the new textbook to think about correlations between physiology and architecture? Does the illustration have too much, too little, or just the right amount of information? Ask the students to summarize the illustration characteristics that communicate ideas and information clearly.

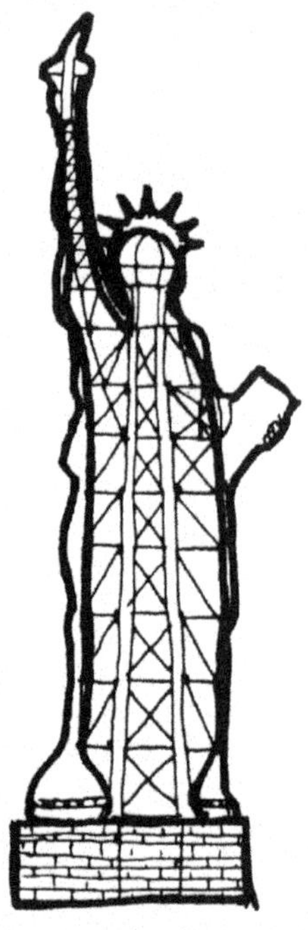

FRAMEWORK OF STATUE OF LIBERTY NEW YORK HARBOR DESIGNED BY GUSTAV EIFFEL

RELATED ACTIVITIES

Redesign the body

Ask the students to write an illustrated essay answering the following questions:

- Can you invent a better body?
- Where would you place the parts?
- What materials would you use?

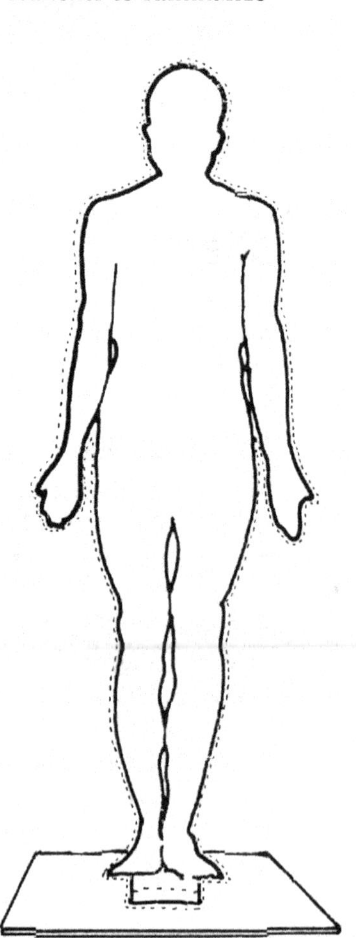

RESOURCES AND BIBLIOGRAPHY

Appendix:

Understanding the Forces of Structure (p. 87)
Energy and Plumbing Survey (p. 102)

Adkins, Jan. How a House Happens. New York: Walker and Company, 1972.
Carratello, Patricia. My Body. Carratello/Smith, 1972. Hanks, Belliston and Edwards. Design Yourself. William Kaufman, Inc. Hawkes, Nigel. Structures: The Making of Architectural and Engineering Wonders. New York: New York: Macmillan, 1990.
Macaulay, David. Underground. Boston: Houghton Mifflin Co., 1976.
Wilson, Forrest. What It Feels Like To Be A Building. Washington D.C.: Preservation Press.

COLORS AND TEXTURES

GOAL

To help students gain an understanding and familiarity with color and textures, how they work and what they express when they are used in interior design.

ARCHITECTURAL VOCABULARY

Interior designer A professional who designs the insides of buildings
Color board A color sample display made by an interior designer for the client
Color wheel A two dimensional model showing the full array of spectrum colors arranged in a circle
Color temperature A psychological impression of warmth or coolness given by colors
Cool colors, receding colors Blue and green are examples of cool, "receding" colors; they are associated with cool water and green trees
Warm colors, advancing colors Red and yellow are examples of warmer, "advancing" colors; they are associated with hot sun, red fire, flames
Hue The color quality of a spectrum color identified by its name
Spectrum The band of colors seen in a section of a rainbow
Intensity or saturation The brightness or dullness of a color
Value The lightness or darkness of a color
Neutral colors Black, white or gray; colors with no hue

PRESENTATION

The power of bubble gum pink

Explain to students that color can affect behavior. Here is an example to share: A color researcher found that if he put a large board with bubble gum pink in front of the eyes of weight lifters, they could not lift the weights. He also found that the color subdued angry prisoners. Now some prison rooms are painted bubble gum pink.

A color brainstorming session

Students will look at twelve colors–the basic spectrum colors of red, orange, yellow, green, blue, purple and six others, if possible bluish grey, yellow green, pink, black, brown and turquoise. Have the students, as a group, consider one color at a time. As they look at each color, one at a time, encourage them to brainstorm, telling their spontaneous associations with each color. Have a recorder write on the blackboard the title of each color and list all reactions for a period of one minute per color. No response should be left out. At the end, go back to each list and have the group select five or more responses for each color and remove the others. Then have a recorder make a master list of all the colors and the reactions to them. This will help students understand their own and others' reactions to colors.

ASSIGNMENT

Students will make a color board for an interior design client.

MATERIALS

Many old magazines
Scissors
Crayons
Glue
Pencils
Newsprint
Tagboard
Colored fabric samples
Color swatches from a paint store
Mat board scraps from a picture framing shop
Masking tape
Crayola markers

SKILLS AND CONCEPTS

Math
Language Arts
Art
Deductive reasoning
Spatial relationships
Dimensional analysis
Applying knowledge
Classifying
Geometry
Texture
Balance
Aesthetics
Color

SETTING

Classroom

Color survey

Conduct a survey on color responses. Have the students ask people of varying ages, lifestyles and interests a standard set of questions. Sample questions might include some of the following: What color is your favorite piece of clothing? What color would you choose for a car? What color would you like the rug to be in your (room, classroom, office– whatever place the person spends most of every day)? What color of toothbrush would you choose? If you had a little tree house what color would you paint it?

RED RED ORANGE ORANGE YELLOW ORANGE YELLOW YELLOW GREEN GREEN BLUE GREEN BLUE BLUE VIOLET VIOLET RED VIOLET

Color representation exercise

Give the students a list of words that have been used to describe colors. The list might include such words as hot, fresh, natural, feminine, rich, masculine, vibrant, loud, quiet, sophisticated, tranquil, avant garde, traditional. The student should make colored illustration or example of each word. Depending on ability, this might vary from drawing the word in outline letters and coloring them to selecting sample color swatches from old magazines and pasting them next to the descriptive word. This is a valuable exercise for helping the students select colors that will satisfy their client's preferences.

Texture rubbings

Have the students look for a surface with an interesting texture. They may find a surface to rub on the inside of a wall or a floor or perhaps outside on a walking tour of the neighborhood. To make a rubbing they tape down a piece of paper larger than the area to be rubbed. (Brown paper grocery bags have good tough paper for rubbings.) Give them thick crayons for rubbing and tell then to rub in one direction from the center to the edges of the paper and always away from the center to the edge. Encourage them to try several rubbings. Have them draw a picture of the object they rubbed or bring an example of it to class.

Texture word representation exercise

In the following exercise, students will represent word meanings by visual symbols. Assign words from the list of texture words on page 43. Have students fold a sheet of paper in half and write their word in the upper left hand corner of the folded paper. With a large felt tip marker, they should draw a symbol of the word in the upper half of the folded paper. On the lower half of the folded paper, they should create a repetitive pattern using the symbol they made on the upper half of paper. Keep assigning word exercises until all words have been illustrated by the class.

VISUAL SYMBOLS

holes	rough	wrinkly	fireworks
uneven	sharp	waves in sand	coarse
lumpy	basketware	gritty	slippery
curly	knotty	slick	bumpy
bristly	glassy	fat	grainy
glossy	small	prickly	polished
pointed/sharp	pebbly	shiny	soft/rounded
thistly	silken	up and down	thorny
silky	zig-zag	splintery	sleek
downy	gravelly	velvety	barbed
satiny	spiny	fleecy	tacky
smooth	soft	waxy	hairy
oily	furry	greasy	spongy
mossy	slimy	plush	filmy
gooey	shaggy	doughy	delicate

Help the students to articulate the message they see in the visual symbols. Display the drawings. Ask the students questions such as: Which patterns are bold? Which are subtle? Which seem earthy? Which seem manmade? Which seem loud? Which seem quiet? Which are regular? Which are irregular? Does the word symbol make you think of the word it is illustrating?

client

A client wants guidance in choosing colors and textures for a new home and has selected you, the student interior designer to help make good choices. (Note: The description and type of person the client is should be defined by each student.) The client needs a colored drawing and samples of the colors and textures to understand what you are recommending and will need to have you explain why you think these choices will be best for the client's new home.

architectural program

Photocopy the interior design of a room from a magazine.
It is like a color board drawing used by professional interior designers. Give each student two copies of the drawing.
The students should first use the color board to design a room for themselves. They should select the colors and textures that they like. Then they should use them to color in the color board. Have each student write a brief self-description and an explanation of why this design is appropriate for them.

Each student should then write a short description of his or her client. Does the client like loud, noisy colors or cool quiet colors? How does the client like to spend his or her spare time? Is the client young or old? Is the client interested in art or music– what kind? How will colors affect the space?

Each student should make, or select from magazines, the color swatches chosen for his or her client. After moving the swatches around and looking at them in different combinations, they should choose colors and textures appropriate for their client's room. Not all colors on all objects have to be different. Many can be the same throughout the space. The student should color the color board drawing, arrange some swatches around the drawing in an orderly way, and be prepared to explain their choices to the client.

evaluation

Have each student give an imaginary client presentation of his or her project, thoughtfully explaining the reasoning they used in reaching their design solutions. The students should say why they like or dislike certain choices. Quite often when we buy something we may say we like it, but can't say why. We need to help children not only make choices about the material world, but help them articulate why these choices were made.

Related activities

1. Repeat the word representation exercises using movement and then musical sounds to indicate word meanings. Represent the words using one movement or musical phrase - create a repetitive pattern.
2. Visualize a geometric shape. Cut it out of paper and place it on a different background color. Now choose a word and demonstrate it using cut paper geometric forms and the two colors - (instability, motion, anchored, frantic, playful, resting, etc.) Try the exercise again using 5 strips of color.
3. Cut and fold colored and textured paper into 3 dimensional shapes and design a town. The texture can be obtained by using texture rubbings.

RESOURCES AND BIBLIOGRAPHY

Appendix:
Color Wheel (p. 85)

Birren, Faber. Light, Color, Environment. New York: Van Nostrand Reinhold, 1969.
Birren, Faber. Principles of Color. New York: Van Nostrand Reinhold, 1969.
Fine Arts Museum of San Francisco. Rainbow Book, Berkeley: Shambala, 1975.
Porter, Tom. Architectural Color. New York: Whitney Library of Design, 1982.

DESIGN IN NATURE

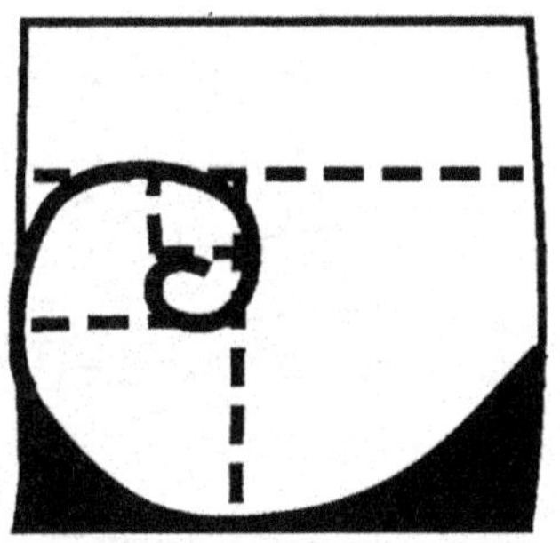

GOAL

To help students understand some of the structures in nature and use some of them in a "fantasy" architectural structure for the moon.

ARCHITECTURAL VOCABULARY

Cantilever A structure which extends into space and is supported on one end only
Chambered Nautilus A sea creature with a chambered spiral shell of perfect Golden Mean proportions
Crystal A natural formation whose atoms are arranged in a definite pattern which is expressed outwardly by a geometric pattern of planes
Fibonacci Numbers A number pattern which demonstrates proportions found in nature. (1+1=2, 1+2=3, 2+3=5, 3+5=8)
Golden Mean A system of proportion in design, based on proportions found in spirals in nature and expressed by Fibonacci Numbers. In the Golden Mean, 8 units divide to a ratio of 5 to 3 rather than the symmetrical division of 4 to 4; the steps illustrated below show how these proportions are reached:

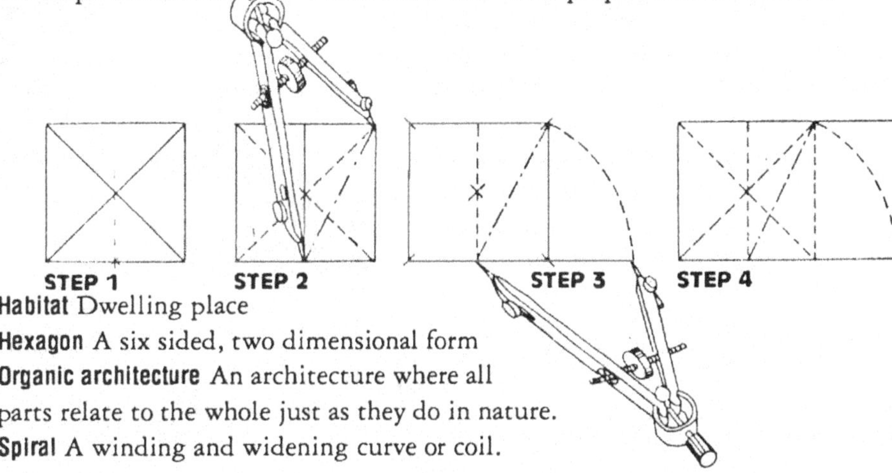

Habitat Dwelling place
Hexagon A six sided, two dimensional form
Organic architecture An architecture where all parts relate to the whole just as they do in nature.
Spiral A winding and widening curve or coil.

PRESENTATION

Architecture in nature

The ideas and information below shows how nature has influenced architecture. (If possible, give each student a photocopied set of Historical Structures/ Famous Buildings from the appendix to look at as you present this material.)

Nature is a grand architect. Nature designs seashells as homes for sea animals. The structure of the Sydney Opera House by Danish architect Jørn Utzon resembles nature's seashell forms.

Crystals in nature have a pattern of flat, smooth surfaces. They grew into that shape because of the orderly pattern of their atoms.

Organic structures such as plants offer wonderful architectural systems. A tree, for instance, has a foundation of

SYDNEY OPERA HOUSE, AUSTRALIA

ASSIGNMENT

The students will design living quarters for moon miners.

MATERIALS

Markers
Paper
Cardboard
Sticks
Stretch fabric (old nylons)
Glue
Sticks
Modular items (film canisters, egg cartons)
Scissors

SKILLS AND CONCEPTS

Math
Science
Social Studies
Art
Approximating/ estimating
Spatial relationships
Geometric construction
Comparing and contrasting
Applying knowledge and evaluating products

SETTING

Classroom

GUGGENHEIM MUSEUM, NEW YORK CITY, FRANK LLOYD WRIGHT, 1954

roots, and branches that cantilever out from the trunk. Architects learn by looking at plants and forms that animals make. Beehives are hexagonal cells grouped together. Does the beehive remind you of apartments? A spider builds its web in a very orderly fashion, beginning with the outer frame and spiraling toward the center.

The spiral is a favorite form in nature. A snail shell, a sunflower's center, a fly's eye, a ram's coiled horn and a coiled snake are spirals. A set of mathematical relationships, called the Fibonacci numbers (1+1=2, 1+2=3, 2+3=5, 3+5=8, and so forth) defines the proportions found in nature's spirals.

The shell of a sea animal called the Chambered Nautilus is a perfect example of these proportional relationships. Architects use Fibonacci numbers to achieve harmonious proportions in their designs. Another name for these proportions is Golden Mean. The Guggenheim Museum in New York City is an application of nature's spiral form in architecture. This museum was designed in the 1940s and completed in 1954 by American architect, Frank Lloyd Wright. Its spiral ramp and walls wind outward from the ground to the top floor under the dome. The Guggenheim's spiral is made of steel-reinforced concrete.

SECTION DRAWING OF TOWER AT JOHNSON WAX CENTER, RACINE WISCONSIN, FRANK LLOYD WRIGHT, 1950

DOUGLAS FIR TREE

The egg is another shape repeated in nature and in architecture. The curved egg shell withstands force even though it is very thin. The egg shell is a thin plate with a curved surface that transmits forces along its curve to the ground. The appendix: Famous Buildings/Historical Structures shows three examples of curved thin-shelled concrete buildings based on natural forms, Los Manantiales in Xochimilco, Mexico by Mexican architect Felix Candela (roof five-eighths inch thick); The Sydney Opera House, Sydney, Australia, by Danish architect, Jørn Utzon; The Olympic Sports Palace in Rome, Italy by Italian architect Pier Luigi Nervi (roof two inches thick).

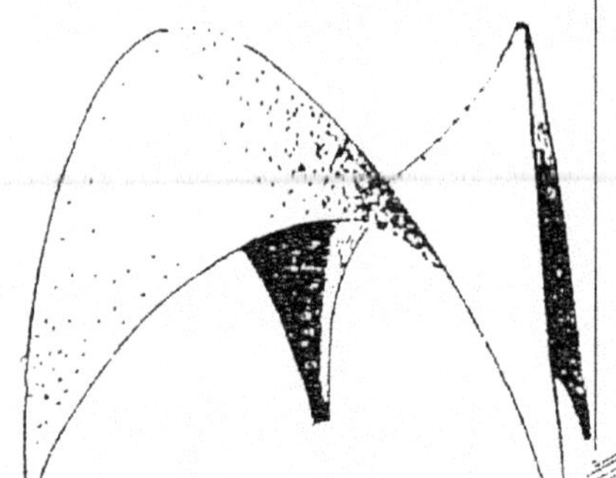

COSMIC RAY RECORDING LAB, UNIVERSITY OF MEXICO, FELIX CANDELA, 1951
HYBERBOLIC PARABOLOID SHELL CONSTRUCTION OF CONCRETE ONLY 5/8" THICK

client

Six astronauts have gone to the moon on an expedition to mine moon rocks. Please design special living quarters for these moon miners.

architectural program

Site requirements

The site is the edge of a crater where a large deposit of pure gold has been "unmooned." Since there is no ozone layer on the moon, you must provide protection from the sun's rays. Since there is very little gravity on the moon, the structure can be placed on the sloping site very easily.

Habitat requirements

An important requirement is that the housing complex must be based on a natural form found on earth. This is to help the moon miners cope with the prolonged periods away from the earth. Any number of natural forms can be employed. The following areas are required:

- Kitchen
- Sleeping bunk areas for 3 men and 3 women
- Living room
- Bathroom
- Exercise area with a sauna
- Laboratory for rock analysis
- Airlock entry for people and a moon vehicle

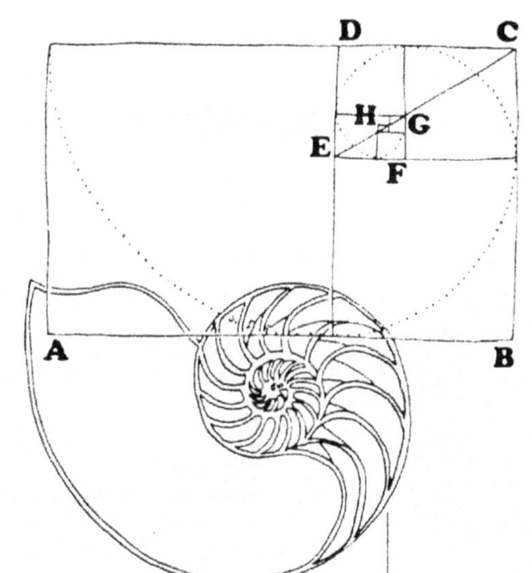

Design procedure

Students should use the design development procedure presented in previous lessons, Plans and Perspectives and Entryways:

1. Schematic drawings:
   - Bubble diagram (they make a "bubble" for each required area listed above)
   - Plan view drawing (see appendix: Drawing a Floor Plan)
   - Elevation drawing
2. Perspective drawing (see appendix: Perspective)
3. Model (see appendix: Model Making)

The scale for the model should be 6" = 1'.

Scale based on Moon Miner

Photocopy Moon Miner on index weight paper or have students trace the figure on cardboard and cut it out.

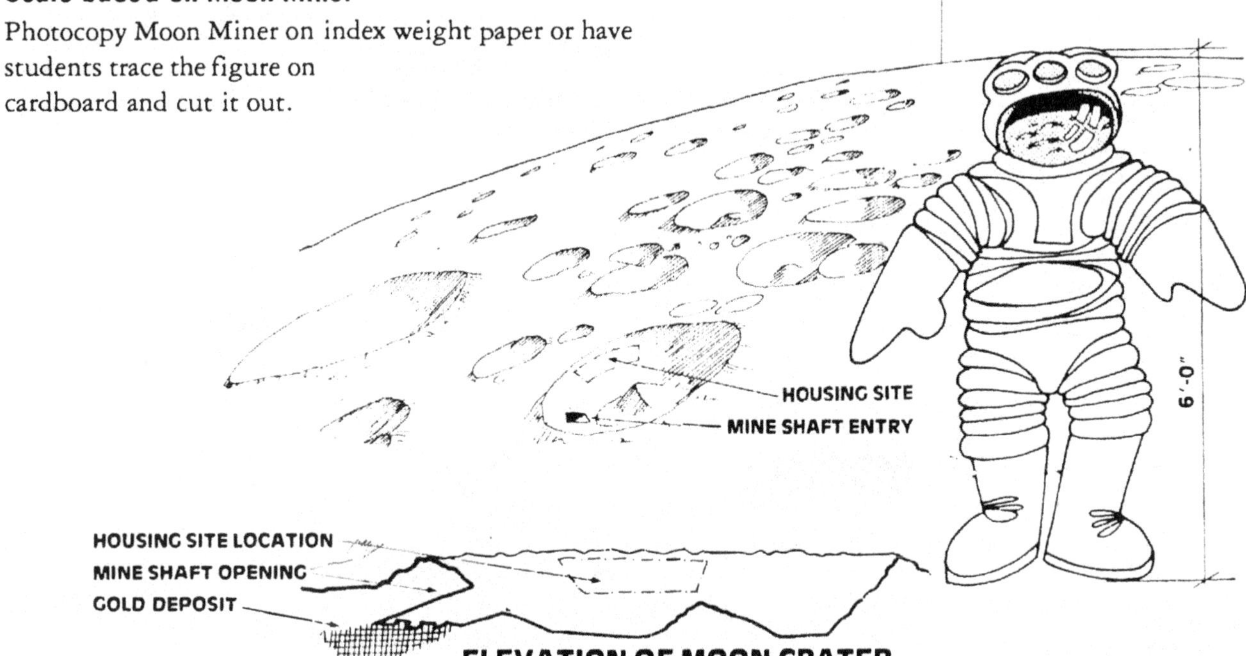

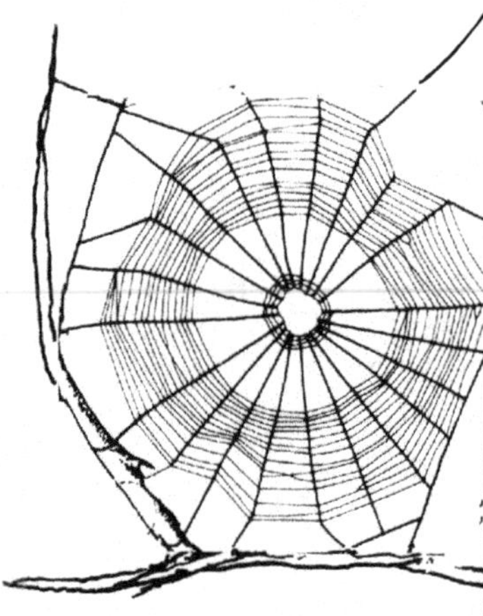

evaluation

Students should present drawings and models to the class and later display their work in a big space so all the projects can be viewed at one time. Review each project. on the basis of the student's success in finding, understanding and using a natural form for the moon housing complex design.

RESOURCES AND BIBLIOGRAPHIES

Appendix:
Historical Structures / Famous Buildings (p. 74)
Visual Vocabulary (p. 77)
Using an Architect's Scale (p. 80)
Drawing a Floor Plan (p. 81)
Understanding the Forces of Structure (p. 89)
Physics of Structure Exercises (p. 94)
Paper Structures for Architectural Models (p. 96)
Paper Patterns for Geometric Forms (p. 97)
Model Building (p. 105)

ICO Crystal Game - Based on an isohedric crystal design, the ICO kit contains four games of increasing complexity, each involving multiple options. Creative Publications Catalog.
Allen, Howard. How Buildings Work: The Natural Order of Architecture. New York: Oxford University Press, 1980.
Doczi and Gyorgy. The Power of Limits: Proportional Harmonies in Nature, Art and Architecture. Boulder: Shambhala, 1981.
Cricone, Lisa and Joseph Cannard. Small Worlds Close Up. New York: Crown Publishers, Inc., 1978.
Forsyth, Adrian. The Architecture of Animals: Equinox Guide to Wildlife Structures. Ontario, Canada: Camden House, 1989.
Goldsworthy, Andy. A Collaboration with Nature. New York: Harry N. Abrams. 1990.
Hildon and Pederson. Build You Own Polyhedra. Menlo Park, CA: Addison-Wesley, 1988.
McCauley, David. Underground. Boston: Houghton, Mifflin, Co., 1973
Morman, Jean Mary. Wonder Under Your Feet. New York: Harper, 1973.
Padwick, Richard and Trevor Walker. Pattern: Its Structure and Geometry. Wates: Ceolfrech Press, 1977.
Stevens, Peter S. Patterns in Nature. Boston: Little Brown and Company, 1974.
Wilson, Forrest. What It Feels Like to Be a Building. Washington, D.C., Preservation Press, 1988.
Zubroski, Bernie. Messing Around With Drinking Straw Construction: A Children's Museum Activity Book, Boston: Little, Brown, & Co., 1981.

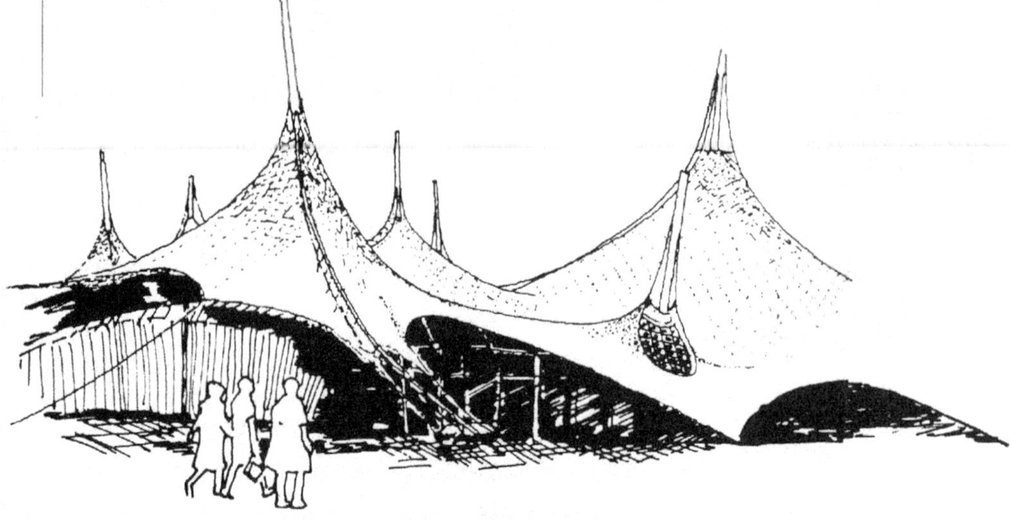

GERMAN PAVILION, MONTREAL EXPO, 1967, FREI OTTO (TENSILE FABRIC STRUCTURE)

FORM IN ARCHITECTURAL HISTORY

GOAL

To encourage observation skills and help students understand that architecture is usually organized around basic geometric shapes and forms they can identify.

ARCHITECTURAL VOCABULARY

Arcade A series of arches on pillars used as the screen and roof support of a covered walkway
Column Vertical beams (posts) used to support a horizontal beam (lintel)
Dome A half-sphere used as a roof
Elevation Two dimensional drawing of the front of a building
Façade The carefully designed front wall of a building; the "face" wall
Portal A doorway or entrance, especially a large, decorated one
Cantilever A form whose load is completely supported at one end
Catenary arch An arch form made by suspending a chain from two points

PRESENTATION

Geometric form drawings

The objective of this activity is to help students analyze how geometric forms are used on buildings. Use examples from Famous Buildings/Historical Structures in the appendix: the Pantheon, Colosseum and Olympic Sports Palace by Nervi in Rome, Italy; the Great Pyramids, Giza, Egypt; a typical wood frame house; a typical early Christian Byzantine chapel; the Morris Store in San Francisco by Frank Lloyd Wright; the Seagram Building in New York by Mies Van der Rohe and Philip Johnson. If you have access to a light table ask students to trace around the major geometric shapes of the building.

Light, shade and shadow drawings:

The objective here is to help the student learn to see and express form and space in buildings using white (of drawing paper), shade (gray marker or chalk) and shadow (black marker). Find images that show buildings from a corner perspective or show a clear shadow and light shading on a wall.
Explain to students that the first quality that our eyes perceive is the value,

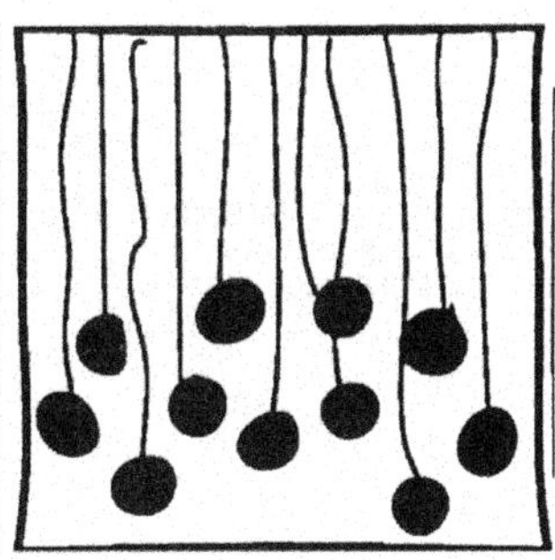

ASSIGNMENT

The students will take a walking tour and will document the architecture of a neighborhood.

MATERIALS

Clipboards
Black Flair pens
Pencils with erasers
Slides of architecture
Projector
Camera (optional)

SKILLS AND CONCEPTS

Math
Art
Language Arts
Vocabulary
Geography
Science
Social Studies
Spatial relationships
Observing
Classifying
Geometric construction
Problem solving
Geometry
Ratio
Scale and proportion
Habitat

SETTING

Classroom
World

KAUFMANN HOUSE, "FALLINGWATER," BEAR RUN, PENNSYLVANIA, FRANK LLOYD WRIGHT, 1937

the relative lightness or darkness of an object. Draw an example of a cube with the sun shining from one side and shade and shadow on the opposite side. Show the light's direction with an arrow. The students should be able to tell which direction the light is coming from in each photo. Ask them to show where they think the light source is. Have them try to shade in the gray and black areas without drawing an outline. It will help them to see the areas of gray and black if they squint their eyes. Have them practice filling in the gray and black areas in a fluid way, omitting details. Allow about three minutes for each drawing.

CHAPEL OF NOTRE DAME DU HAUT, RONCHAMPS FRANCE, LE CORBUSIER, 1954

Language Arts - Write a poem about architectural features

Consider the concepts of "façade" and "arcade." Consult a dictionary for their pronunciation, meaning, and etymologies. Do the words rhyme? Why or why not? Write a poem, using the names of parts of buildings. Here are some additional architectural parts: hip roof, gambrel roof, attic, dormer, turret, dome, cupola, doorway, entrance, portal, casement, mullion, spandrel, balcony, canopy, verandah, porch, portico, column, capitol, pilaster, parapet, gable, brackets, cornice, pediment, quoin, fanlight, shutter, belt course, lintel, shingles, shakes, etc.

Three famous architects

Three of the world's most famous architects experimented with using a combination of simple geometric forms and complex organic forms in their designs.

Le Corbusier was a Swiss-French architect who studied human proportions and the logic of machines. In his early designs, he made extensive use of the "basic box" and concentrated on inventive ways to arrange the interior space. In his later designs, he experimented with sculptural ways to use concrete. His chapel of Notre Dame du Haut at Ronchamps, France is made of concrete shaped in a sculptural way.

Antonio Gaudi was a famous Spanish architect who used many organic rounded forms and shapes in his architecture. He made waves of shimmering color by embedding tiles, cups, bowls and bottles into his walls. He used catenary arches, the same type of arches found in suspension bridges. When he designed the Church of La Sagrada Familia, he created an upside down model made of heavy strings suspended from the ceiling to get the catenary arch forms he desired. Invite students to form catenary arches by suspending heavy string or keychain from two points. Ask them what distinguishes a catenary arch from a rounded arch.

CHURCH OF LA SAGRADA FAMILIA, BARCELONA, SPAIN, ANTONIO GAUDI, (UNDER CONSTRUCTION SINCE 1883)

Frank Lloyd Wright, an American architect got ideas for his architecture by studying nature— the rocks, hills, trees and plants— and the view— that existed on the building site. He called his architecture "organic architecture." His house design, called "Fallingwater" has concrete terraces that appear to float over a waterfall. These are supported on one end in the bedrock behind the house. The terraaces are like the rocks around the house in form and color.

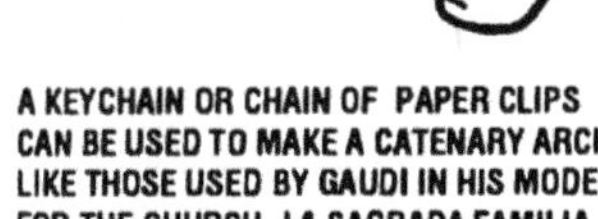

A KEYCHAIN OR CHAIN OF PAPER CLIPS CAN BE USED TO MAKE A CATENARY ARCH LIKE THOSE USED BY GAUDI IN HIS MODEL FOR THE CHURCH, LA SAGRADA FAMILIA

client

The local historical society believes that it is very important to document the architecture of your school neighborhood so that people in the future will know how this area looked in the 20th century. They have asked for your help. Since there is so much construction and change occurring now, it could be that people in the future will forget what this area looked like. You will need to record the shape of the buildings and their details–dormers, turrets, domes, entrances, windows; facades; arcades; balconies; columns.

architectural program

A walking tour

Younger children can learn to identify geometric forms in architecture. Pick a locale with examples of architecture with a variety of geometric forms. Preview the trip before you take the children to find key places where the group can stop and observe vistas of several buildings at once. You can help the students prepare for the tour by making homemade "clip boards" consisting of paper stapled to a scrap of matboard. Photocopy the Geometric Shape and Form Chart from the poster. As you walk along, ask the students to search for and sketch structures which use geometric forms. Show them how the elements of architecture can be distilled to their geometric essence - the cone, triangle, pyramid, square, cube, circle, semi-circle, cylinder, dome. If the students have enough confidence, they should use felt tip pens for these sketches.

EXAMPLE OF A SCAVENGER HUNT

Variations on a walking tour

Older elementary students may enjoy a scavenger hunt. In a preview trip, using the Visual Survey Form, you should find a series of interesting features for your students to seek out.Working in teams, for safety, have students hunt for features which you found on your preview trip.

The Visual Survey Form

The Visual Survey Form is a useful tool for older students to observe and record details of architecture. They should use one form to document each building in a selected neighborhood. They may also photograph buildings. In this way they will actually produce a record of the neighborhood as it looks now.

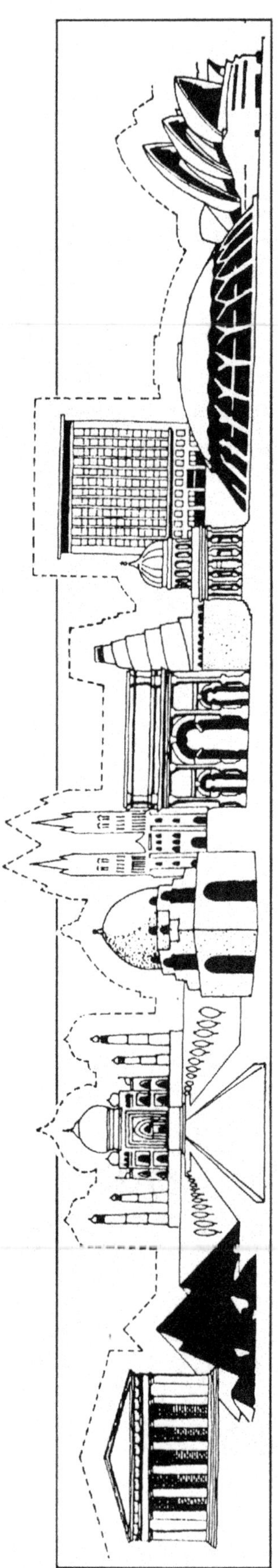

Rural area walking tour substitutes:

1. Tour the school, looking for internal and external geometric shapes and forms.
2. Take a field trip to a nearby city for a walking tour.
3. Collect magazine pictures and construct a collage of buildings for analysis.
4. Copy appendix Famous Buildings pages and have children analyze them.
5. Give students geometric shapes and have them work independently to locate buildings which reflect those shapes.

evaluation

Display all the drawings and/or photographs made by the students. Have them tell you how geometric shapes and forms and other architectural features they became aware of were used to create the shape of the neighborhood. Encourage students to tell (1)what they preferred, (2) what they did not like and (3) articulate the reason. Evaluate the drawings and photographs for their value as a historical record of the neighborhood that was studied.

RESOURCES AND BIBLIOGRAPHY

Appendix:
Historical Structures / Famous Buildings (p. 74)
Visual Notetaking (p. 104)
Visual Powerpoint Presentation (p. 109)
How to Develop a Walking Tour (p. 107)
Visual Survey Form (p. 119)

Allied Arts of Seattle. Lydia S. Aldredge, ed. Impressions of Imagination: Terra Cotta Seattle, 1986.

Andrews, J.J.C. The Well-Built Elephant and Other Roadside Attractions. New York: Congson & Weed, Inc., 1984.

D'Alelio, Jane. I Know That Building! Washington, D.C. : The Preservation Press, 1989.

Denison, Allen and Huntington, Wallace. Victorian Architecture of Port Townsend, Washington. Hancock House Pub. Inc., Seattle, 1978.

Hernandez, Xavier and Pilar Comes. Barmi: A Mediterranean City Throught the Ages. Boston: Houghton Mifflin, 1990.

Isaacson, Philip. Round Buildings, Square Buildings and Buildings That Wiggle Like a Fish. New York: Knopf Books, 1988.

Kostof, Spiro. American By Design. New York: Oxford University Press 1987.

Maddux, Diane, Ed. Master Builders: A Guide To Famous American Architects. The Preservation Press, 1985.

McAlester and McAlester. A Field Guide to American Houses. New York: Alfred A. Knopf, 1984.

Macaulay, David. Great Moments in American Architecture. Boston: Houghton Mifflin Co., 1978.

Macaulay, David. Pyramid. Houghton Mifflin Co., 1975.

Pevsner, Fleming and Honour. A Dictionary of American Architecture. Woodstock, New York: The Overlook Press, 1976.

Pomada and Larsen. Daughters of Painted Ladies: America's Resplendent Ladies. New York: E.P. Dutton, 1987.

Poppeliers, Chambers and Schwartz. What Style Is It? A Guide to American Architecture. The Preservation Press, 1983.

Salvadori, Mario. The Art of Construction. Chicago: Chicago Press Review, 1990.

Young, Caroline and Colin King. Castles, Pyramids and Palaces. London: Osborne Publishing, Ltd., 1989.

BRIDGES

GOAL

To familiarize students with types and principles of bridge construction.

ARCHITECTURAL VOCABULARY

Arch A curved structure built so that the stones or other component parts support each other by mutual pressure

Cantilever A form whose load is completely supported at one end

Catenary arch A type of arch shaped like the "pointed" end of an egg; inverted arch formed by suspended cables of a suspension bridge

Keystone A wedge-shaped block which forms the top part of an arch and "locks" the other stones in the arch

Post and beam (also called *post and lintel*) Construction which uses vertical posts supporting a horizontal beam to carry a load over a space

Spandrels Spaces between a series of arches with a straight beam above

Suspension Structural system in which cables hanging from towers carry a beam

Truss Apparatus of parts fastened together to support a beam

Voussoirs Wedge shaped stones or bricks of an arch

Girders The main beams to support a bridge

PRESENTATION

Introduce students to the following types of bridges and the principles they use.

Natural bridges

A fallen tree provided a way to span a stream. A rock fall allowed people to cross a stream, and later the water eroded some rocks away forming a simple arch over the stream. In areas warm enough to grow large vines, a natural cable bridge was formed by intertwining vines to form suspension chains on which people could move across gorges or rivers. Thus the beam bridge, the arch bridge, and the suspension bridge all evolved from people observing the three basic natural bridges found in nature.

Arch bridges

The first arch bridges were made of wedge shaped cut stones (*voussoirs*) or bricks set side by side on temporary timber supports until the top piece (keystone) was in place. An arch is supported by compression. The weight of the bridge and the things that move across it are pressing down along the curve of the arch to the foundation and then to the ground.

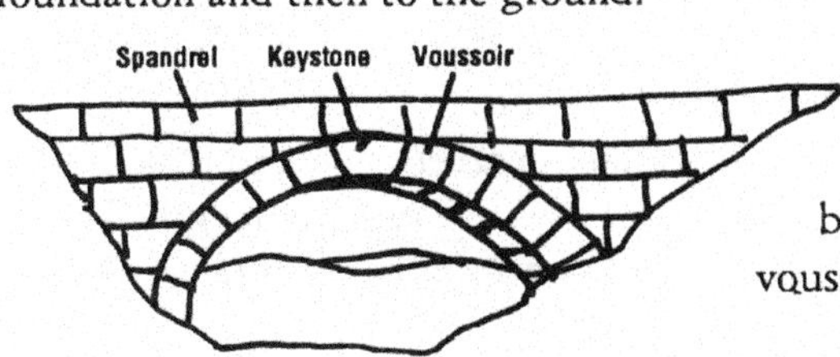

Roman stone bridge This is a typical Roman stone bridge showing basic arch bridge components: spandrels, voussoirs, and keystone.

ASSIGNMENT

Each student will (1) learn to identify types of bridges (2) write an environmental impact statement, and (3) design, draw, and build a model of a bridge.

MATERIALS

Newspaper
Scissors
Glue
Toothpicks
Cardboards
String
Masking tape
Model building materials

SKILLS AND CONCEPTS

Math
Physics
Social Studies
Earth Science
Art
Measurement
Scale
Schematic drawing
Mapping
Problem solving
Mechanical systems
Gathering data
Environmental impact
Balance
Aesthetics

SETTING

Classroom
Home

ARCH BRIDGES

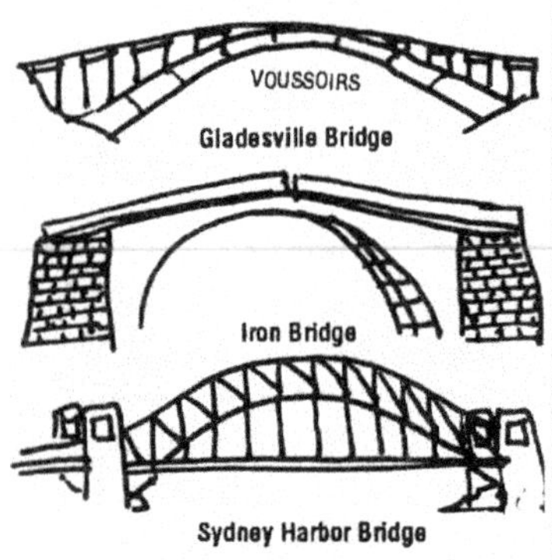

Gladesville Bridge This arch bridge in Sydney, Australia is made of reinforced concrete with hollow concrete *voussoirs* and a hollow box section arch that spans 1000 feet.

Iron Bridge Near Coalbrookdale, England, this bridge opened in 1779. The first cast-iron bridge with 5 iron rib arches spans 70 feet across and is still standing today.

Sydney Harbor Bridge This is an example of a steel arch bridge in Sydney, Australia which spans 1650 feet.

BEAM BRIDGES

Beam bridges

Beam bridges are slabs or beams supported by piers. The weight or load on the beams is transferred to the pier and the pier transfers the load to the ground. Most concrete freeway overpasses are beam bridges.

Post bridge

Post bridge This clapper type bridge, found in England, is made of stone formed into slabs and piers.

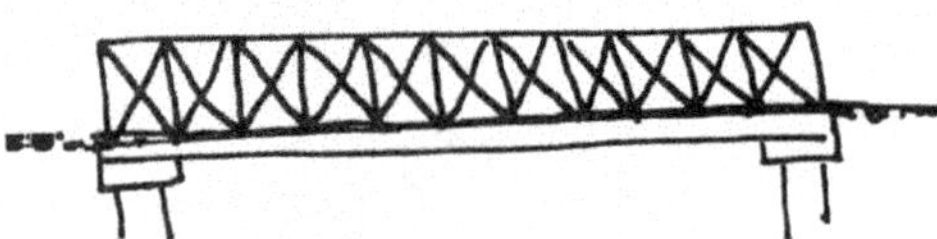

Howe Truss Bridge

Howe truss bridge Originally, the vertical members were wrought-iron rods. This design influenced railroad bridges in America throughout the 18th and 19th century.

Britannica Tubular Bridge

Britannica Tubular Bridge Opened in 1850, this bridge spans from pier to pier with rectangular tube sections through which the trains passed. It is a wrought-iron beam structure.

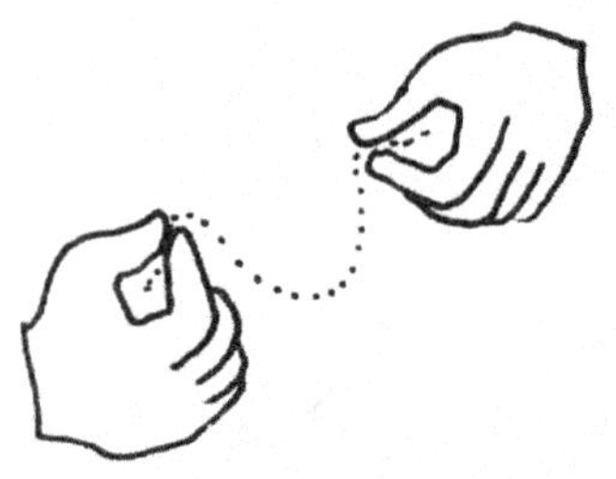

CATENARY CURVE
A chain or cable suspended from two points will form a catenary curve, which acts like an inverted arch. Suspension bridges use this inverted arch for support.

Suspension bridges

A continuous cable supports the deck by means of metal suspenders. This is very lightweight bridge construction. The cable members hold up the roadway through tension. The roadway is usually a truss that keeps the deck stiff so the traffic load is spread out over the whole bridge structure. Suspension bridges have four basic parts: towers, cables, suspenders and anchorages.

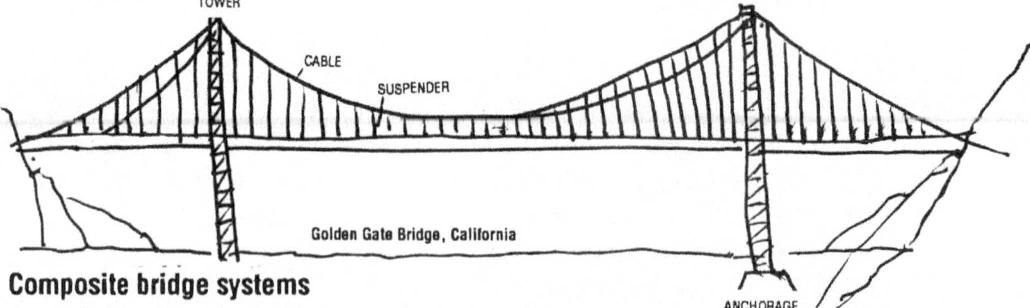

Golden Gate Bridge, California

Composite bridge systems

Some bridges use a combination of structural systems.

Maracaibo Bridge The Maracaibo Bridge near Zulia, Venezuela, opened in 1963. It is made of prestressed concrete and stretchers over five miles in length. The structure combined V and H trestle piers for the main spans and tied cantilever beams.

BRIDGES

GOAL

To familiarize students with types and principles of bridge construction.

ARCHITECTURAL VOCABULARY

Arch A curved structure built so that the stones or other component parts support each other by mutual pressure

Cantilever A form whose load is completely supported at one end

Catenary arch A type of arch shaped like the "pointed" end of an egg; inverted arch formed by suspended cables of a suspension bridge

Keystone A wedge-shaped block which forms the top part of an arch and "locks" the other stones in the arch

Post and beam (also called *post and lintel*) Construction which uses vertical posts supporting a horizontal beam to carry a load over a space

Spandrels Spaces between a series of arches with a straight beam above

Suspension Structural system in which cables hanging from towers carry a beam

Truss Apparatus of parts fastened together to support a beam

Voussoirs Wedge shaped stones or bricks of an arch

Girders The main beams to support a bridge

PRESENTATION

Introduce students to the following types of bridges and the principles they use.

Natural bridges

A fallen tree provided a way to span a stream. A rock fall allowed people to cross a stream, and later the water eroded some rocks away forming a simple arch over the stream. In areas warm enough to grow large vines, a natural cable bridge was formed by intertwining vines to form suspension chains on which people could move across gorges or rivers. Thus the beam bridge, the arch bridge, and the suspension bridge all evolved from people observing the three basic natural bridges found in nature.

Arch bridges

The first arch bridges were made of wedge shaped cut stones (*voussoirs*) or bricks set side by side on temporary timber supports until the top piece (keystone) was in place. An arch is supported by compression. The weight of the bridge and the things that move across it are pressing down along the curve of the arch to the foundation and then to the ground.

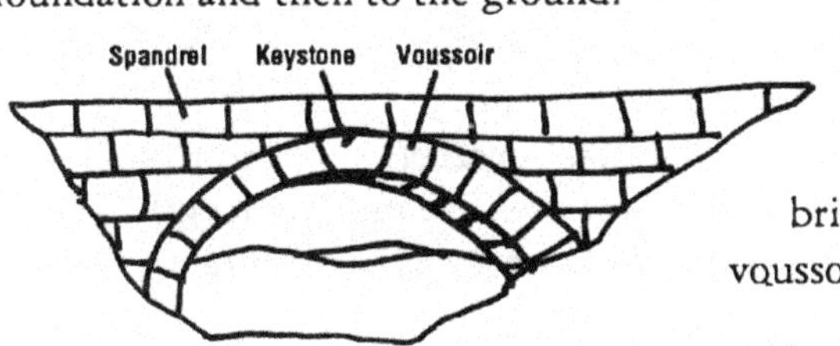

Roman bridge

Roman stone bridge This is a typical Roman stone bridge showing basic arch bridge components: spandrels, voussoirs, and keystone.

ASSIGNMENT

Each student will (1) learn to identify types of bridges (2) write an environmental impact statement, and (3) design, draw, and build a model of a bridge.

MATERIALS

Newspaper
Scissors
Glue
Toothpicks
Cardboards
String
Masking tape
Model building materials

SKILLS AND CONCEPTS

Math
Physics
Social Studies
Earth Science
Art
Measurement
Scale
Schematic drawing
Mapping
Problem solving
Mechanical systems
Gathering data
Environmental impact
Balance
Aesthetics

SETTING

Classroom
Home

ARCH BRIDGES

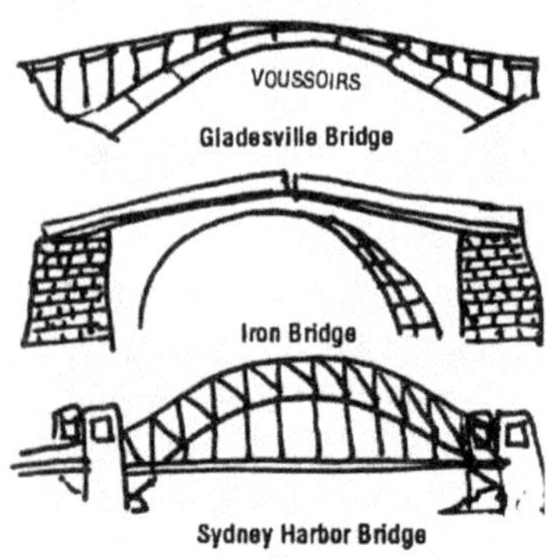

Gladesville Bridge This arch bridge in Sydney, Australia is made of reinforced concrete with hollow concrete *voussoirs* and a hollow box section arch that spans 1000 feet.

Iron Bridge Near Coalbrookdale, England, this bridge opened in 1779. The first cast-iron bridge with 5 iron rib arches spans 70 feet across and is still standing today.

Sydney Harbor Bridge This is an example of a steel arch bridge in Sydney, Australia which spans 1650 feet.

BEAM BRIDGES

Beam bridges

Beam bridges are slabs or beams supported by piers. The weight or load on the beams is transferred to the pier and the pier transfers the load to the ground. Most concrete freeway overpasses are beam bridges.

Post bridge

Post bridge This clapper type bridge, found in England, is made of stone formed into slabs and piers.

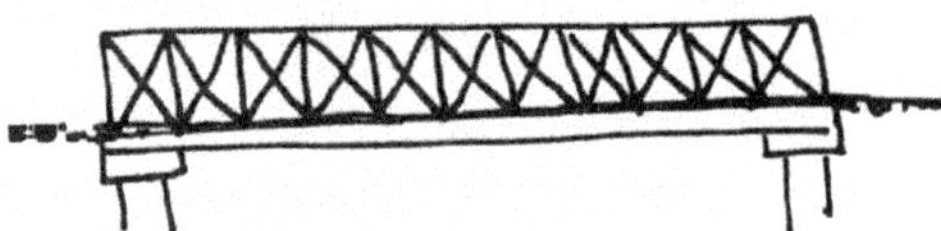

Howe Truss Bridge

Howe truss bridge Originally, the vertical members were wrought-iron rods. This design influenced railroad bridges in America throughout the 18th and 19th century.

Britannica Tubular Bridge

Britannica Tubular Bridge Opened in 1850, this bridge spans from pier to pier with rectangular tube sections through which the trains passed. It is a wrought-iron beam structure.

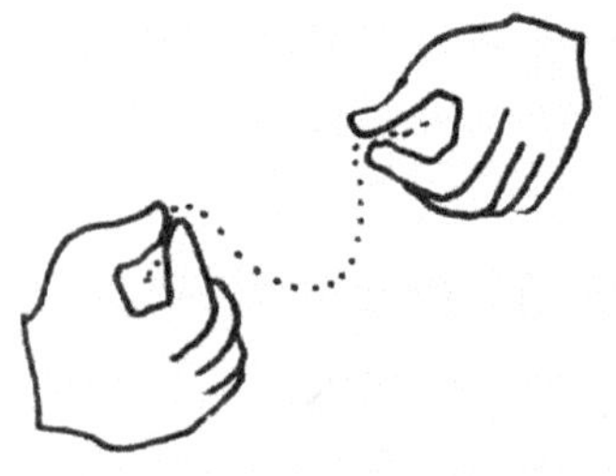

CATENARY CURVE
A chain or cable suspended from two points will form a catenary curve, which acts like an inverted arch. Suspension bridges use this inverted arch for support.

Suspension bridges

A continuous cable supports the deck by means of metal suspenders. This is very lightweight bridge construction. The cable members hold up the roadway through tension. The roadway is usually a truss that keeps the deck stiff so the traffic load is spread out over the whole bridge structure. Suspension bridges have four basic parts: towers, cables, suspenders and anchorages.

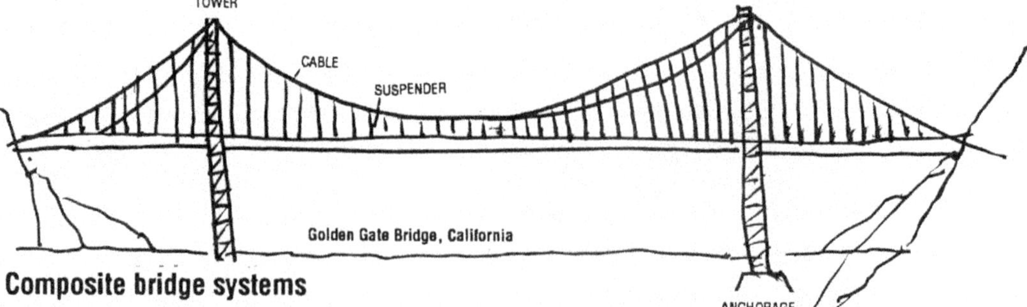

Golden Gate Bridge, California

Composite bridge systems

Some bridges use a combination of structural systems.

Maracaibo Bridge The Maracaibo Bridge near Zulia, Venezuela, opened in 1963. It is made of prestressed concrete and stretchers over five miles in length. The structure combined V and H trestle piers for the main spans and tied cantilever beams.

The Fourth Railway Bridge This bridge in Scotland was constructed in 1890 of steel and is a combination of girders and cantilever truss structural systems.

Understanding bridges through other parts of our enviornment

Many things we do every day and things we see in our environment also act like bridges. Give students copies of the appendix pages, Understanding the Forces of Structure. Then give them examples below and ask them for words that interpret the forces that are illustrated: COMPRESSION (chewing), TENSION (carrying suitcases), A SIMPLE BEAM (pushups), A CANTILEVER BEAM (tree branch). Some other examples to interpret are horse-drawn ploughing, pushing a baby stroller, carrying books, carrying groceries, a balance beam, a gangplank, a draw-bridge, a diving board, and an extended arm.

client

A bicycle club has successfully raised enough money to build a jogging and bike path. A part of the path must cross a small but very deep canyon. The club has commissioned you to design a "people's" bridge across the canyon. This bridge should be as beautiful as the landscape that surrounds it and should appear to gracefully cross the canyon.

architectural program

Site analysis

Each student should draw a map to show where his or her bridge will be built. They should list the characteristics of the site. (Is it flat land? Is it rocky? Etc.) Older students should draw a contour map using the lesson. Appendix Contour Map Exercise on page 103.

SITE PLAN

Environmental impact statement

Challenge the students: Do you want to preserve trees and wildlife? If so, how will you do it? Have the students write and environmental impact statement. Here are some sample quesions to get them started:

- Are there animals or birds living in the canyon? What type?
- What type of habitat do they need? What are their food sources?
- Is there a streambed in the canyon? What steps should be taken to protect it?
- What plants naturally occur in the canyon? Do they prevent erosion?
- What types of rocks or soil are at the site? Is there evidence of landslides? Is there evidence of flooding?

TRUSSES CAN BE MADE BY JOINING POPSICLE STICKS WITH BRADS

A "STONE" ARCH CAN BE MADE WITH STONES CUT FROM A SEMI CIRCLE OF FLORIST'S STYROFOAM

A CHAIN OF PAPER CLIPS CAN BE USED TO FORM A SUSPENSION BRIDGE'S CATENARY ARCH

Schematic drawings

Each student should draw a site plan and an elevation drawing of his/her bridge.

Model

Using clay, toothpicks, wood blocks, sugar cubes, cardboard strips, drinking straws with paper clips and/or other materials, have each student build a model of his/her bridge. The recommended size is at least 18" long and at least 12" high.

evaluation

Display all bridge drawings and models and have the students present their designs to the class. Ask them to discuss their solutions to the design problem. In addition, have each student describe the environmental impact of his or her proposed bridge.

RESOURCES AND BIBLIOGRAPHY

Appendix:

People (p. 84)
Paper Structures for Architectural Models (p. 96)
Paper Patterns for Geometric Forms (p. 97)
Understanding the Forces of Structure (p. 87)
Physics of Structure Exercises (p. 94)
Model Making (p. 105)
Contour Map Exercise (p. 103)

Croad, Stephen. London's Bridges. Royal Commission, 1983.

Corbett, Scott. Bridges. New York: Four Winds Press, 1978.

Goldwater, Daniel. Bridges and How They Are Built. New York: Young Scott Books, 1965.

Leonhardt, Fritz. Brucken: Bridges. Cambridge, MA: The MIT Press, 1984.

McGregor, Anne and Scott. Bridges: A Project Book. New York. Lothrop, Lee and Shepard Books, 1980.

Silverberg, Robert. Bridges. Philadelphia: MacRae Smith Co., 1966.

Whitney, Charles S. Bridges: Their Art, Science, and Evolution. New York: Greenwich House, 1983.

Wilson, Forrest. What It Feels Like to Be A Building. Washington D.C.: Preservation Press, 1988.

Zubrowski, Bernie. Messing Around With Drinking Straw Construction. Boston: Little, Brown and Company, 1981.

SUPER WALL GRAPHICS

GOAL

To give students the technical knowledge that will enable them to design and paint a large scale design on a wall of their school.

ARCHITECTURAL VOCABULARY

Proportion The relation of one size to another
Scale Numeric scheme for sizing a design
Enlarge Increase in size to reproduce in a larger scale
Color In this context, coloring matter or pigment
Supergraphic A large design applied to a wall
Design A pre-planned outline, symbol or pictorial representation
Representation Drawing or painting that accurately records what we see
Abstraction Drawing or painting that simplifies the way we represent what we see or represents our attitudes or emotions about what we see
Symbolism Designing that substitutes another image for what we actually see
Grid pattern logic Regular parallel vertical and horizontal lines are used as reference points for a design; by enlarging grid, the design can be easily enlarged
Transfer of images Moving a linear composition from one surface to another
Figure/ground relationship Perception of positive form and negative space, such as black letters on white paper
Part to whole perception Perception of the relationship of a fragment of a figure to the whole figure

PRESENTATION

Show students examples of graphic or sculptural ornamentation and painting techniques. Try a walking tour that looks at supergraphics, a visit to an art museum, a slide presentation, a visit with a stage set painter, a visit to a billboard company, a muralist, stained glass artist, relief sculptor; or have students find examples in books or magazines in the art and architecture section of the public library.

client

Your school principal has commissioned you to design and paint a supergraphic for your school, which will represent your community. It can include symbols that represent the geographic and cultural heritage of your school. The supergraphic can be placed on a flat wall, around a corner, or around a doorway.

architectural program

Class participation in the design process

In a class brainstorming session, the students should present their ideas for symbols which might be used to represent their community. The class should select the symbols that they prefer, then work on individual design ideas for the project. The class's preferred symbols should guide but not limit the individual designs.

ASSIGNMENT

Students will create a super wall graphic for the school.

MATERIALS

For designing the graphic you may need: 45° triangle, T-square, shape templates, a scale, large and small felt tip markers, acetate (for overhead projector), white drawing paper 16"x18", large roll of white butcher paper, scissors, scotch tape, tracing paper.

For painting the graphic you will need: Colored water-based paints, paint, brushes, 1" (2.5 cm), 4" (10 cm), a variety of small brushes, drop cloth, spackling compound, pet food cans, sponges, coffee cans, chalkline
Flexible or French curve (optional)
Parallel rule (optional)
Slide, overhead or opaque projector

SKILLS AND CONCEPTS

Math
Art
Grid system
Spatial relationships
Ratio, scale proportion
Measuring
Problem solving

SETTING

School

Students should each prepare a carefully colored design. Using an overhead or opaque projector, project each design on the wall in the selected location. After all the proposals have been presented, the class should select three or four designs to present to the principal of the school.

Surface preparation

Be sure that the wall that will receive the graphic is clean and patched and that you select paints that will adhere to the paint that is already on the wall. Assemble the appropriate materials and equipment. Paint a fresh background.

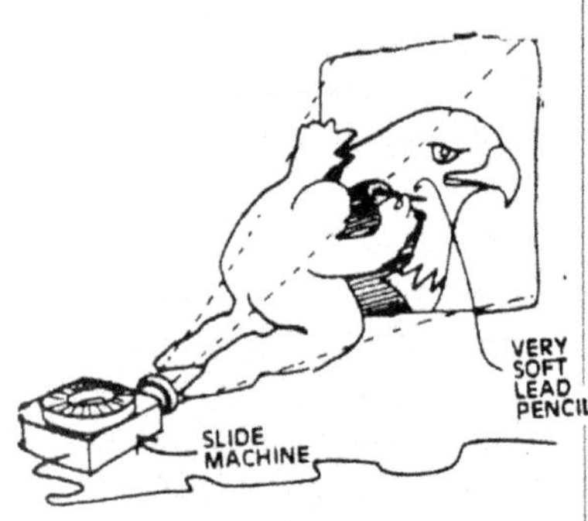

Projecting a design on the wall

Slide projection Using a camera (loaded with slide film) on a copy stand, make a 35mm slide of the design chosen by the class. Project the slide directly on the wall. Have the students trace around the projected image with a soft pencil.

Overhead projector Make a color or black and white photocopy of the design on acetate. Using an overhead projector, project this image on the wall where you want to trace the design. Move the projector forward or backward to reduce or enlarge the image. This is an especially useful way to put words and letters on a wall. Students trace around the projected image with a soft pencil.

Opaque projector Using an opaque projector, project an image on the wall and have students trace around it with a soft pencil.

Using a grid pattern enlargement system

With your students, determine a scale to use to enlarge the selected design. Once the scale is determined, draw a grid on tracing paper or acetate. Superimpose the grid over the artwork and trace the artwork and trace the outline of the design on the grid with a clear, simple contour line. For better visibility, the design and the grid may be taped to a portable light table or a window to backlight the design.

If you plan to use the grid pattern enlargement system, pay careful attention to the points where the traced line of the design crosses the grid lines. It is these intersection points that locate the points necessary to accurately enlarge the design when it is being transfered to the wall.

Once the design is traced on the grid, lay out an enlarged scale grid on the wall that will be receiving the supergraphic. Mark points 12" apart along the top and bottom and side edges of the supergraphic area. Lay out the lines of the grid.

Grid pattern enlargement: A Humpback whale graphic, Eagle River Elementary School, Eagle River, Alaska. Hall graphics can communicate such things as the real size of things like this whale designed and painted to actual scale (1'0"= 1'0").

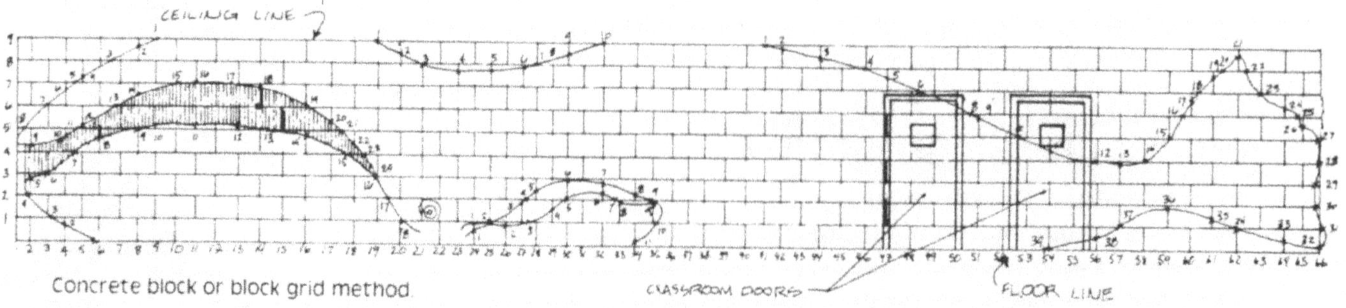

Concrete block or block grid method

Straight lines can be laid on the wall with a contractor's chalk snap line. This will create a washable grid covering the wall with one foot squares. Number the lines on the pattern. Transfer the intersection points traced on the 1/4" grid to their corresponding positions on the wall grid. Draw the enlarged graphic designed by connecting the intersecting points on the large grid with a soft lead pencil.

Concrete block or brick grid method

Many school hallways have bricks or concrete blocks which form their own grid. If this is the case, set up the grid pattern corresponding to the blocks or bricks laid in the wall and make it work for you as in the preceding method. Mark each point where the graphic line intersects with a wall block.

Other pattern making ideas

Trace human forms in various positions. Cut out. Tape to the wall, trace image, remove paper. Use a pencil or chalk to trace graphics on the walls.

Make a composite of of children's drawings. Have the children make large drawings. Paint a background color on the wall. Cut out the drawings and trace around the edges to transfer the drawings to the wall. Arrange them into a composite design and have the children paint them.

Drawing hints

To draw a straight line for a short distance, use either a straight piece of wood or a yardstick. To draw large circles, use either a chalkboard compass or a length of string looped around a pencil.

To make a straight line between two points which are far apart, stretch the string of a contractor's chalk line-marker between two marked points. Have someone pull the string away from the wall and snap it against the wall, leaving a line of chalk dust.

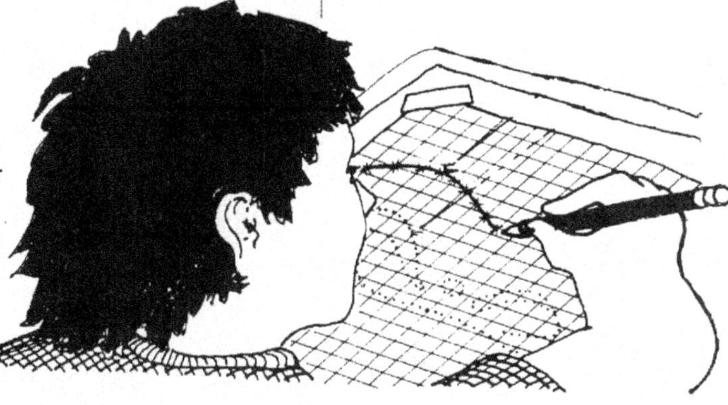

Painting techniques

There are several ways to paint graphics. The overall design can be broken up into small parts, to be painted in sections. In this way "part-to-whole" and other visual relationship skills can be taught along with basic painting techniques. Have students make preliminary studies on paper with colored pens and then look at them from a distance to see how the larger design will appear.

Freehand edge To paint a freehand edge, grasp the brush as you do when you hold a pencil. Dip the brush into the paint and wipe off the excess. Set the brush on the surface, apply slight pressure and move the brush smoothly along the surface. Relax. The paint will form a bead that can be controlled, leaving a crisp, even edge of paint. Look a little beyond the line you are painting so you can push the paint up to the line as the brush is moving.

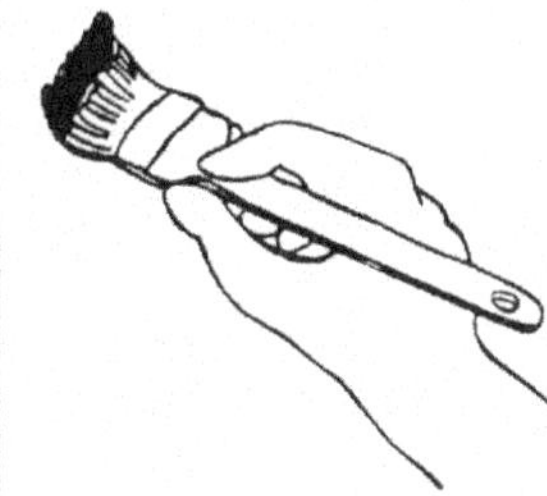

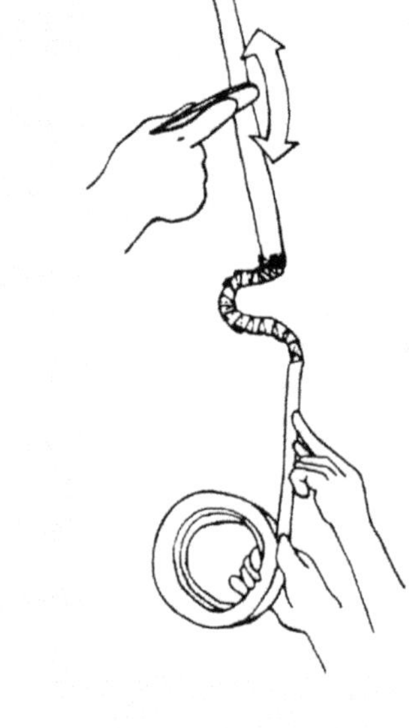

Painting straight and curved lines Clean, crisp lines are easier for inexperienced painters to achieve when they mask the edges of the area that they will be painting. Apply masking tape along marked lines to mask the edges. To mask a curved line, use a continuous piece of masking tape that is still connected to the roll. As you unroll the tape, fold it in small tucks to follow the curved line on the wall. After it is laid along the curve, have an adult cut a smooth curve along the tucked edges with a sharp utility knife. Press down the edge of the tape with a popsicle stick to seal it to the wall so that paint will not seep under it. Remove the tape within two or three days or it will leave a gum residue.

Flat single color application In some cases, the graphic images look best applied as a flat color. This method will result in a two-dimensional appearance. It is a good method to use for letters and signs.

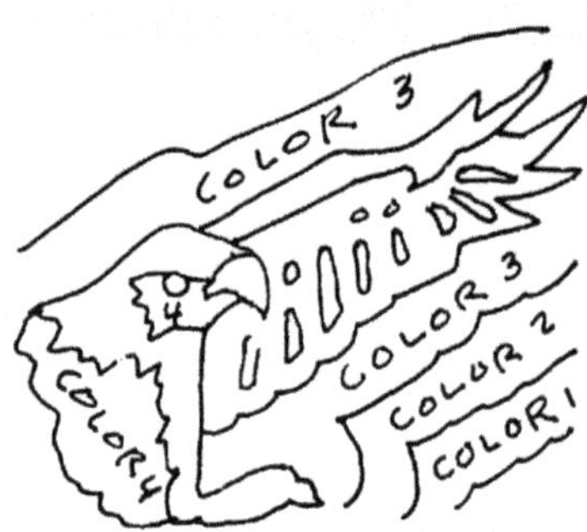

Polarization With this technique, many people can paint at one time. Instead of blending, the colors are divided into little shapes as in a paint-by-number painting. Breaking up of the color gives the composition dramatic characteristics with flat single color application. Give each color a number. Then place corresponding numbers in areas of the traced pattern that will become the supergraphic. Paint the areas numbered with the corresponding colors.

evaluation

Students should gather around the completed wall graphic and express what they learned through this large project. They should assess teamwork, design process, techniques of production and how they used principles of design. They should tell what they think worked well and how they think some parts of the process could be improved.

Related activities

•Have students enlarge or reduce their originals to a uniform scale to create a mosaic mural. Each reproduces a section of the grid.
•Experiment with different shading techniques used by architects. Using a selected part of a supergraphic reproduced on paper, have the students shade each object with a different type of shading technique— stipple, smudge, sketch, parallel line, line contrast, transparent color overlays.

RESOURCES AND BIBLIOGRAPHY

Appendix:
Hand Lettering (p. 79)
People (p. 84)
Perspective (p. 83)
Color Wheel (p. 85)
Visual Notetaking (p. 104)

Ching, Frank. Architectural Graphics. New York: Van Nostrand Reinhold, 1985.
Crowe, Norman and Paul Laseau. Visual Notes for Architects and Designers. New York: Van Nostrand Reinhold, 1984.
Laseau, Paul. Graphic Thinking for Architects and Designers. New York: Van Nostrand Reinhold, 1980.

PREFERENCES

GOAL

To help students evaluate the ambiance of certain environments, understand reasons for their preferences and to apply knowledge in designing a classroom as a studio.

ARCHITECTURAL CONCEPTS AND VOCABULARY

Aesthetics The philosophical principles of art and design
Ambiance The mood, character, quality, or atmosphere of a place, an environment, or surrounding
Bubble diagram Circles or "bubbles" which represent spaces and relationships
Elevation The front view of an object such as a house front
Model A miniature, built copy of something
Plan view A diagram of a site or building as seen from above
Scale Proportion of a plan or model in relation to the actual size of the object
Spatial relationship Relation of objects, people or spaces to one another

PRESENTATION

My favorite place— a creative visualization

In order to create a new design, it helps to forget the way things are and open up one's imagination to all the possibilities it can invent. This creative visualization exercise will help stimulate creative, imaginative suggestions that could be integrated into the design of the classroom of the future.

Clear a large area in the room–enough space for the whole class to lie down on the floor. Students should have near them some large paper and a set of colored large felt tip markers. Have the students lie down on the floor with their eyes closed. If you can find a tape of ocean wave sounds, play it while reading the following very quietly:

"Close your eyes and relax your head. Make your neck loose. Now make your arms go limp like a doll. Now relax your trunk, relax your feet. Take some deep breaths and listen to the sounds of this room. Try to imagine yourself walking along a beach. The sun is warm on your body. The sand feels warm to your feet. The waves are crashing in on the shoreline. A sea gull cries. You are alone. You are the only person on the beach. You begin a walk and you walk along this beautiful beach. Listen to the waves crashing." (Pause) "All at once you see a dot on the horizon. You can't make out what it is. You keep walking. Soon you realize that the figure coming down the beach is you yourself. Yourself takes hold of your hand and crosses over a sand dune through time and space to the special place that you would like to be. Try to see this place in your mind;

ASSIGNMENT

Students will design and build a model of a new classroom.

MATERIALS

Large drawing paper
Colored marker sets
Model building materials
Cardboard
Scissors
Glue
Masking tape
Construction paper

SKILLS AND CONCEPTS

Math
Science
Art
Social Studies
Dimensional analysis
Spatial relationships
Geometric construction
Scale, ratio, proportion
Experimentation
Evaluation
Communication
Geometry
Problem solving
Cause, effect
Socialization
Space
Harmony
Aesthetics

SETTING

Classroom

imagine the colors and textures and smells. Think about it for a minute and put yourself in this place. Now quietly begin to draw this place. Spend as much time as you need to draw a complete picture, showing all the objects and all the colors. Is your place outdoors or indoors? What does the sky or ceiling look like? Are there trees? Is there furniture? Is there water? Sunshine, light? What is on the ground? What is on the floor?"

Class discussion

Display all the students' drawings and have them break up into groups of four to talk about their special places. Have each group pick features of their special places which could be incorporated into a classroom of the future.

client

A classroom teacher is the client. She wants the students in your school to help her create the ideal classroom. She wants to know the students' likes and dislikes concerning their present classroom and wants them to design a new classroom using their best ideas. She wants the classroom of the future to be very different from the classroom of today. She believes students learn best when the classroom offers lots of hands-on materials and experiences and a studio workshop atmosphere.

architectural program

This is an involved design project that will last through several classroom periods.

Analysis of the classroom as it it now

Floor plan Have the students measure and draw a plan view of the classroom and its furniture as it is now, using a scale of 1/4"=1'0".

Tally likes and dislikes Make a list of features of the classroom such as furniture, lights, windows, floor covering, and so on. Have each student copy the list on a sheet of lined paper folded into four columns. Have them write features on the left, "do like" and "don't like" in the next two columns and "tally" in the right column. Write the sum of "likes" for each feature in the "do like" column, the sum of "don't likes" in the "don't like" column. Subtract the "don't like" sum from the "do like" sum for to give each item a score. Record the score in the "tally" column. Then rank the features from the most liked to the most disliked according to the scores.

Requirements of the new classroom

The new classroom should be designed in such a way that many activities can harmoniously go on at once. The students and teacher do not have to have their own desks, and furniture can be organized in different ways to change the way or increase the ways the classroom can be used. They should all have individual cubby holes in which to store their papers and books, and portable toolboxes with handles in which to carry school supplies and other tools.

Ideas from the students The class as a group should make a list of teaching/learning areas which they would like to see in their classroom. Some zones might include the following:

- Entryway
- Portable student storage
- Student cubby holes
- Personal space zone
- Soft area
- Library and reference zone
- Plants and living things
- Sink and wet zone
- Technological zone
- Teacher zone with drop-down table
- Tables and closets
- Mini-museum display space
- Writing surfaces
- Open space
- Access to outside (patio)
- Supergraphic
- Banners

Group design process

Design teams After establishing the zones needed for a working classroom, the class should break into teams of four. The teacher assigns all the zones among the teams. Each team will make a list of items needed in their zones, design the zones and illustrate their designs with clearly labeled bubble diagrams. (See bubble diagram information in Entryways and Plans and Perspective lessons.)

Team presentation of bubble diagrams All teams should display their bubble diagrams. The designers of each presentation should explain their work and participate in a class discussion to determine which designs are the most successful. In the discussion the class should decide upon four or five zones that will be included in the new classroom. When the presentations end each team accepts a zone to design.

Study model construction

Each team will now make a study model to show its design concept for its zone. These models are not meant to be complete or done in fine detail. Study models are usually built in a short period of time (one hour is usually enough). Tell the students that these will be pinned on the wall when complete, so they should glue the parts down securely. Simple tools and materials such as scissors, white glue, paste, drafting tape and construction paper will do nicely. Each study model should be built to a scale of 1/2"= 1'0". Give each student a photocopy of the 1/2"= 1'0" scale on pg. 120. Scale model people, like those on pg. 84, should be used for visual reference. Tell the students to use their time wisely. After they begin working, you should announce the time left to complete the model every ten minutes. The students are encouraged to work quickly in order to develop fluid thinking and visual representation skills. Each model and the drawing that it was based on should be displayed on the wall.

The classroom can be thought of as an architectural design studio, with students working cooperatively towards solutions. Cooperative learning occurs when students help one another solve problems creatively and see and listen to several points of view.

RELATED ACTIVITIES

Redesign another environment for the future, such as a recreational center that serves different age groups.

evaluation

Display all bubble diagrams, plans and models made during the various steps of this project. Discuss the pros and cons of new ideas the students have incorporated in their designs for the classroom. Review a checklist of the client's specifications and have the students determine if the final design solutions meet his or her needs and dreams of a classroom for the future.

RESOURCES AND BIBLIOGRAPHY

Appendix:
Visual Vocabulary (p. 77)
Visual Verbal Journal (p. 78)
Hand Lettering (p. 79)
Drawing a Floor Plan (p. 81)
People (p. 84)
Arrows and Multiple Views (p. 86)
Paper Structures for Architectural Models (p. 96)
Paper Patterns for Geometric Forms (p. 97)
Model Building (p. 105)

Dattner, Richard. Design for Play. Cambridge: MIT Press, 1969.

Frost, Joe L. and Barry Klien. Childrens Play and Playground. Boston: Allyn and Bacon, Inc., 1979.

Loughlin, Catherine and Joseph Suma. The Learning Environment. New York: Teacher's College Press, 1982.

Nelson, Doreen. Transformations: Process and Theory, Santa Monica, Center for City Building, 1984.

Rouard, Marguerite and Jacques Simon. Children's Play Spaces. Woodstock: Overlook Press, 1977.

Sanoff, Henry. Learning Environments for Children. Raleigh, Sanoff.

Taylor, Anne and George Vlastos. School Zone: Learning Environments for Children (2nd Edition). Albuquerque: Horizon Communications, 1983.

Weiss, Harvey. Model Buildings and How to Make Them. New York: Thomas Crowell, 1979.

LANDSCAPE

GOAL

To help students learn techniques to analyze their natural environment, create a landscape design and work cooperatively.

ARCHITECTURAL VOCABULARY

Contour map A map in which the configuration of the land is shown through contour lines

Ecology Relationship between environment and living creatures

Form follows function A phrase coined from architect Louis Sullivan, meaning that design is based on use

Landscape design A planned scheme for the development of an outdoor site with plants and other items such as paths, paving, outdoor recreation amenities or outdoor furnishings

Physical fitness Exercise and care of the body

Site analysis Study of a natural and/or built environment and its impact on design

PRESENTATION

Contour drawing exercise

This exercise shows how to make a section drawing from a topographic map of a site. It will enable students to show changes in land contour in a new playground that they will design. On the upper half of a chalkboard, draw a map of a site with a lake, a hill and some trees. Draw two or three concentric contour lines within the base of the hill and the edge of the lake. Draw seven parallel horizontal lines under the map. Call the fourth line 0. the lines above it +10 feet, +20 feet, and +30 feet. Label the lines below zero -10 feet, -20 feet, and -30 feet. Draw a horizontal line across the site map. Have students show the shape of a section under the line by drawing a dotted line from each intersection on the straight line above to a line below. The point from the edge of the lake goes to the "0" line. The next line in the lake goes to "-10." The base of the hill starts at "+10." When all the points are charted below, connect them in the manner of a graph that shows the shape of the land. You can photocopy this exercise from page 103 of the appendix so that all students can try it.

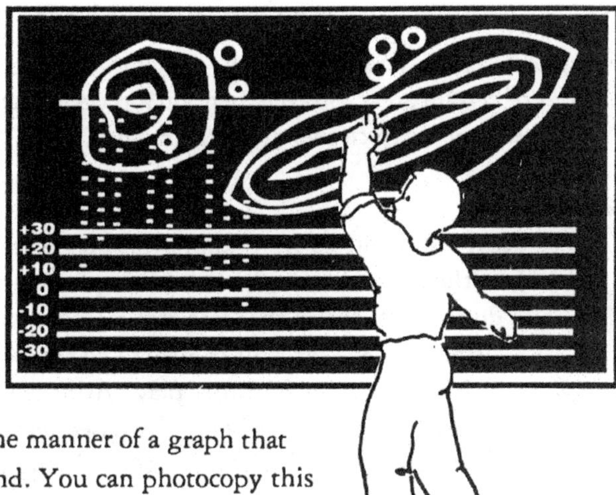

ASSIGNMENT

Student teams will design playground equipment or other settings for a playground and integrate individual designs into a total playground plan.

MATERIALS

Sketchboards
Masking tape
Pens
White glue
Camera
Push pins
Construction paper
Cardboard
Scissors
Small tree branches
Moss, dried grass
Camera
Architect's scale

SKILLS AND CONCEPTS

Math
Social Studies
Science
Art
Statistics
Estimating
Dimensional analysis
Graphing
Observing
Communicating
Evaluating products
Problem solving
Scale, proportion, ratio
Weather and climate
Environmental impact
Socialization
Contour mapping

SETTING

Classroom
Playground

client

A group of environmentalists has commissioned the class to redesign your school's playground as a creative play park for the surrounding community and the school. The group wants the new play park to be a good place to develop physical fitness and awareness of the environment.

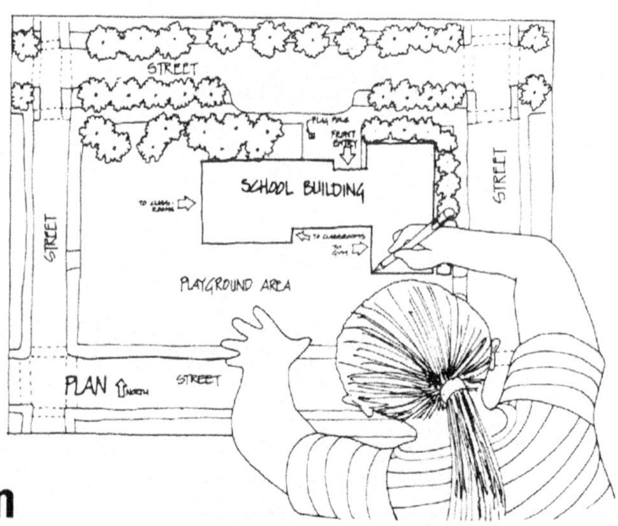

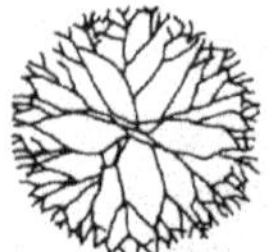

Tree symbols
Tree symbols in plan view and elevation give character to a site and sense of scale and place.

architectural program

Students will work in teams to design specific places and pieces of equipment for the new park. They begin with a site analysis. They collect data on the present playground, looking at existing characteristics and evaluating playground use before redesigning the area and its equipment into a more functional and beautiful for all people in the community.

Site analysis

Have the students prepare an analysis of the present site. The following steps will facilitate the task:

Schematic drawing

All students should draw a plan view of the way the playground and the school buildings are now. The site plan view of the school playground should show every physical object that is in place, including the building, property lines, trees, fences. play equipment, roadways, walkways, electrical vaults and so on.

Photography

Have students take photographs of the playground as it now is. They also can take slides of certain areas, project them on a piece of paper taped to the wall and have the students trace them (photo tracing).

Data collection

Instruct the students to study the ways the playground is now used. Have them observe how the children play on the playground? Where do students spend the least and most amount of time at recess? Where do the girls play? Where do the boys play? What do they play? Is there a place for quiet play? Ask the students to locate all the information that is being discussed with clearly labeled bubble diagrams on their plans of the existing playground. They should locate

all the "knowns" on their playground, such as areas where there are windy or sunny spots, cold spots, trees, bushes, fences. Are there fences? How would they change them? Map the way children move around the playground. What entrances and exits are used and where do students wait for the bus or a ride home?

Frequency count

Lead a "chalk talk" about the present playground's activity areas, equipment and landscaping. Count and tally students likes and dislikes about their playground. Arrange them in order from the most liked to the least liked item. Count the "votes" for each "like" and "dislike." pg. 33 (See Entryways lesson for a sample tally chart.)

Determining the new play park requirements

Continuing the discussion, make lists of equipment and landscaped places necessary for the various activities that could take place in the creative play park. Ask the students to think about active and passive play, imagination and fantasy, physical fitness and ecological awareness.

Forming design teams

Divide the class into teams of two or more students. Each team should design one component for the playground that would foster the activity with which they have been working. Assign each team at least one activity place to design for the new play park from different items listed under the "equipment and place list." Make sure each item in the list is assigned to a team. Many activities could use the same equipment so encourage them to work together with other design groups and share equipment.

Schematic drawings of individual designs

Assign a scale for the groups to use in all the drawings and models for this exercise. If you wish, give each student architect's scale, found on pg. 80 for measuring. Each team first prepares a plan view of the design they propose for their component. The team members should then draw elevations of two or more sides of their design, shown in its surroundings. Students should label every drawing they make.

Working models

Have the students make "working models" of their parts of new playground. (See Preferences lesson for working models.) Give the teams one to two hours to construct a working model of the place or piece of equipment on which they are working. Have them show trees, paving or plants as an integral part of the design. Tell them that these models should be made of light

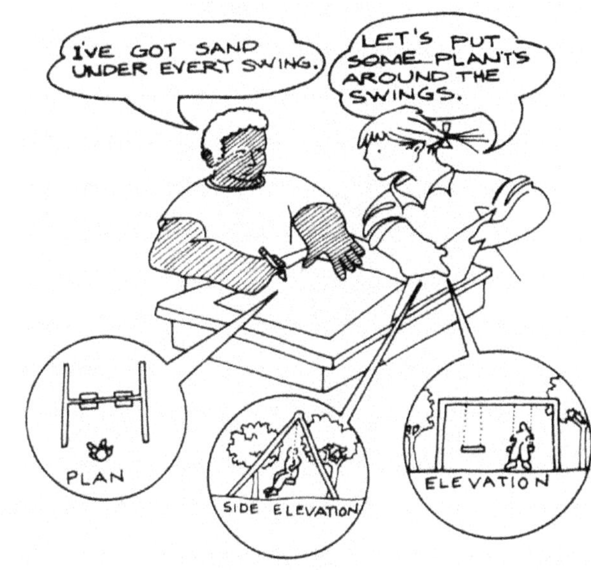

weight material, securely fastened to a cardboard base, as they are going to be hung on the wall for evaluation.

evaluation

Design teams display their models on the wall. Have each team present its model and explain what the equipment or area does as a learning tool about the environment and how it helps students and people in the community to keep physically fit.

New site plan

After presentations are made, take models off the wall and rearrange the parts of the proposed playground on the floor. At this point, the students will need to evaluate how the activities at each part of the site fit together. Once the class has arrived at a consensus on the arrangement, organize a team of enthusiastic students draw a neat, well-organized and clearly labeled site plan for the new playground. Present this playground plan to the principal and tell him your class would like to help build this playground. Display the model and drawing on the hall walls of your school so everyone can see them.

RESOURCES AND BIBLIOGRAPHY

Appendix :
Visual Vocabulary (p. 77)
Visual Verbal Journal (p. 78)
Drawing a Floor Plan (p. 81)
Perspective (p. 83)
People (p. 84)
Arrows and Multiple Views (p. 86)
Paper Structures for Architectural Models (p. 96)
Paper Patterns for Geometric Forms (p. 91)
Model Making (p. 105)
Contour Map Exercise (p. 103)

Dattner, Rich. Design for Play. Cambridge: MIT Press, 1969.
Frost, Joe L. and Barry Klein. Childrens Play and Playground. Boston: Allyn and Bacon, Inc., 1979.
Loughlin, Catherine and Joseph Suma. The Learning Environment. New York: Teacher's College Press, 1982.
Nelson, Doreen. Transformations: Process and Theory, Santa Monica, CA: Center for City Building, 1984.
Rouard, Marguerite and Jacques Simon. Children's Play Spaces. Woodstock: Overlook Press, 1977.
Sanoff, Henry. Learning Environments for Children. Raleigh: Sanoff.
Taylor, Anne and George Vlastos. School Zone: Learning Environments for Children (2nd Edition). Albuquerque: Horizon Communications, 1983.
Morrow, Baker. Dictionary of Landscape Design. Albuquerque: University of New Mexico Press, 1987.
Lane Publishing. Western Garden Book, Menlo Park, California: Lane Publishing Co., 1985.

CITY PLANNING

GOAL

To help students understand how cooperation and collaboration contribute to the design and development of cities.

ARCHITECTURAL VOCABULARY

City plan An organized arrangement of places and systems for densely populated areas

Walled city A city protected by a continuous wall

Random city plan A city with clusters of neighborhoods, each with its own center

Grid city plan A plan with city streets that cross each others at right angles

Linear city plan A city plan with business and industry stretched along arterial streets

PRESENTATION

A discussion of human settlements

Explain that human settlements develop from the needs and interests of their inhabitants. Show students the African tribal village. The houses in African tribal villages were arranged in a circle. This type of plan works well for the members of the village because they share the food they hunt and gather and live much like one big family. Ask the students, "Would this be a good plan for a modern city?" Next show the castle and the walled medieval city. Help students to see that these were designed to protect people from unfriendly neighbors. Ask them if a modern city should have walls and towers like this or should a modern city be different? Explain that planners direct and shape the way a city grows, based upon the needs and interests of the community. They make plans that look like views from an airplane flying over a town or city. The patterns of squares, rectangles, and circles are streets, homes, and parks.

client

Your state's governor has selected your class to design a new capital city for your state. The governor addresses the class: "Students of today should be involved in the design for the new capital. Many of you will live and work in this new city in the not-too-distant future. I want a wonderful new city for the center of the state's business. I want the new capital to be a city for the future. I want this city to take advantage of the things that are special about our state."

ASSIGNMENT

The class will assemble a model city from parts built by small teams.

MATERIALS

Drawing Paper
Tape
Markers
Model building materials
Glue

SKILLS AND CONCEPTS

Math
Earth Science
Art
Social Studies
Real life problems
Spacial relationships
Scale
Predicting
Valuing
Geometric construction
Problem solving
Cause-effect
Habitat
Enviornmental impact
Cultural awareness
Aesthetics
Systems analysis

SETTING

Classroom

RANDOM CITY
ROME, ITALY
This kind of city is the most comfortable city to live in. It evolved and most people needs as it grew.

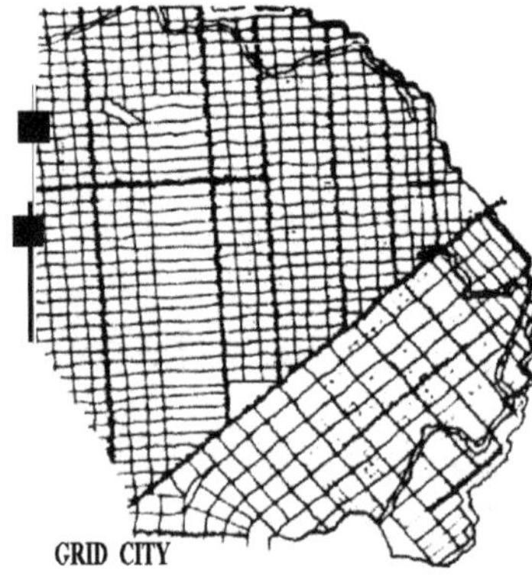

GRID CITY
SAN FRANSISCO
The grid city looks like a game of tic-tac-toe with lines in horizontal and vertical patterns. It allows easy access and circulation to every part of the city.

Architectural program

The students should brainstorm ideas for the needs of a new capital city. Ask the students to make two lists on the chalkboard. One list should include the students' ideas for good living and working conditions in the new capital city. The other list should include things the new capital city should avoid, like pollution, poor traffic patterns and slums. Keep a record of the two lists so that good conditions can be incorporated into the plan and poor conditions can be avoided as the plan is developed.

Design program requirements

The site for the new capital city is far away from other large cities. This new city must be designed to have all the things that make a community a livable place for 20,000 people. The new capital city requires the following elements:

1. Transportaion

Good transportation systems to and from the city. An airport, a bus station-, a train station, a mass transit system, and a system of parking lots that allows the center of the city to be free from automobiles.

2. Residential areas

Single family home sites, multiple family home sites, apartment and condominium living complexes, large estates if desired, and a mansion for the governor.

3. Business district

Shopping center, office buildings, cafes, supermarkets, banks, movie theaters.

4. Recreation and open spaces

These should be located throughout the city: parks, running and bike paths, a golf course, lakes, swimming pools, soccer and baseball fields, a band shell.

5. The capitol complex

An assembly building for both the houses of the legislature; a building for the state supreme court; a building for all other government agencies a building for the state library and museum; an auditorium for the pertorm1ng arts.

Urban pattern

The students should agree on a general pattern for the city they will build. As a group they should make a bubble diagram and rough plan view of the new city, then break up into five design teams, each of which will be responsible for designing the physical aspects of one of the five design programs for the new city.

Design teams

Each group will take responsibility for fulfilling the requirements of one of the five headings under the heading "Design program requirements." Three of these categories are areas (residential, business, capital complex) and two are citywide systems (transportation, recreation/open space).

Preliminary design schemes

Working individually, students should analyze how to meet the design requirements in the category for which his or her group is responsible. They do this by developing bubble diagrams and using other schematic devices, such as arrows. When each student has made bubble diagrams, the groups should reassemble and resolve their design plans with each other. Then they should proceed to the next step: developing a plan view that shows how they propose to fulfil the requirements for their area or system for the capital city. Be sure that a uniform scale is used for all drawings and models so that all parts will fit together. Suggested scales are 1"=20', 1"=40' or 1"=50'.

Interfacing with other groups

As teams develop plans that fulfill their part of the design program requirement. they should consult with other groups wherever different areas of the city might overlap. The students should now understand something about how urban planners work cooperatively to solve problems for their city.

Model of the New Capital City

When the five groups have completed their respective plans of each area of the city, they are ready to build a model of the new capital city they have designed. The same student groups should build models from the plans they have prepared. The models need not be elaborate. Paper, cardboard, clay, construction paper, and/or rigid plastic foam will be sufficient. Again: Be sure that a uniform scale is used by everyone so the model parts will all fit together. An easy way to keep everyone working on the same scale is to have each group make scale model people and cars as a way of visualizing the size of things to be designed. Use carpet squares (often available inexpensively or free from carpet stores) as a base for the city model segments. They are sturdy and provide good moveable modules for students to use when they design city plans. Finally, have the whole class put the city together in the center of the classroom and discuss the completed design.

Related activities

1. Mapping

Have students draw a map of the routes they would take from their houses to school. Tell them to draw important buildings or and name important streets on their routes. Display the maps and have them compare their maps with one another. Have them try to put their maps together into an overall map.

2. Walking tour

Take the class on a walking tour of a neighborhood near the school or a field trip to an area of the city. First identify the kind of area you are visiting, such as a residential area, a business/commercial area, or an industrial zone. Next have a discussion about how the building designs fit in to their surroundings. You might point out buildings that don't seem to work very well. Make the children aware of what kind of things are used to create the architecture of different buildings, such as color, form, shape, texture, line, and materials. Ask younger students how many triangles, circles, half circles or rectangles they see. Give older students copies of the Visual Survey Form from the appendix.

Encourage the students to think about the different kinds of structures as if they have been arranged as a piece of artwork and have the class discuss the total streetscape or view in terms of balance, proportion, unity. Have the students try to detect how the form of the building has been shaped by its function. As you walk along, see if the students can express their feelings about the architecture they are seeing– happy, sad, active, passive, loud, quiet, slow, fast. Have someone photograph the buildings on the tour and later show them. When you return to class, have the students draw a scene from their tour or take sketch boards with them and draw details of the tour.

evaluation

The evaluation for this exercise can take place while the class assembles the city. Ask questions about the appropriateness of the placement of various buildings in the city. Does the capitol complex relate to the rest of the city? How will people travel to different parts of the city? How did the students decide where to put the parks and open spaces? Where are the schools? Talk about your design decisions as you go about creating the new capital city for your state.

RESOURCES AND BIBLIOGRAPHY

Appendix:
Visual Vocabulary (p. 77)
Hand Lettering (p. 78)
People (p.84)
Using an Architect's Scale (p.80)
Paper Structures for Architectural Models (p. 96)
(Paper Patterns for Geometric Forms (p. 97)
Model Building (p. 105)
How to Develop a Walking Tour (p. 107)

Bryfogle, Charles. ETAL. The Teacher and the City. Toronto: Mentuen, 1971.
Faberstein, Jay and Min Kantrowitz. People in Places, Englewood Cliffs: Prentice Hall, 1979.
Giblin, James. The Skyscraper Book. New York: Thomas Crowell, 1981.
Group for Environmental Education (GEE). Our Man-Made Environment. A collection of experiences, resources, and suggested activities. Philadelphia: Group for Environmental Education, 1971.
Group for Environmental Education. Introductory Unit to the Urban Environment (GEE), 1971.
McGregor, Anne and Scott. Skyscrapers: A Project Book, 1980. New York: Lothrop, Lee and Shepard Books, 1980.
Nelson, Doreen. City Building Education. A Way to Learn, 1982.
Nelson, Doreen. Classroom City (Film). 1981. Center for City Building, 2210 Wilshire Blvd., Suite 303, Santa Monica, CA 90403, (213) 208-1332.
Sandak, Cass. Skyscrapers. New York: Franklin Watts, 1984.
Sanoff, Henry and others. Seeing the Environment: An Advocacy Approach. Raleigh, North Carolina; Learning Environment, 1975.
Wilson, Forrest. City Planning Games of Human Settlement, New York: Van Nostrand Reinhold, 1975.

APPENDIX

Historical Structures / Famous Buildings 74
Sketches which can be photocopied on sheets or labels and given to students

Visual Vocabulary 77
Examples of exercises in contour, schematic, section and cognitive map drawings.

Visual Verbal Journal 78
A book that students can make for sketches and notes by George Vlastos

Hand Lettering 79
Lessons in hand lettering from the book *Architectural Graphics* by Frank Ching

Using an Architects Scale 80
Instruction in using an architects scale by Mike Smith

Drawing a Floor Plan 81
Instruction in plan and section drawing from *Architectural Graphics* by Frank Ching

Perspective 83
A few notes on drawing in perspective by Mike Smith

People 84
Lesson in architectural drawings of people from *Architectural Graphics* by Frank Ching

Color Wheel 85
A basic tool for learning about color

Arrows and Multiple Views 86
Some ways of communicating through drawing from *Notes on Architecture* by Berryman

Understanding the Forces of Structure 87
Force, stress, load path, beams, loads, trusses explained by Rick Parker

Physics of Structure Exercise 94
An exercise in identifying and applying structural concepts

Design a Column Capital 95
An exercise in designing an ornamental column capital

Paper Structures for Architectural Models 96
How to make architectural shapes from paper and other materials by Stephanie Jurs

Paper Patterns for Geometric Forms 97
Patterns in instructions by John Tubbs for making cube, cylinder, pyramid, cone and sphere

Energy and Plumbing Survey 102
Questions to aid students in understanding electrical, ventilation and plumbing systems

Contour Map Exercise 103
A map to give students exercise in translating a map view to a land section drawing

Visual Notetaking 104
Learning ways to sketch architecture, from *Notes for Architects and Designers* by Crow and Laseau

Model Building 105
Concepts, techniques and materials used in making models by Nancy Evans

How to Develop a Walking Tour 107
Strategies for a successful walking tour

Powerpoint Presentation 109
How to help students prepare a powerpoint presentation

Visual Survey Form 111
Visual and verbal clues to help students "read" a building by Carolyn Purser

Portfolio Assessment 115

Chart 119
Relationship of Architecture and Children themes to science, math and technology learning goals

1/2" Grid Page 120

HISTORICAL STRUCTURES/FAMOUS BUILDINGS (1)

MONTICELLO, VIRGINIA • 1770-1808 • THOMAS JEFFERSON

SYDNEY OPERA HOUSE, AUSTRALIA, 1957-73, JØRN UTZON

TYPICAL NORTH AMERICAN INDIAN SKIN HOUSE

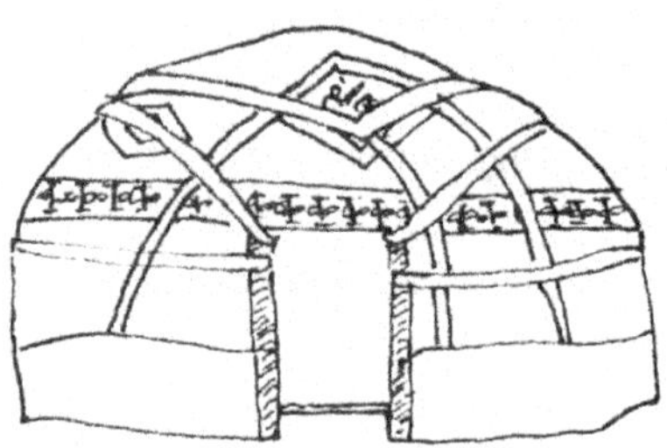

TYPICAL NOMAD TENT NORTHERN ASIA

TAJ MAHAL MAUSOLEUM, AGRA, INDIA

TEMPLE OF APOLLO, DIDYMA, TURKEY, 300 BC

ARC DE TRIOMPHE, PARIS, FRANCE, 1806-1936

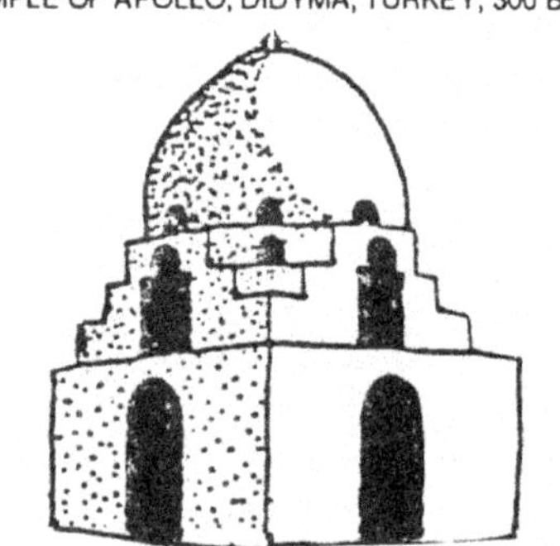

TYPICAL EARLY CHRISTIAN BYZANTINE CHAPEL

OLYMPIC SPORTS PALACE, ROME, ITALY 1957, VITELLOZZI AND NERVI

TAOS INDIAN PUEBLO, NEW MEXICO

HISTORICAL STRUCTURES/FAMOUS BUILDINGS (2)

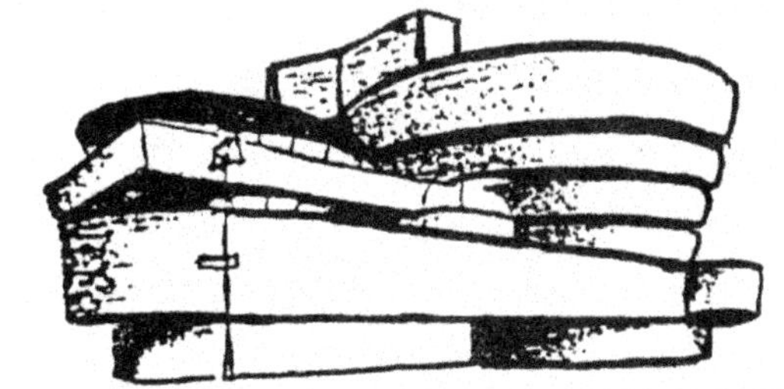

GUGGENHEIM MUSEUM, NEW YORK, 1846-1959, FRANK LLOYD WRIGHT

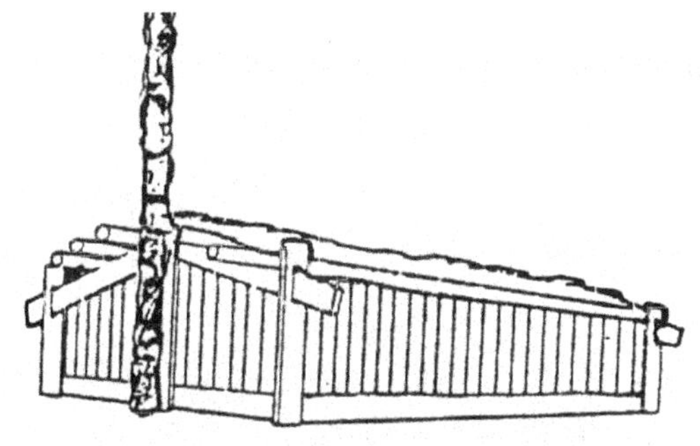

TYPICAL TLINGIT/HAIDA MEETINGHOUSE, SOUTHWEST ALASKA

THE COLOSSEUM, ROME, ITALY, A.D, 70-82

STONEHENGE, GREAT BRITAIN, PRE-RECORDED HISTORY

A TYPICAL SUSPENSION BRIDGE

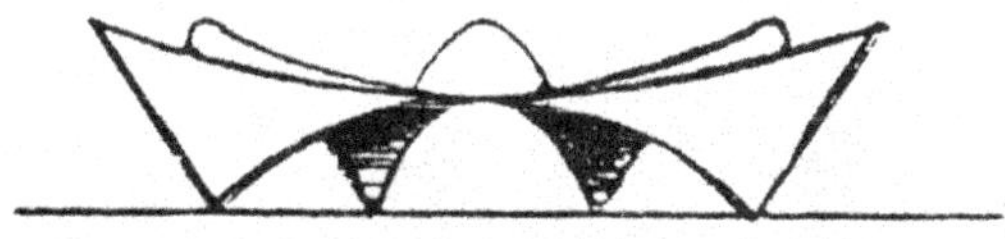

LOS MANANTIALES, XOCHIMILCO, MEXICO, 1957, FELIX CANDELARIO

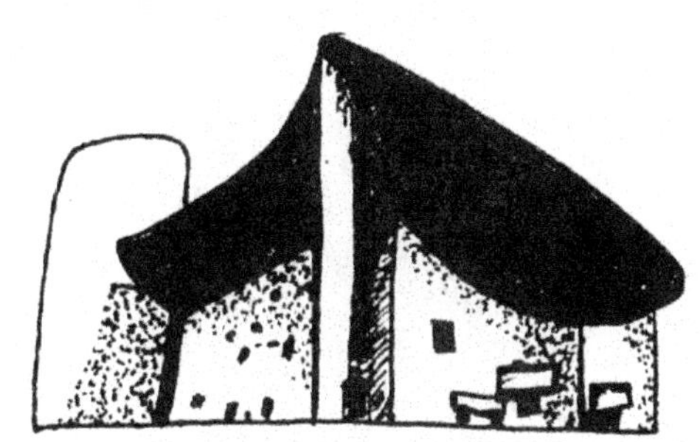

NOTRE DAME DU HAUT, RONCHAMP FRANCE, 1951-1955, LE CORBUSIER

GREAT PYRAMIDS AT GIZA, EGYPT, CIRCA 4000 BC

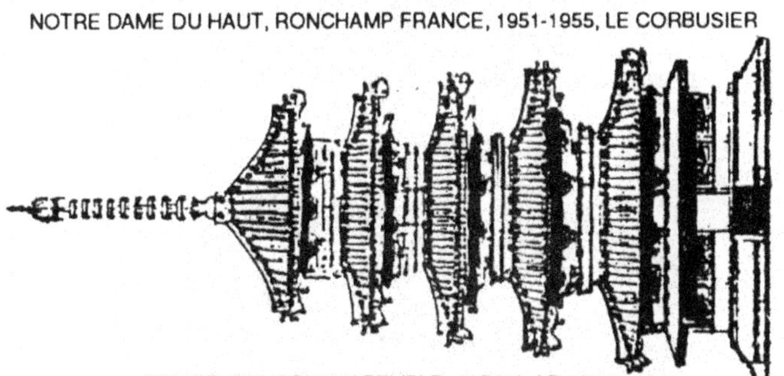

TOWER OF HORYU-JI TEMPLE, JAPAN, AD 607-746

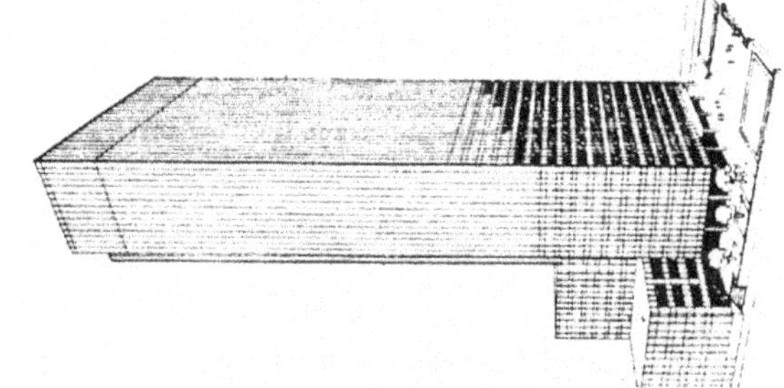

SEAGRAM BLDG, NEW YORK, NY, 1958, MIES VANDER ROHE/ PHILIP JOHNSON

HISTORICAL STRUCTURES/FAMOUS BUILDINGS (3)

TYPICAL IROQUOIS LONGHOUSE

KAUFMANN HOUSE 'FALLINGWATER,' BEAR RUN, PA, 1936, FRANK LLOYD WRIGHT

MOSQUE ENTRANCE, MALI, AFRICA

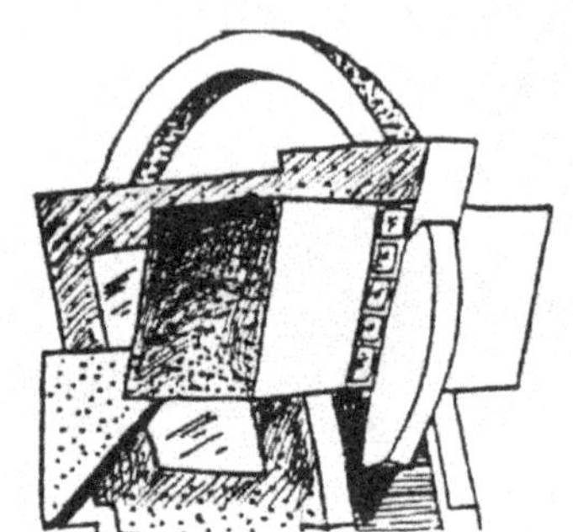

COOKIE EXPRESS BUILDING, CALIFORNIA, 1985

THE PANTHEON, ROME, ITALY, AD 118-128

TYPICAL LOG CABIN OF AMERICAN PIONEERS

ST. BASILS CATHEDRAL, MOSCOW, USSR, 1550-1560

TYPICAL QUEEN ANNE VICTORIAN HOUSE, USA, 1890

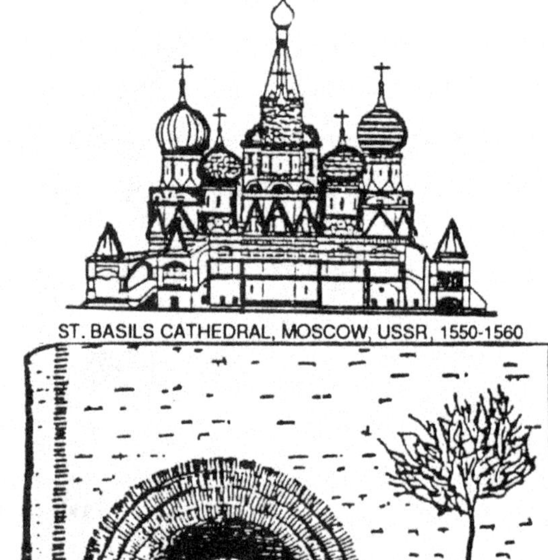

MORRIS STORE, SAN FRANCISCO, CA, 1949, FRANK LLOYD WRIGHT

TYPICAL WOOD FRAME HOUSE, EARLY ANCHORAGE, AK, 1930

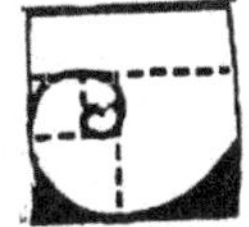

VISUAL VOCABULARY

Examples of student exercises in contour, schematic and section drawing.

Enlarging details

An easy way to help students enlarge a drawing detail is to have them use a piece of paper with a "window" cut in it to look at parts of their drawing and draw what they see in the "window."

SCHEMATIC DRAWING EXAMPLES

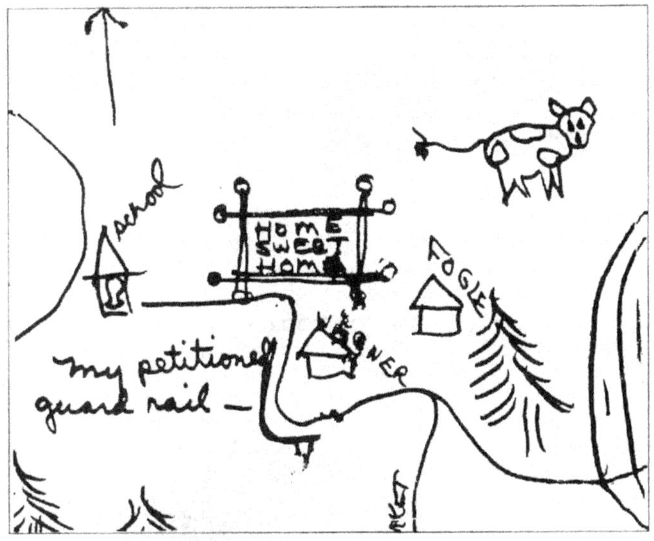

COGNITIVE MAPPING EXAMPLE

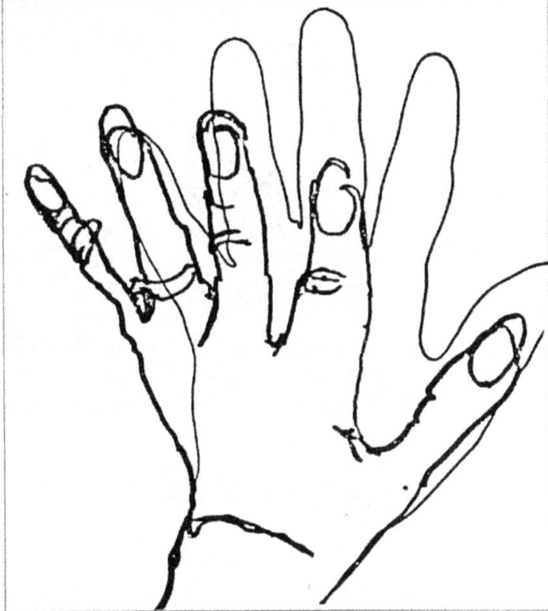

HAND CONTOUR DRAWING EXAMPLE

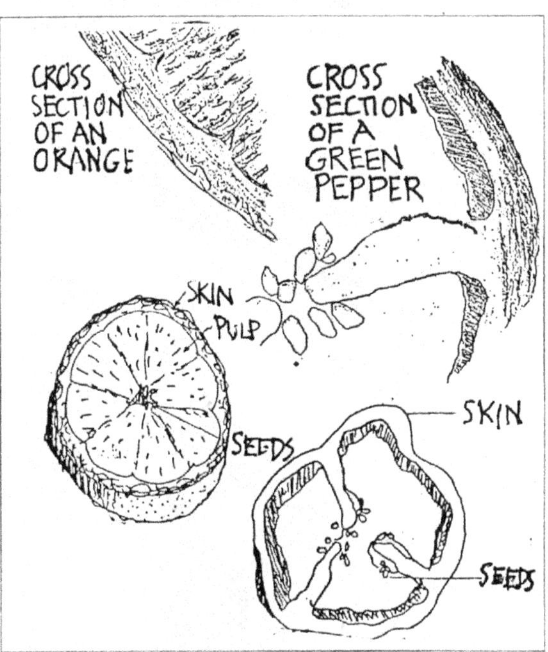

FRUIT AND VEGETABLE SECTION DRAWING EXAMPLES

VISUAL-VERBAL JOURNAL

by George Vlastos of Design Synthesis

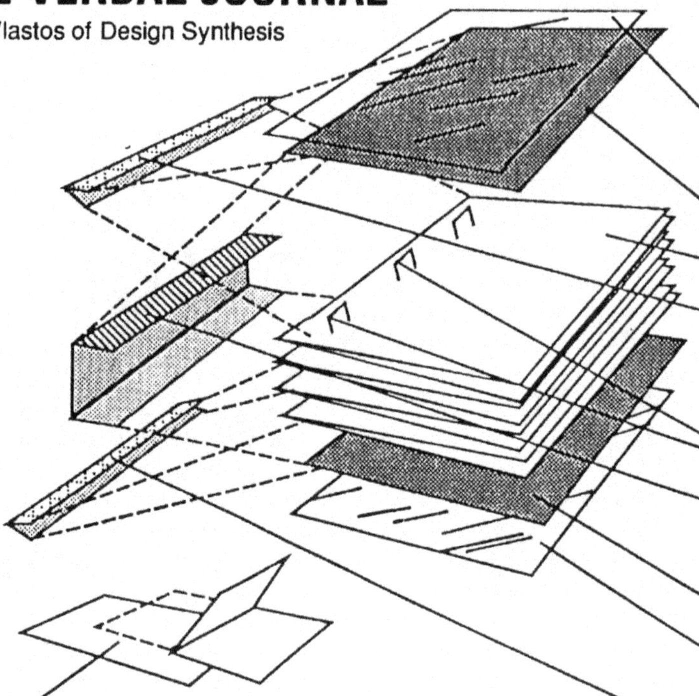

AN EXPLODED VIEW OF THE DUCT TAPE JOURNAL
showing the elements needed to build the book.

Clear plastic adhesive protective covering.

Cardboard front cover.

Folded paper

1" wide masking tape set to both the back of the front cover and the stapled folded paper sheets.

Staples

3" silver duct tape set onto the back of the journal to protect the binding.

Cardboard back cover.

Clear plastic adhesive protective covering.

1" wide masking tape set to both the back of the back cover and the stapled folded paper sheets.

1 8 -1/2"x 11" paper is folded as shown to create the page size for the journal.

2 Stack the folded sheets of paper so the folded edges are all at one end..

3 Staple the folded side of the sheets together to bind the pages of the journal.

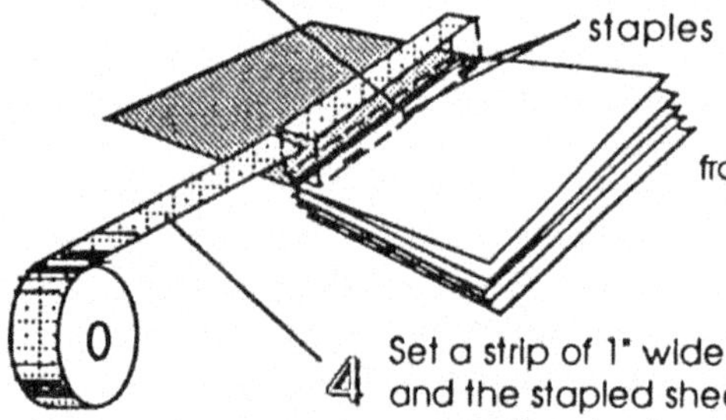

staples

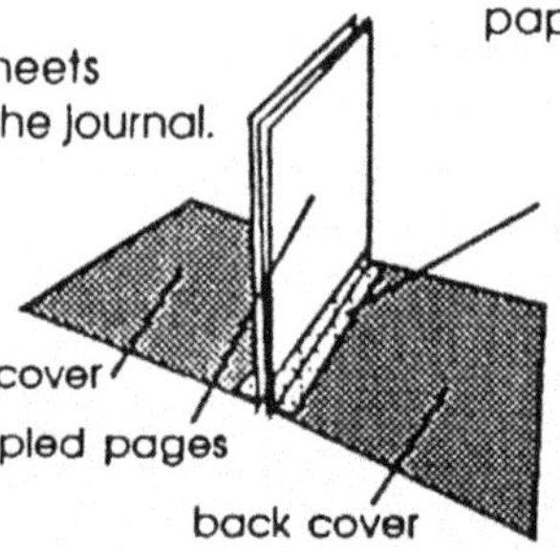

front cover

stapled pages

back cover

5 Masking tape holds the stapled folded sheets of paper to both the front and back cardboard covers.

4 Set a strip of 1" wide masking tape on the cardboard journal covers and the stapled sheets of paper as shown. Note that the masking tape covers the staples on both sides of the bound pages.

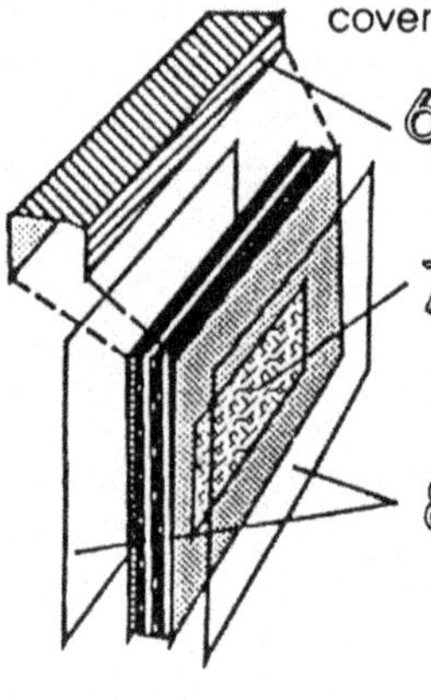

6 once the bound pages and the cardboard covers are taped together then a strip of 3" silver duct tape can be laid over the back of the journal and protect the binding.

7 Create a graphic art statement on the front cover to personalize the journal.

8 Set a clear plastic adhesive covering over both front and back cardboard covers to protect the art work on the journal covers.

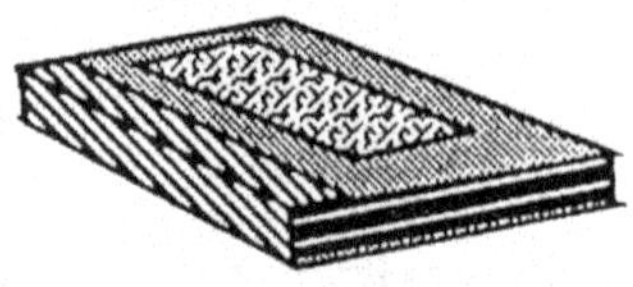

Finished duct tape journal ready for use.

HAND LETTERING

(from Architectural Graphics by Frank Ching)

ABCDEFGHIJKLMNOPQRRSTUVWXYZ 1234567890

ABCDEFGHIJKLMNOPQRSTUVWXYZ 1234567890

The use of guidelines is mandatory for letters to be consistent in height.

For letters to communicate and not to distract or detract from the drawing itself:

① keep lettering vertical
a small triangle is a quick and efficient way to keep vertical lettering strokes consistently vertical

straightedge
MNPTEIIII O

slanted lettering is directional; this movement is generally distracting in a rectilinear drawing scheme

② maintain oblong proportions for the most stable lettering

ABC — normal; A — too broad; ABCD — too vertical

Everyone inevitably develops an individual style of lettering. The most important characteristics of a lettering style are: readability and consistency, in both style and spacing.

Letter spacing is not based on equal spacing between the extremeties of the letters but on equal areas.

SPACING — equal areas correct; SPA — equal spacing incorrect

lowercase lettering can be appropriate if it is sympathetic to the drawing style and if it is executed consistently throughout the presentation. It is generally easy to read, because we recognize the distinctive differences among the characters from its widespread use in the printing industry.

abcdefgghijklmnopqrstuvwxyz

SERIFS enhance the recognition and readability of an alphabet. They too should be used consistently. Perhaps the best example of the use of serifs is the classic roman alphabet, which is the model for the single-stroke alphabet below:

ABCDEFGHIJKLMNOPQRSTUVWXYZ · 1234567890

The maximum-sized single-stroke letter or numeral that should be used is 3/16". Beyond this size a letter or numeral should have width and substance to its strokes so it doesn't appear too weak.

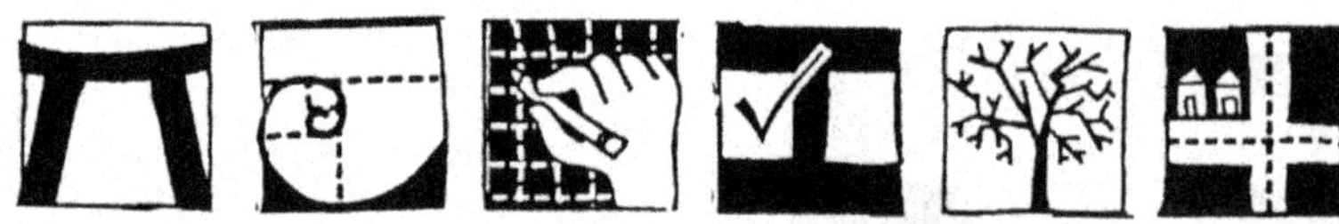

USING AN ARCHITECTS SCALE

by Mike Smith

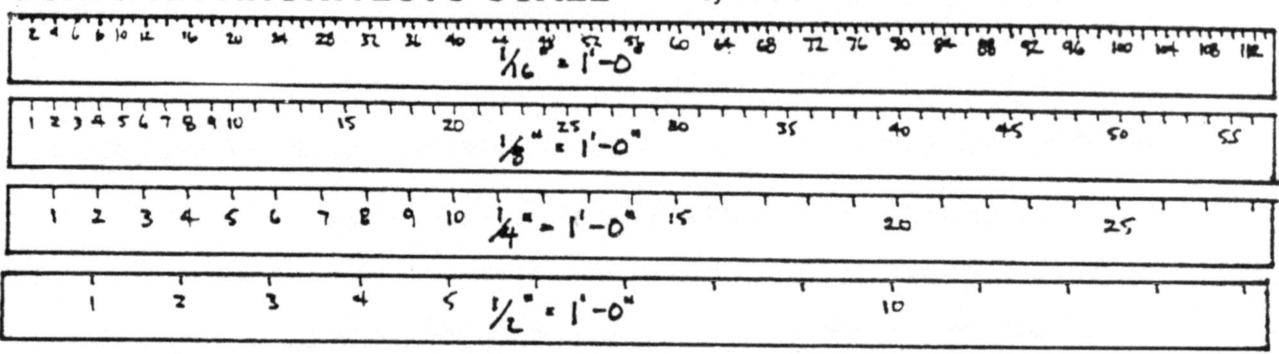

Above are four examples of architect's scales. Each one has different divisions, or *increments*, representing feet. When reading a scale it is important to understand exactly what "scale" means! For example, if a drawing says that the scale is 1/4 inch = 1"-0', it means that for every 1/4 inch of length on the drawing, there is exactly that number of feet. So if you measure 10 -1/4 inch marks, it is 10 feet long.

If you wish to change scale, say from 1/4" = 1'-0" to 1/8" = 1'-0" just remember that two -1/8" marks = one -1/4" mark; or two 1/4" marks = one -1/2" mark; or two 1/6" marks = one -1/8" mark.

EXERCISES

1. Measure the drawing below at (a) 1/4"=1'-0" (b) 1/16"=1'-0" (c) 1/2"=1'-0"

Answers: = ________ = ________ = ________

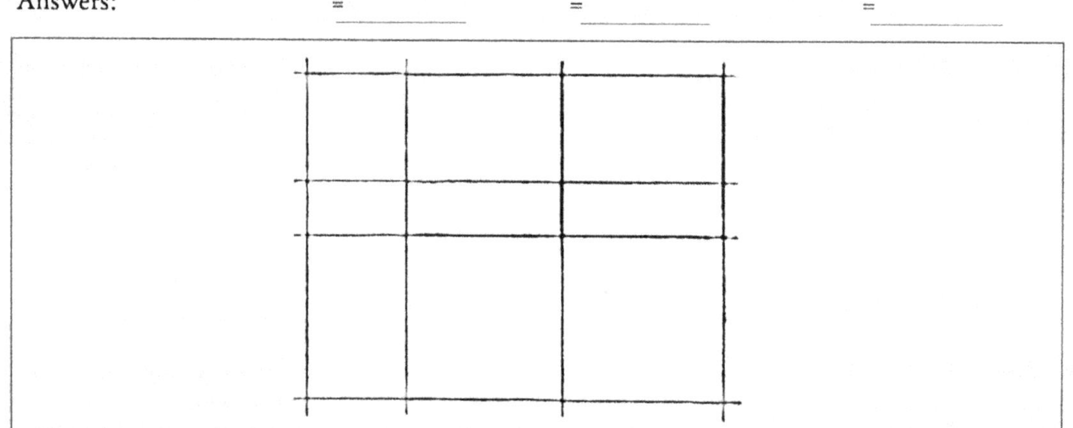

2. If you wanted to cut pieces of paper to the size and shape of a room, what would they be if the scale of the room was (a) 1/4"=1'-0" and the room was 15' by 18'? = ________ (Answer)
(b) 1/16"=1'-0" and the room was 32'x18'? = ________ (Answer)
(Hint: How many scale increments are there in each dimension?)

3. If a room measured 12'-0" x 16'-0" at 1/4"=1'-0" scale what would the same room measure at 1/8"=1'-0" scale?________________(Answer)

4. If a room measured 12'-0" x 16'-0" at 1/8"=1'-0" scale what would the same room measure at 1/4"=1'-0" scale?________________(Answer)

VOCABULARY LIST

Increment - Systematic amounts of increase
Scale - Measuring stick with varying sets of dimensions
Manipulate - To give a drawing a different size by changing the size of the increments

DRAWING A FLOOR PLAN

(from Architectural Graphics by Frank Ching)

This series of drawings illustrate the sequence in which a plan drawing is executed. Although the sequence can vary depending on the nature of the building design being drawn, always try to work from the most continuous elements to those that are contained or defined by them.

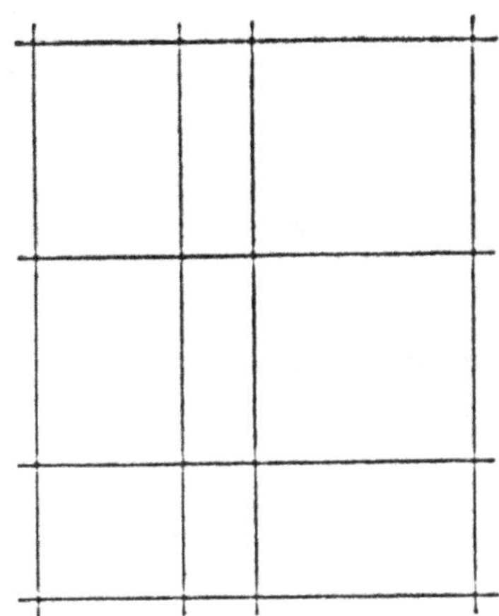

First the major outline and those lines that regulate the position of structural elements and walls are drawn.

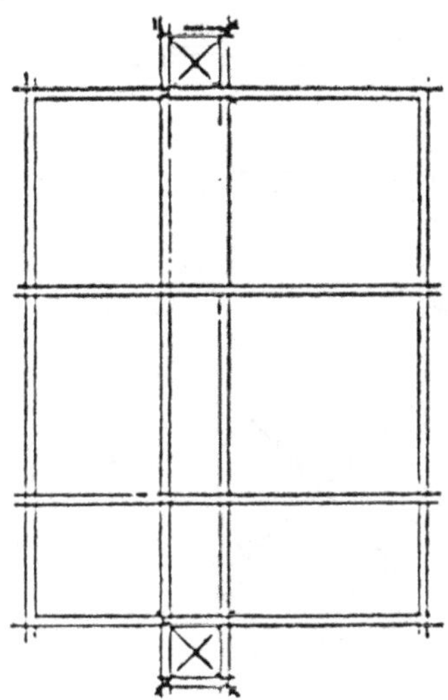

Next the major walls and structural elements such as posts and columns are given proper thickness

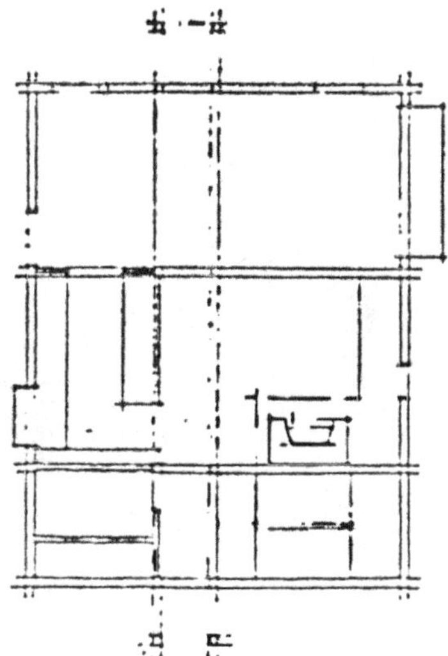

Major built in elements such as windows, doorways and fireplaces are drawn next.

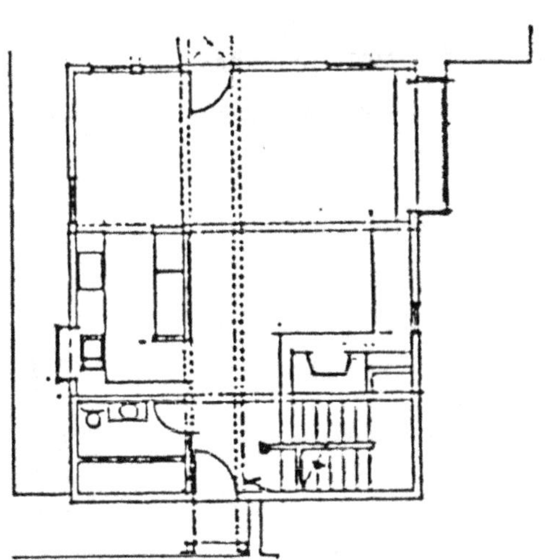

Finally, details such as fixtures and stair treads are drawn.

DOORS AND WINDOWS IN PLAN

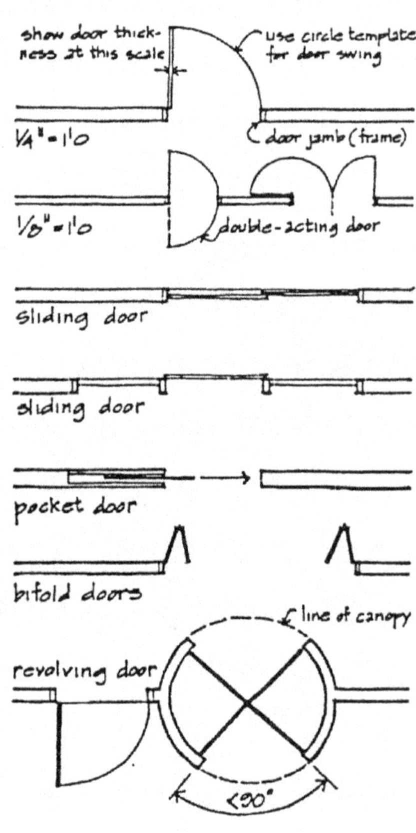

• door type (solid wood, wood frame and glass, storefront, etc) is not illustrated in plan, only in elevational views

• show normally swinging doors at a 90° opening, as illustrated

• note that door swings are shown with light lines and quarter circles

STAIRS

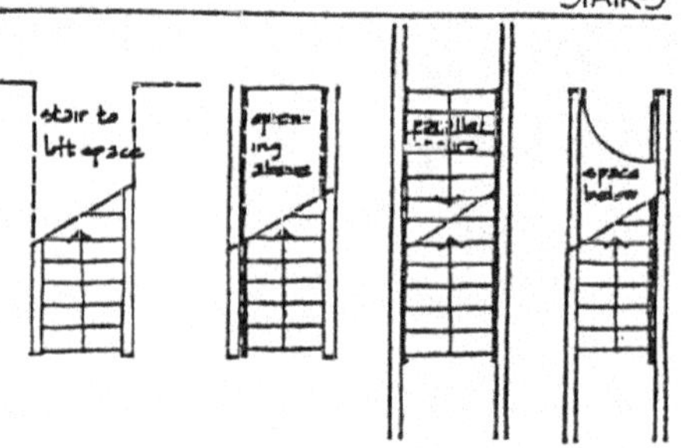

• show detail such as handrails and toe spaces where scale of drawing permits

• convention to indicate direction of stairs: arrow indicates direction (up or down) from level of floor plan

• straight-run stairs

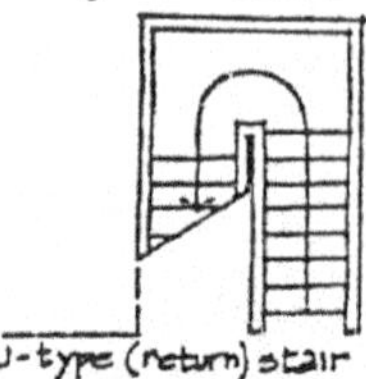

• U-type (return) stair

• spiral stair

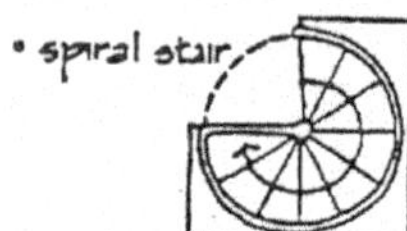

BUILDING SECTION DRAWINGS

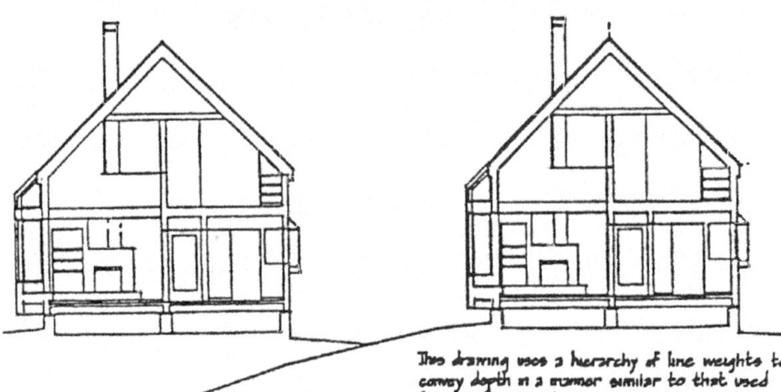

This drawing is a sectional view of a building using a single-line weight. It is difficult to discern what is cut and what is seen in elevation.

This drawing uses a hierarchy of line weights to convey depth in a manner similar to that used for plan drawings (see page 30). These elements that are cut in section are outlined with a heavy line. Those elements that are seen in elevation beyond the section cut are outlined with intermediate line weights. The further back an element is from the section cut, the finer the line weight should be.

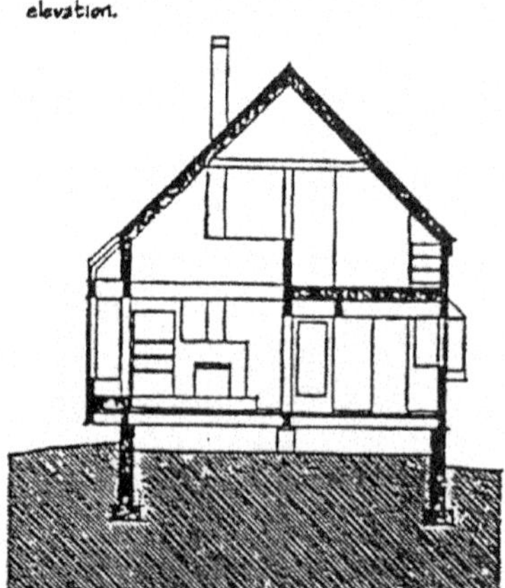

This drawing illustrates how the elements that are cut in section can be given a tonal value to heighten their contrast with elevational elements seen beyond the cut. This is particularly necessary when many elements are shown in elevation.

This last drawing shows how the value system can be reversed when what is seen in elevation is rendered along with the background for the drawing. In this case, the section cut can be left white or given a fairly light value to contrast with the drawing field.

DRAWING A FLOOR PLAN

(from Architectural Graphics by Frank Ching)

This series of drawings illustrate the sequence in which a plan drawing is executed. Although the sequence can vary depending on the nature of the building design being drawn, always try to work from the most continuous elements to those that are contained or defined by them.

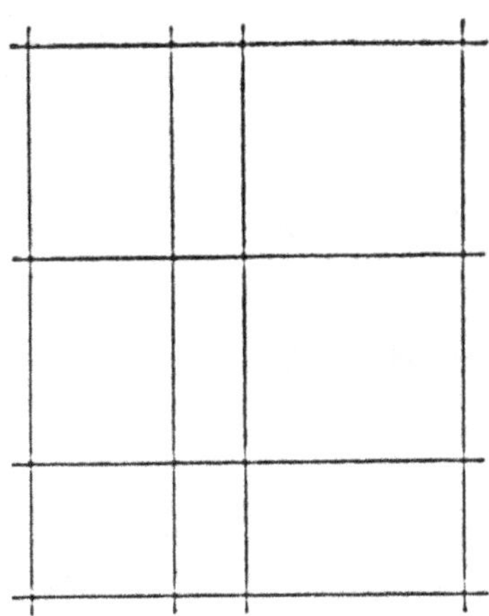

First the major outline and those lines that regulate the position of structural elements and walls are drawn.

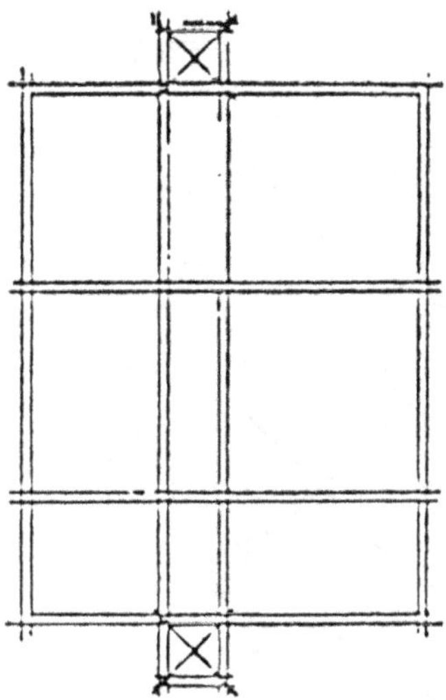

Next the major walls and structural elements such as posts and columns are given proper thickness

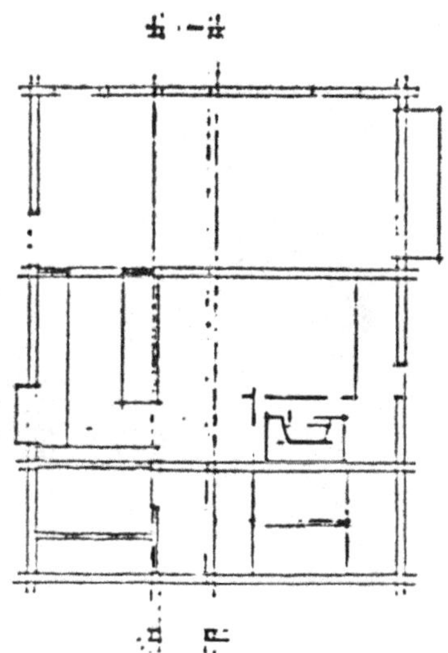

Major built in elements such as windows, doorways and fireplaces are drawn next.

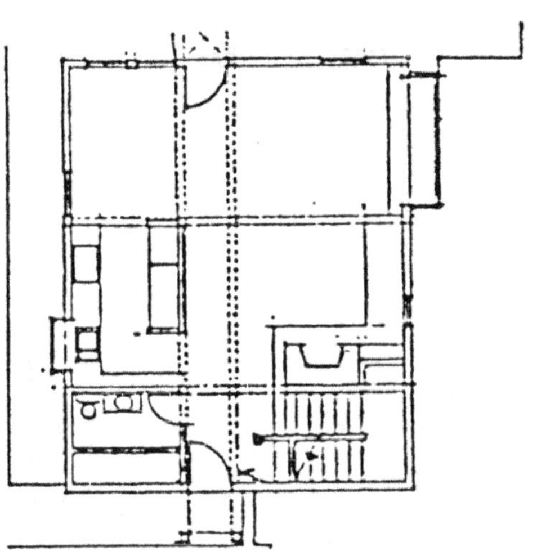

Finally, details such as fixtures and stair treads are drawn.

DOORS AND WINDOWS IN PLAN

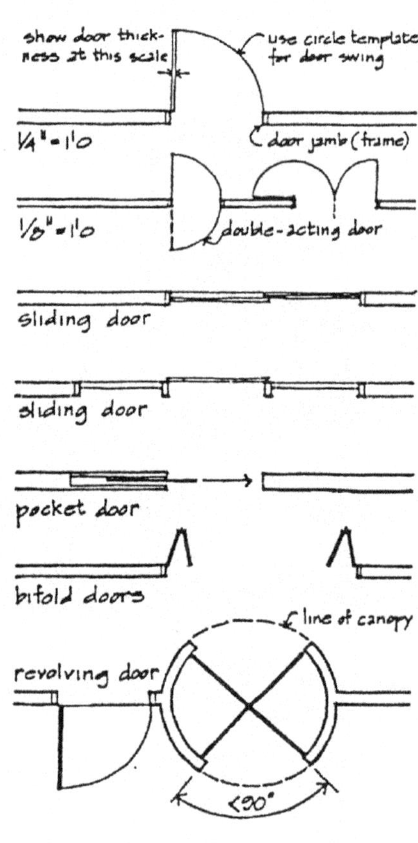

- door type (solid wood, wood frame and glass, storefront, etc.) is not illustrated in plan, only in elevational views

- show normally swinging doors at a 90° opening, as illustrated

- note that door swings are shown with light lines and quarter circles

STAIRS

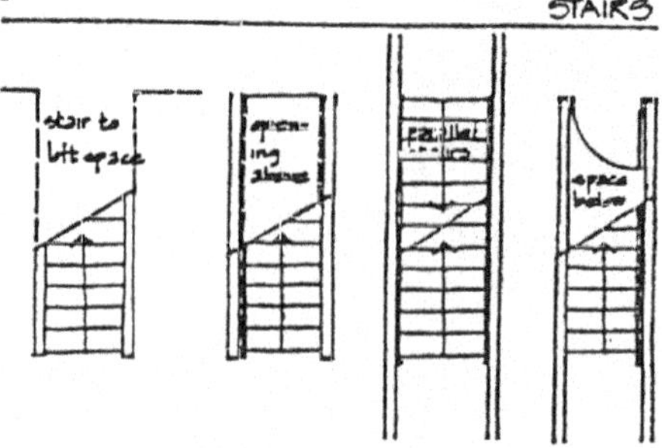

- show detail such as handrails and toe spaces where scale of drawing permits

- convention to indicate direction of stair: arrow indicates direction (up or down) from level of floor plan

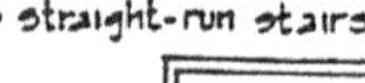

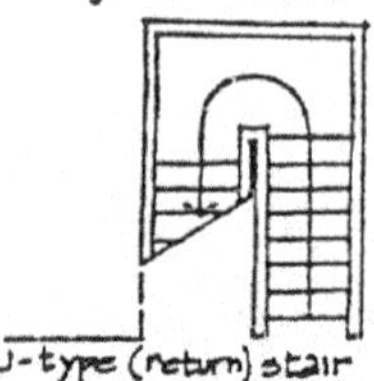

• U-type (return) stair

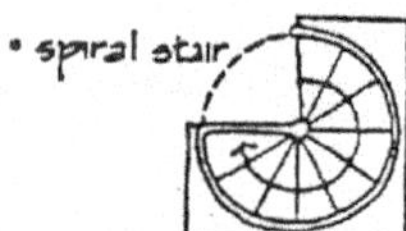

BUILDING SECTION DRAWINGS

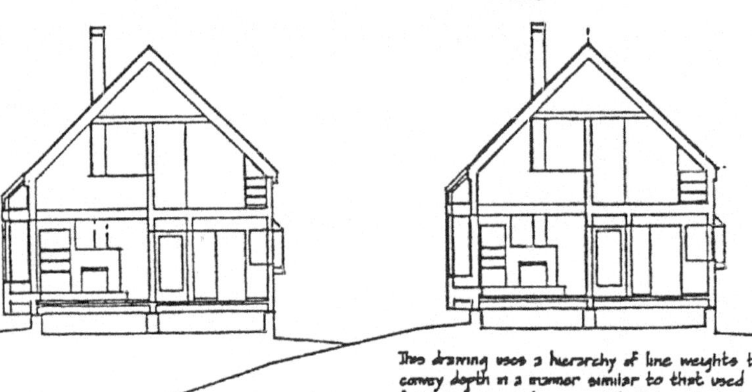

This drawing is a sectional view of a building using a single-line weight. It is difficult to discern what is cut and what is seen in elevation.

This drawing uses a hierarchy of line weights to convey depth in a manner similar to that used for plan drawings (see page 30). Those elements that are cut in section are outlined with a heavy line. Those elements that are seen in elevation beyond the section cut are outlined with intermediate line weights. The farther back an element is from the section cut, the finer the line weight should be.

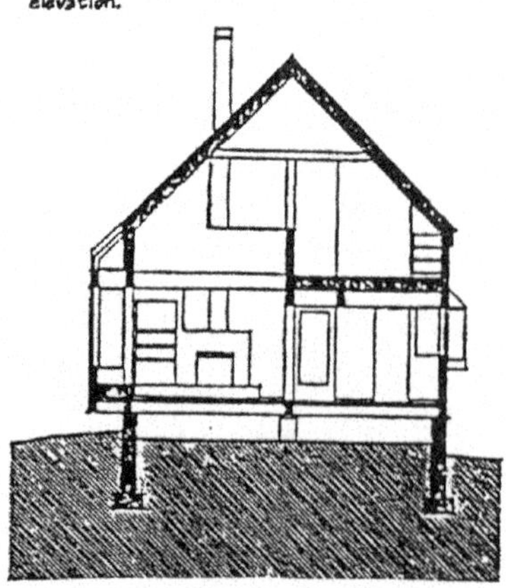

This drawing illustrates how the elements that are cut in section can be given a tonal value to heighten their contrast with elevational elements seen beyond the cut. This is particularly necessary when many elements are shown in elevation.

This last drawing shows how the value system can be reversed when what is seen in elevation is rendered along with the background for the drawing. In this case, the section cut can be left white or given a fairly light value to contrast with the drawing field.

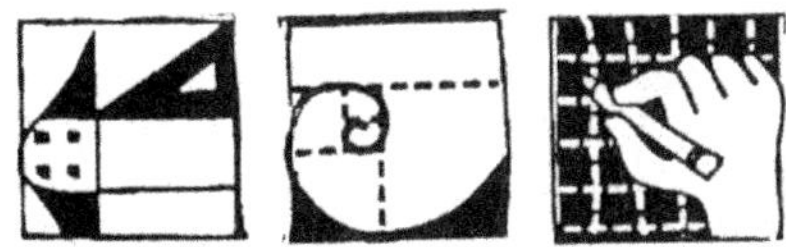

PERSPECTIVE

by Mike Smith

1. As one observes the scene, there is an imaginary line drawn at eye level. This line is known as the HORIZON LINE.

2. All lines not parallel to an imaginary plane in front of the viewer will appear to recede to an imaginary point of infinity on the horizon line. This point is called a VANISHING POINT. Depending on the type of view taken, there may be one or two vanishing points.

3. All horizontal or vertical lines in front of the viewer will appear horizontal or vertical but will foreshorten as they recede in the scene. In a one-point perspective, this applies only to vertical lines in a two-point perspective.

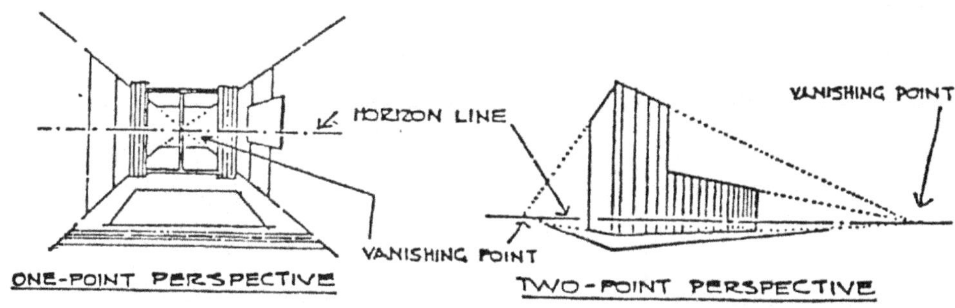

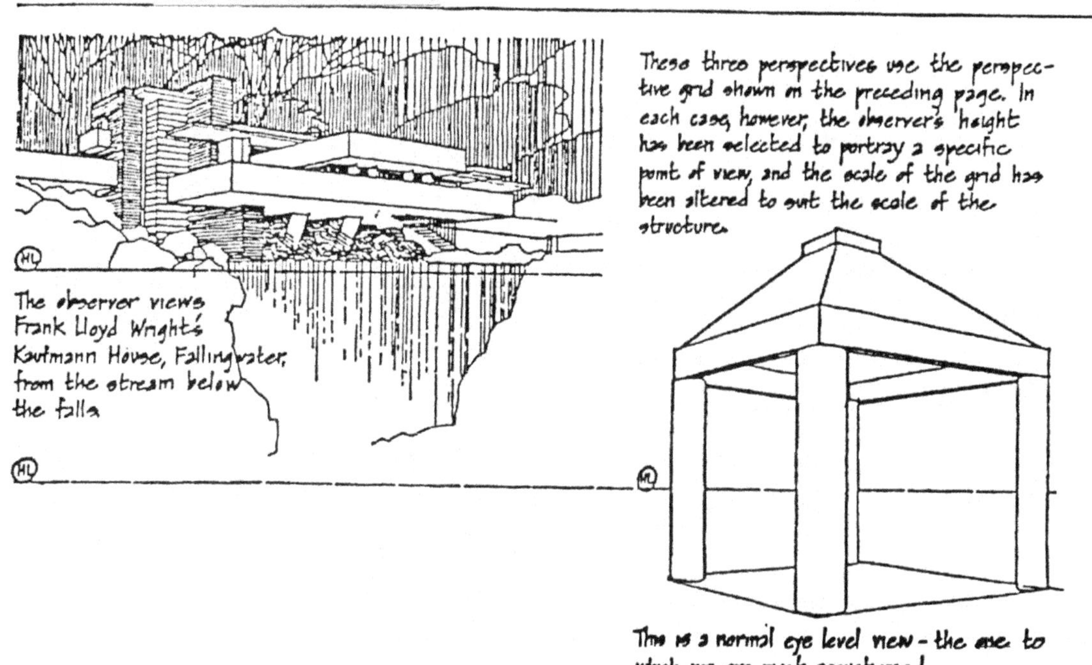

PEOPLE

(from Architectural Graphics by Frank Ching)

The viewer of a drawing relates to the human figures within it; he becomes one of them and thus is drawn into the scene.

- the purpose of placing human figures in an architectural drawing is to indicate scale

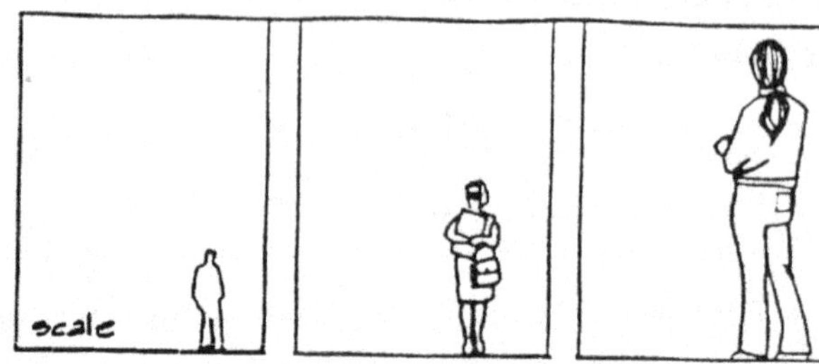

- the placement of human figures can indicate spatial depth and levels

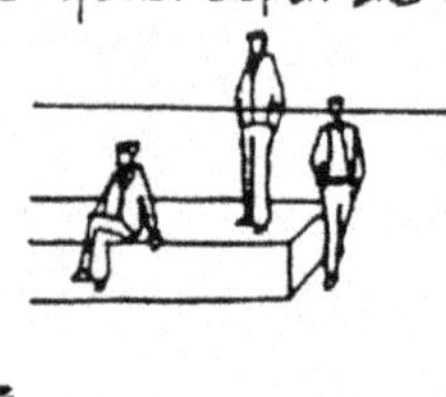

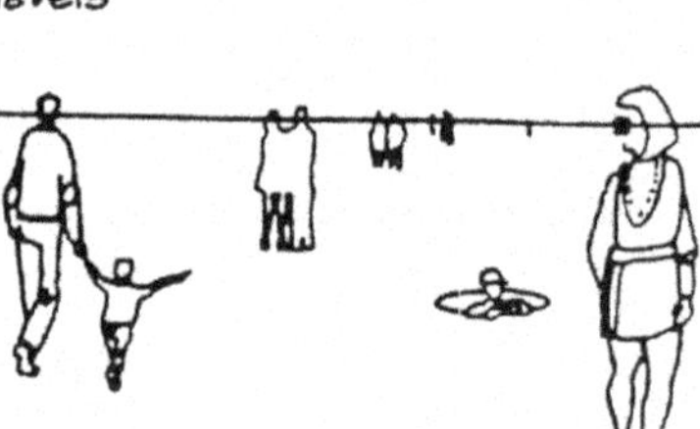

- the number, disposition, and dress of human figures can indicate usage of a space

The important features of human figures, aside from their disposition, are:

- proportion
- size
- attitude

The human figure can be broken down into seven equal parts; the head is one-seventh of the total body height.

It is generally easiest to start human figures with the head at eye level. In orthographic and paraline drawings the 6'-0" height can be scaled. In perspectives the horizon line is at the viewer's eye level, so we can start at the horizon line. Figures above or below the level of the viewer can first be sized as if on the same level and then shifted up or down as required.

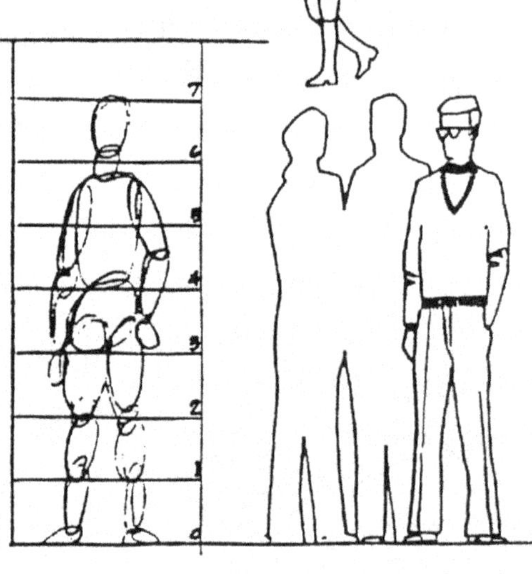

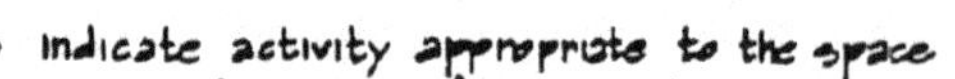

- indicate activity appropriate to the space
- avoid stiff, upright figures and hyperactive groups
- in composition, utilize both groups and solitary figures that are consistent with the usage of the space

COLOR WHEEL

RED, YELLOW and BLUE are primary colors. Orange, green and violet are secondary colors. Neighboring colors are called "analogous" colors. Pastel colors can be made by adding white or extra water. Colors at opposite sides of the wheel are called "complementary" colors. When mixed with each other they make muddy colors like some of the colors found in nature or architecture. Muddy colors can also be made by adding black.

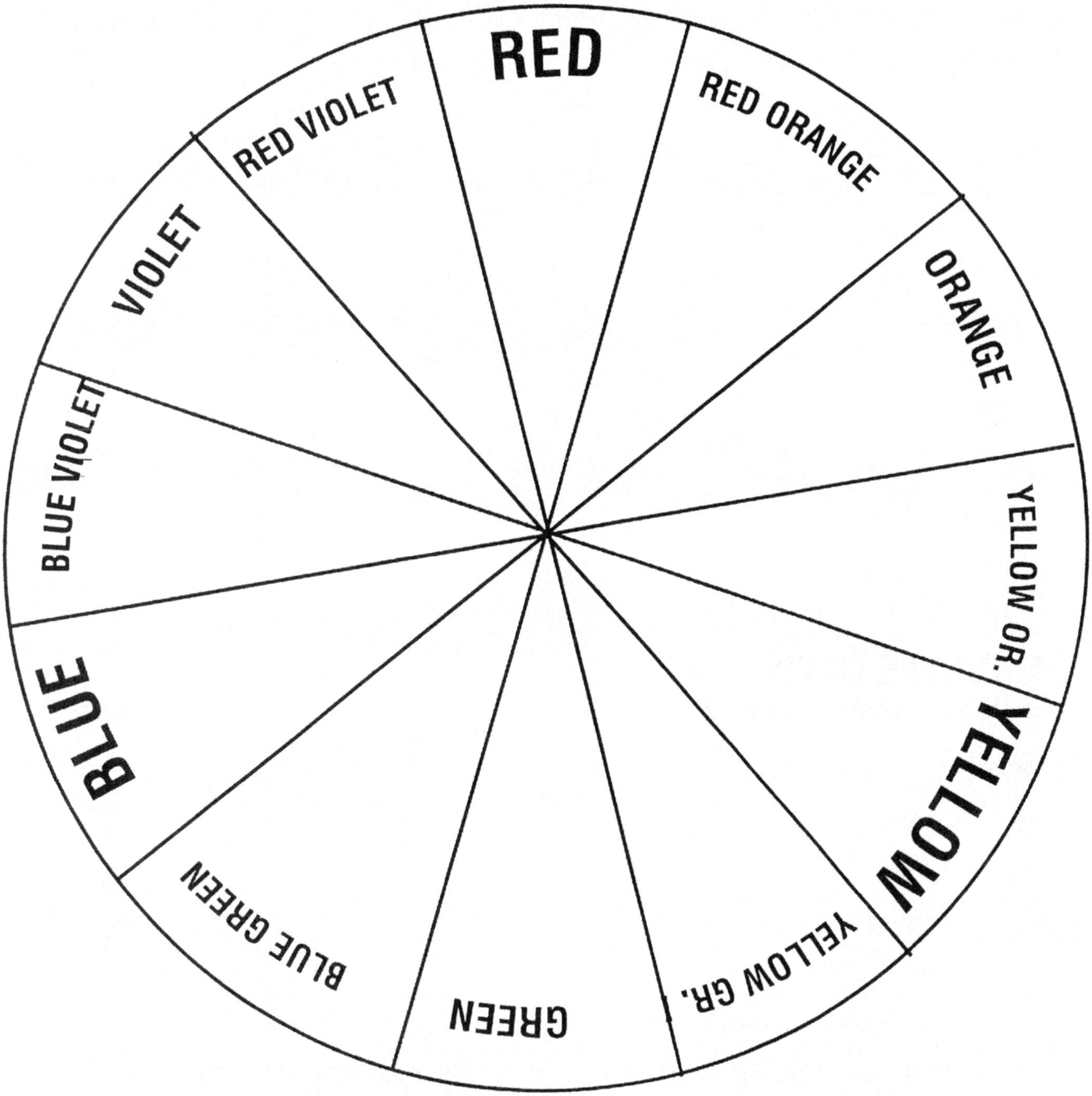

RED
RED ORANGE
ORANGE
YELLOW OR.
YELLOW
YELLOW GR.
GREEN
BLUE GREEN
BLUE
BLUE VIOLET
VIOLET
RED VIOLET

ARROWS

from Notes on Architecture by Berryman

You will find that knowing how to draw interesting arrows can aid you in drawings that communicate concepts, i.e. designing buildings or products. Learn how to draw a great many arrows. Draw arrows with curves in them, three-dimensional arrows, arrows in groups, large arrows, fat arrows, small arrows, wavy arrows. Draw arrows that turn, arrows that spin, arrows that come out of boxes at different angles. Try drawing positive arrows (black arrows with a white background), negative arrows (white arrows with a black background), dark arrows or light arrows. You will find that knowing how to draw different arrows can help you explain points in your drawing and visually enhance your drawings.

MULTIPLE VIEWS

How to show spatial relationships

Vocabulary

Height - Top to bottom

Width - Side to side

Depth - Front to back

Top - Plan view; width and depth

Elevation - Front view; width and height

Elevation - Right side view; depth and height

OBLIQUE VIEW

PLAN VIEW

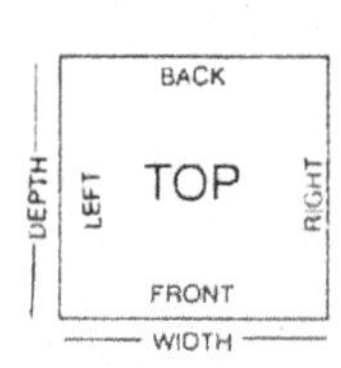

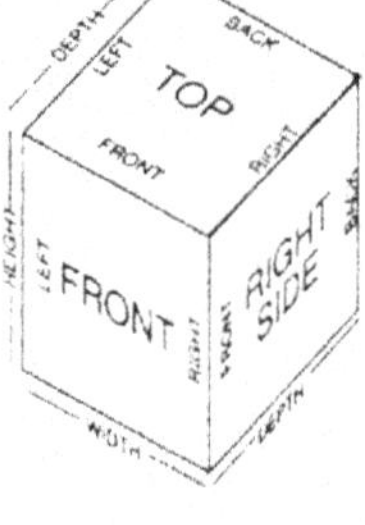

FRONT AND SIDE ELEVATIONS

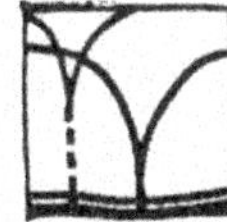

UNDERSTANDING THE FORCES OF STRUCTURE

by Rick Parker (Illustrations adapted from Notes on Architecture by Berryman)

FORCE

Force is an influence on an object which tends to affect its shape or motion or both. Force is commonly measured in pounds. (SI: Newtons)

When forces act on an object directed **toward** each other in the same plane, the arrangement of forces is called **compression.** Compression tends to shorten an object. When forces act on an object, directed **away from** each other in the same plane, the arrangement of forces is called **tension.** Tension tends to elongate an object.

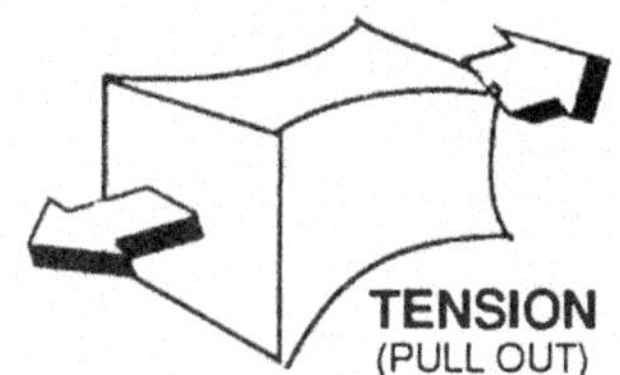

When force is applied to an object some distance from the support, the force produces a bending or twisting called **moment** or **torque.** The magnitude of the moment is equal to the product of force and distance. Moment is usually measured in foot pounds.

When forces (tension, compression or torsion) act on an object in adjacent planes, the arrangement of forces is called **shear.**

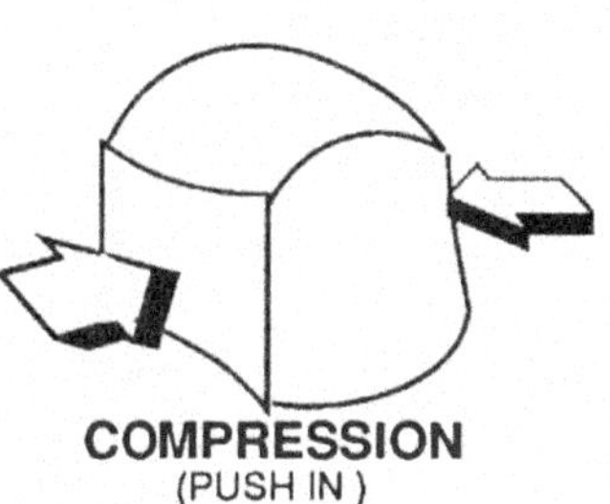

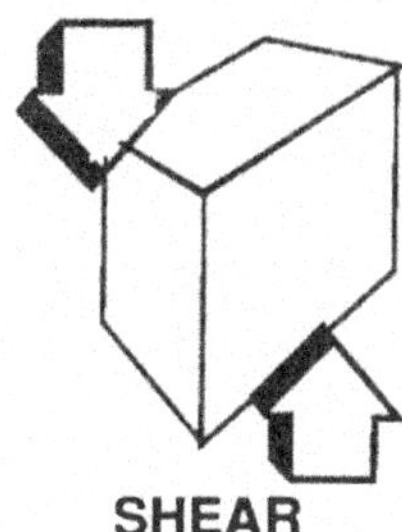

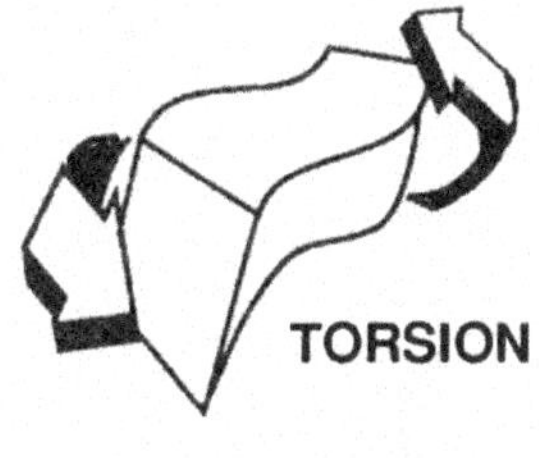

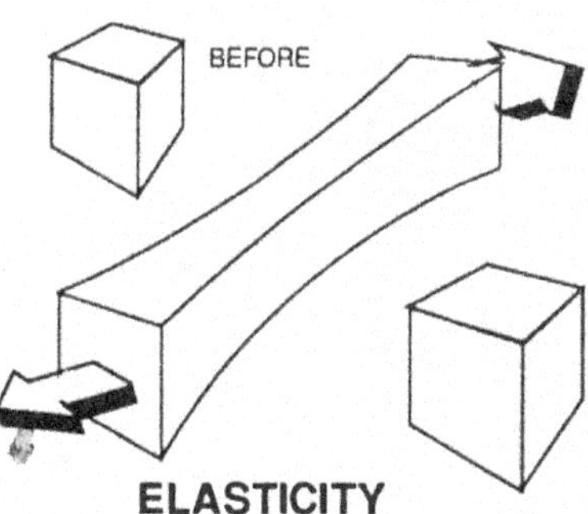

EXERCISE

Describe the forces in the following:

A belt	A twistoff bottle top	A diving board
A ladder	The chain of a swing	A tree in the wind
A rubber band	A ball being hit by a bat	Rubbing your hands together
A piece of paper being cut with scissors		The femur while standing

UNDERSTANDING THE FORCES OF STRUCTURE

by Rick Parker

STRESS

Stress is the concentration of force in a load path. Each person shown here is a "load path."

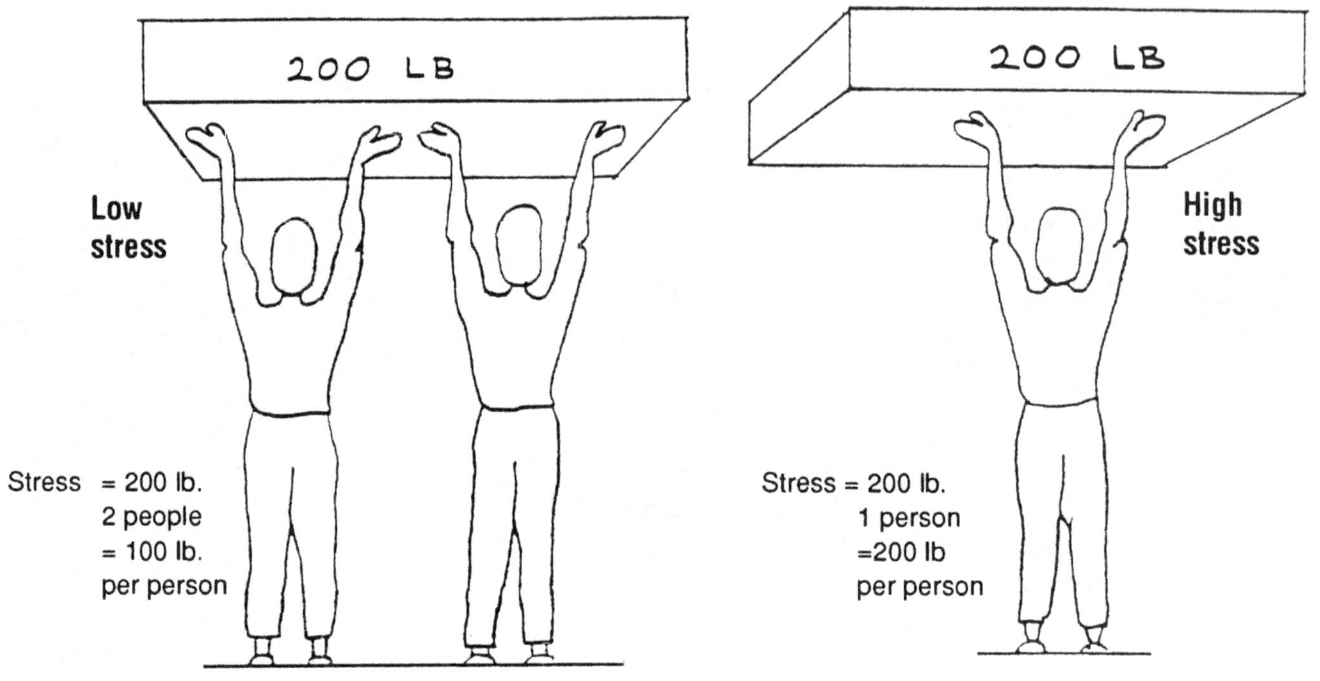

Weight of rock = 200 lb.

Weight of rock = 200 lb.

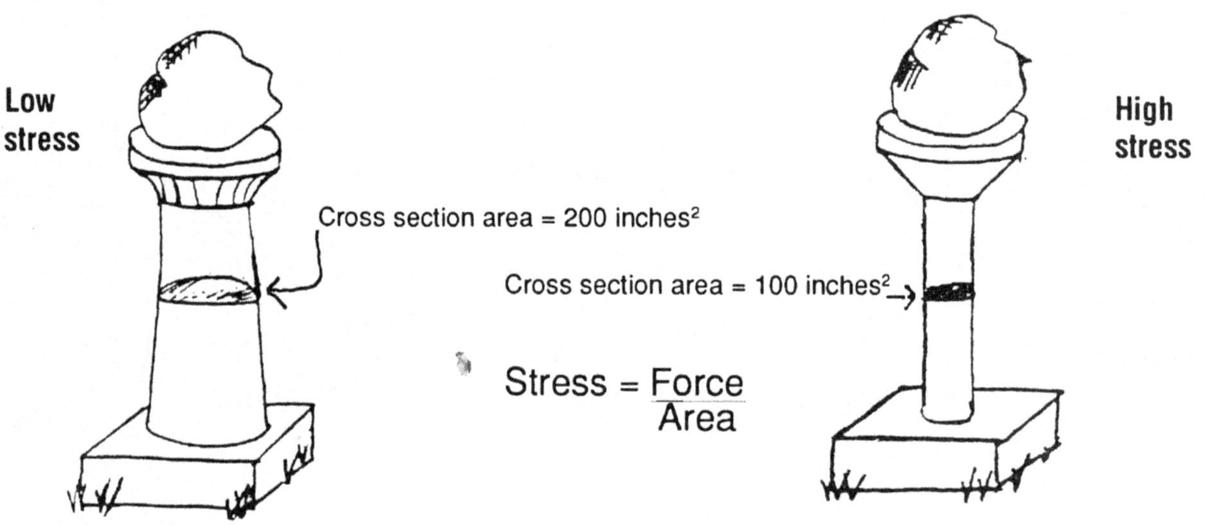

$$\text{Stress} = \frac{\text{Force}}{\text{Area}}$$

$$\text{Stress} = \frac{\text{Force: 200 lb.}}{\text{Area: 200 in}^2} = 1 \text{ PSI}$$

$$\text{Stress} = \frac{\text{Force: 200 lb.}}{\text{Area: 100 in}^2} = 2\text{PSI}$$

PSI = **P**ounds per **S**quare **I**nch

UNDERSTANDING THE FORCES OF STRUCTURE

by Rick Parker

LOAD PATH

Load path is the route forces travel to get from the load to the support.

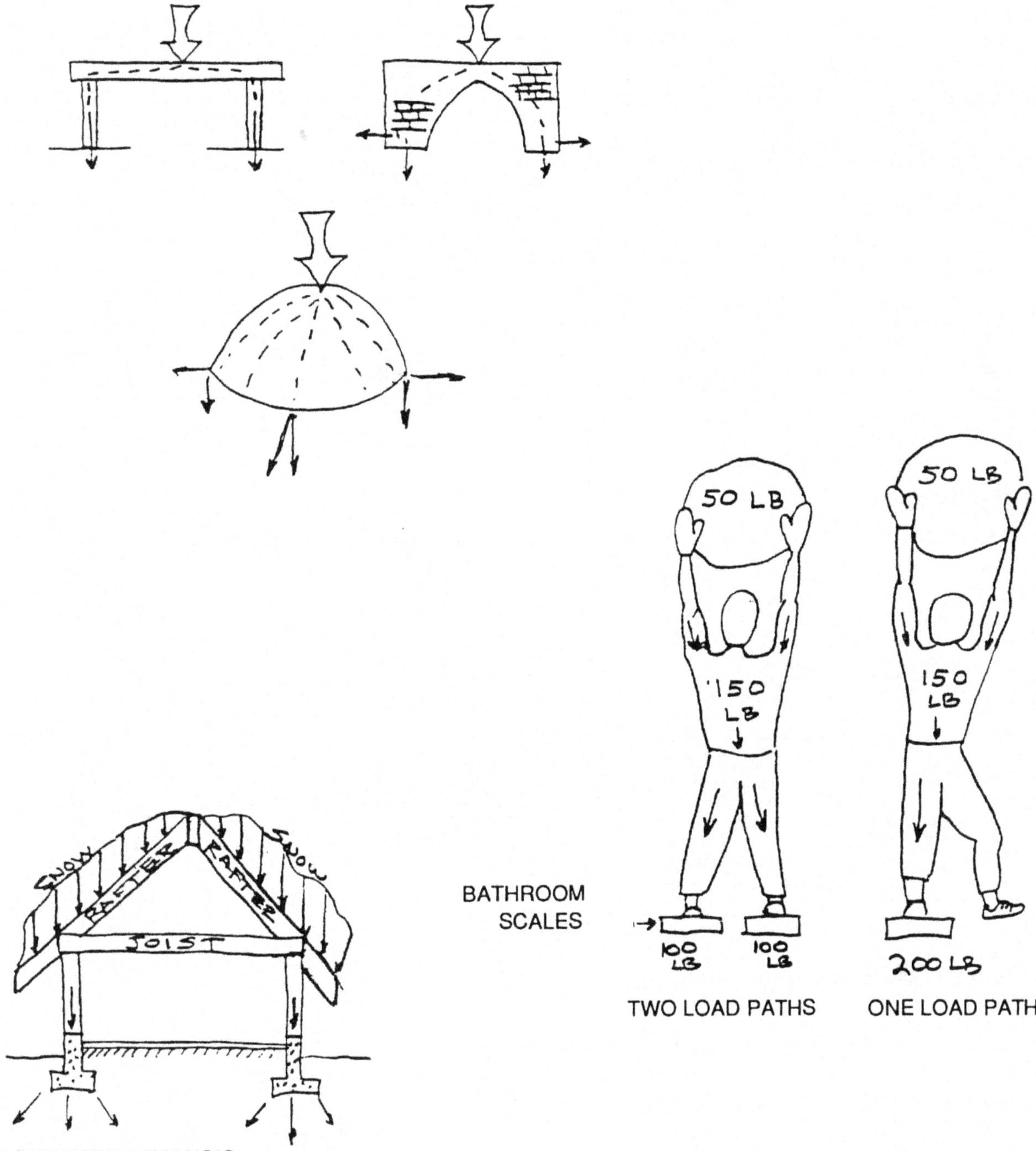

LOAD PATH ANALYSIS

Snow load is transmitted to the wall through the bending of the rafter. The joist counteracts the thrust of the rafter through tension. The rafters bear on the walls, putting them in compression. This transmits the load to the foundation, which distributes the load into the soil by compression.

UNDERSTANDING THE FORCES OF STRUCTURE

by Rick Parker

BE A BEAM

SIMPLE BEAM

A simple beam is supported at each end and the ends are free to rotate when the beam is loaded.

•The top of a simple beam is in compression.

•The bottom of a simple beam is in tension.

•The greatest stress is in the middle of the beam.

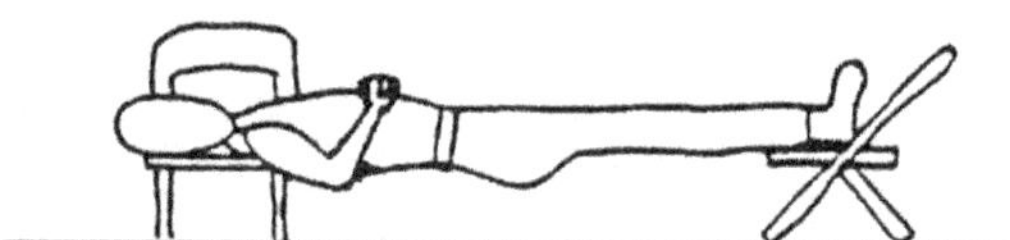

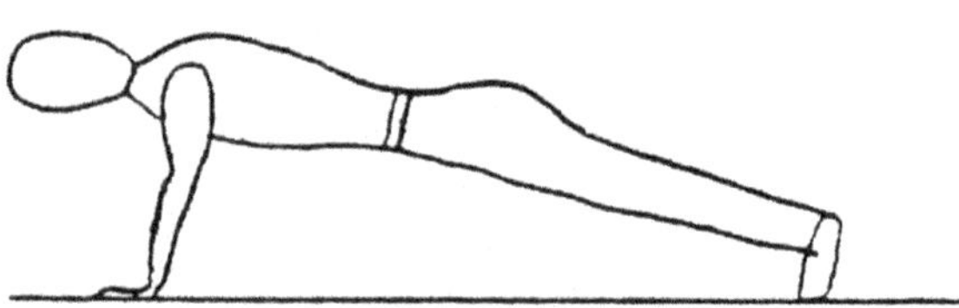

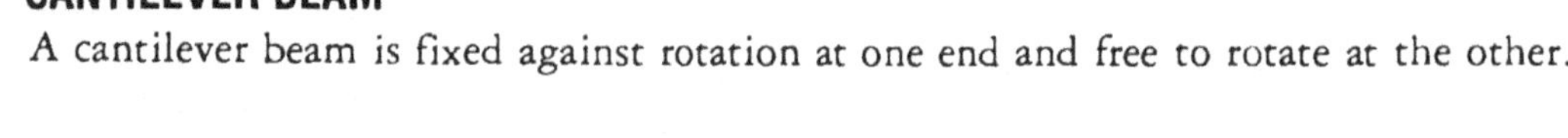

CANTILEVER BEAM

A cantilever beam is fixed against rotation at one end and free to rotate at the other.

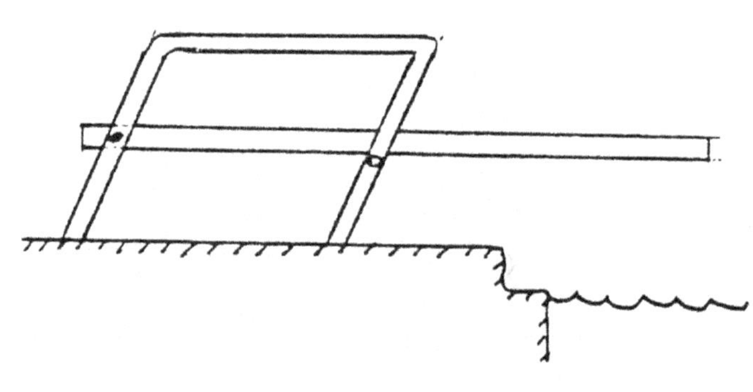

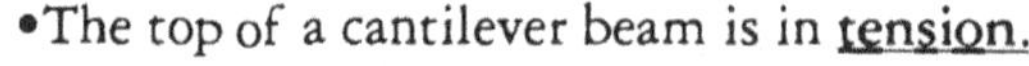

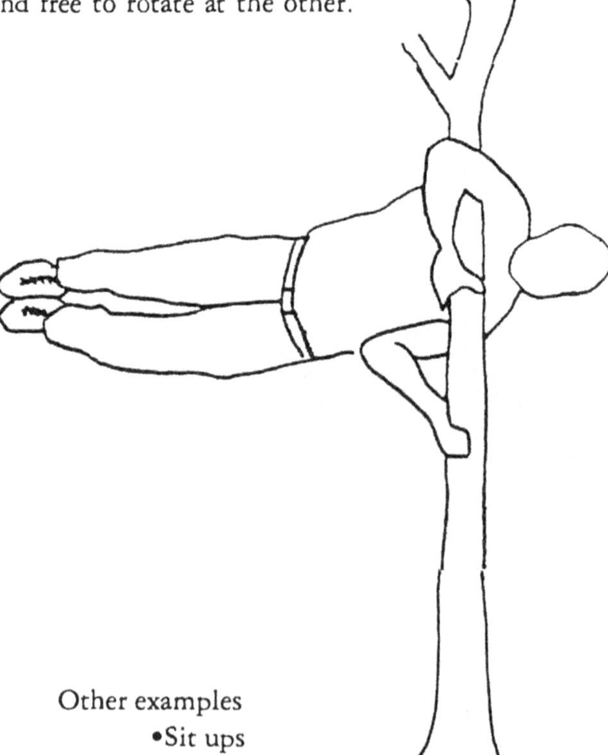

•The top of a cantilever beam is in tension.

•The bottom of a cantilever beam is in compression.

•The greatest stress is at the support of the beam.

Other examples

•Sit ups

•Leg lifts

UNDERSTANDING THE FORCES OF STRUCTURE

by Rick Parker

BE A DOME

Compression ring

Students all lean into the center basketball with feet apart, touching their neighbor's feet. Both the tension ring and the compression ring are essential to keep this dome from collapsing.

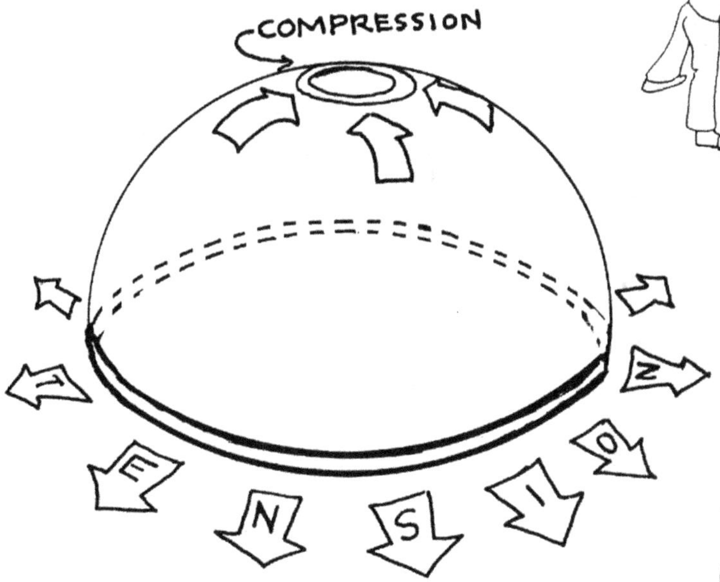

COMPRESSION

T E N S I O N

Tension ring

Students join arms in a circle, intertwining their arms, with their feet together. Everyone then leans back as shown.

Notice how the dome can be thought of as a series of arches arranged in a circle.

UNDERSTANDING THE FORCES OF STRUCTURE

by Rick Parker

BE A SUSPENSION BRIDGE

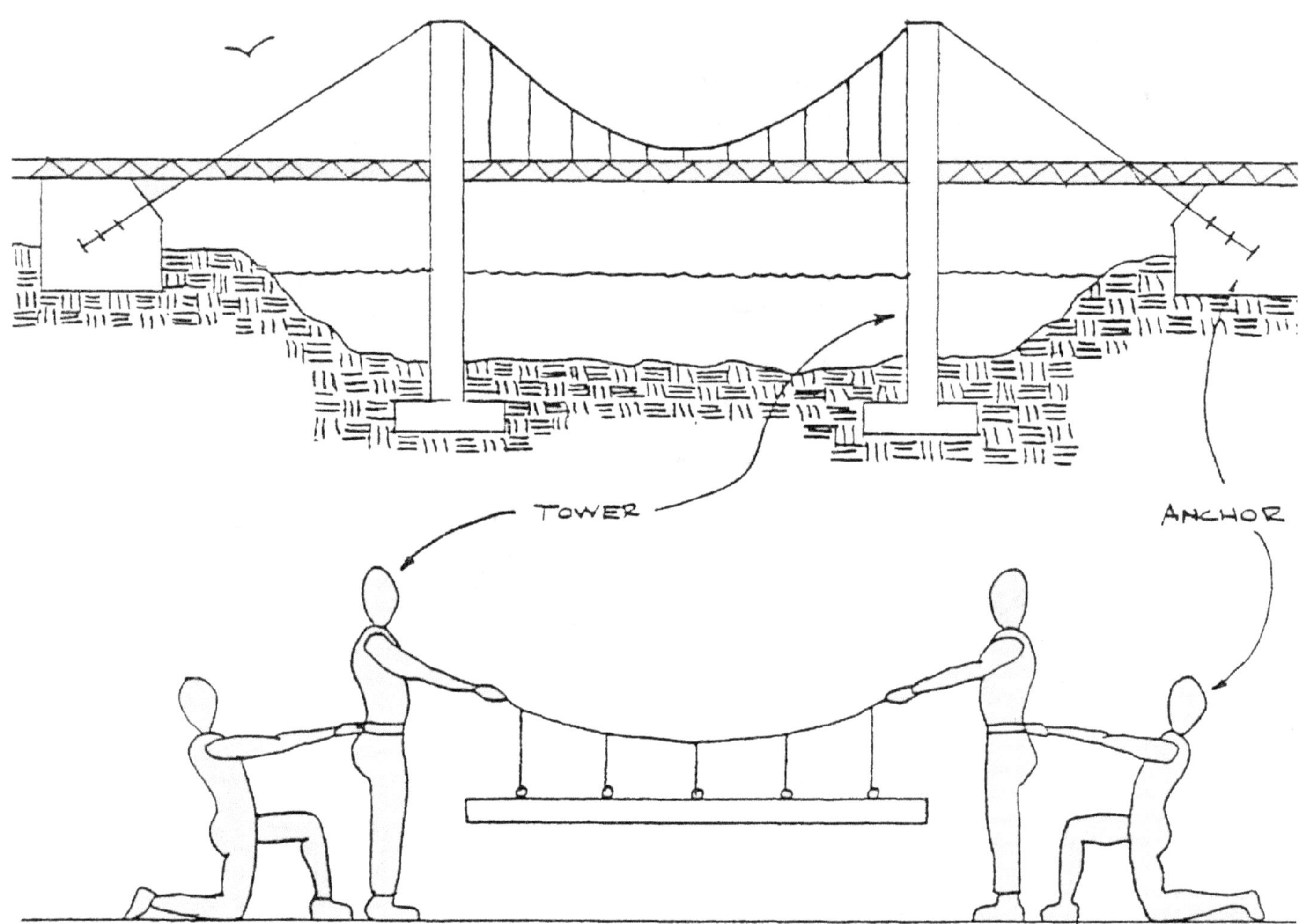

1. Stand with feet together
2. Pull rope between two "towers."
3. Notice how difficult it is to resist the pulling.
4. Have the "anchors" pull on the "towers'" belts.
5. Notice how much easier it is for "towers" to pull the rope.

UNDERSTANDING THE FORCES OF STRUCTURE

by Rick Parker

TRUSSES

A truss behaves the same as a beam. It has diagonal members. It transfers load by ending. When it carries a load, each of its elements can only be in tension or compression.

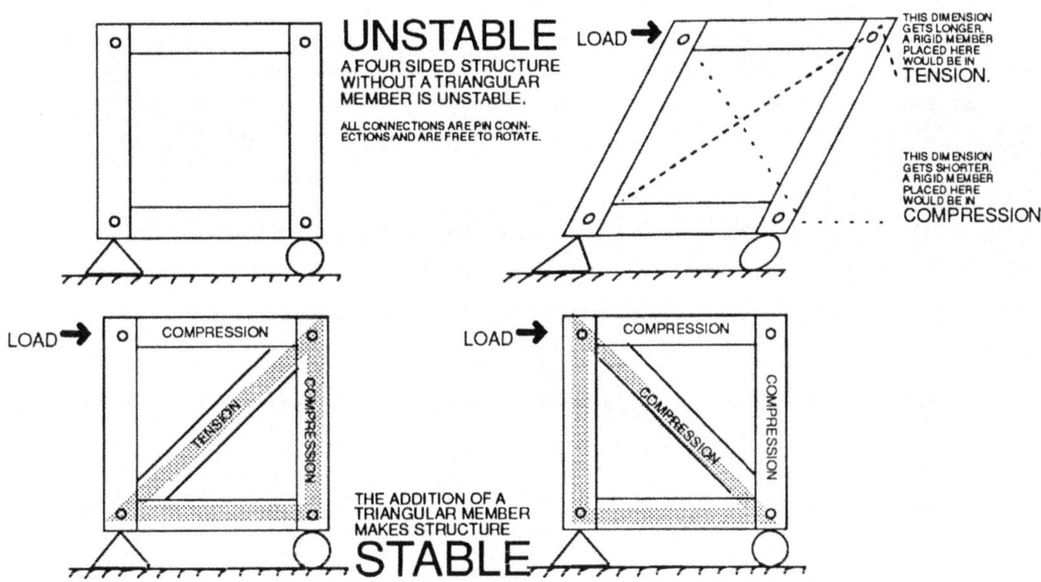

- Look for trusses. Bring in pictures of different types of trusses. Why were the diagonals put in the way they were? Where is the tension? Where is the compression?

Bridge trusses All connections behave as pin connections.

Pratt

Howe

Warren

K

Roof trusses

Fink

Pratt

Howe

Warren

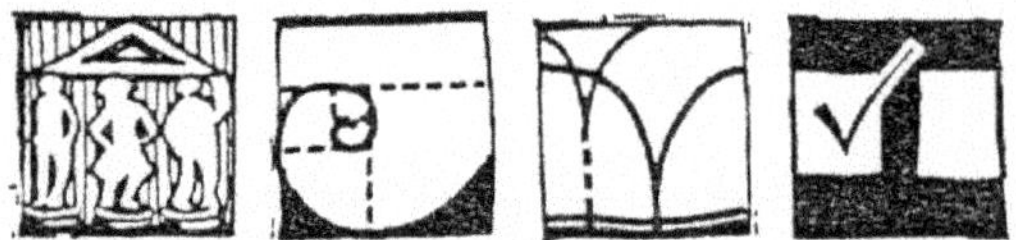

PHYSICS OF STRUCTURE EXERCISE

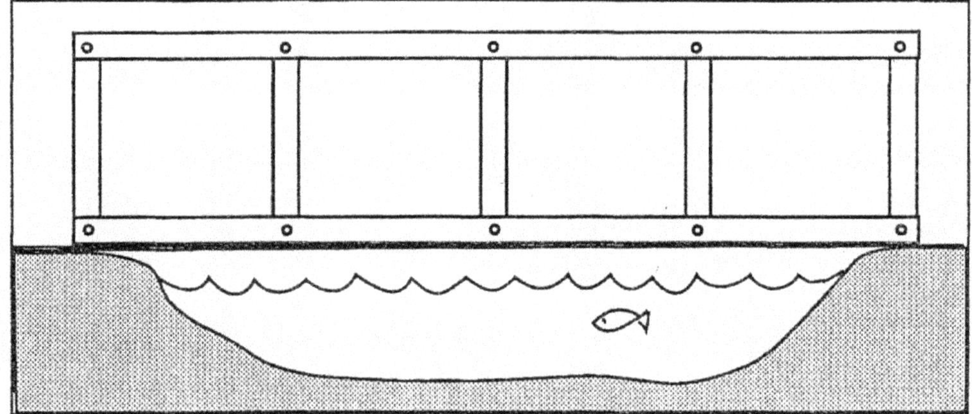

Is this bridge stable? ________ Please explain your answer.

____

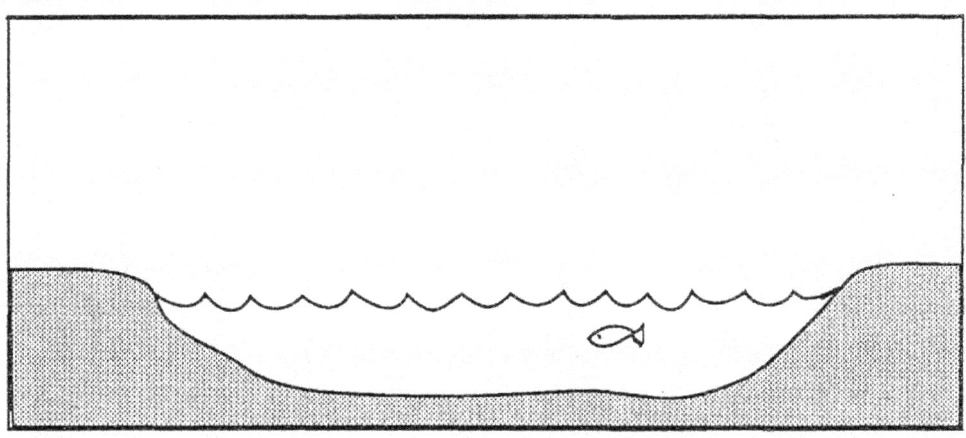

A truck drives to the middle of the bridge. Please show how the bridge stretches.
What force does the truck put on the road? ______________________
What force is put on the top of the bridge? ______________________

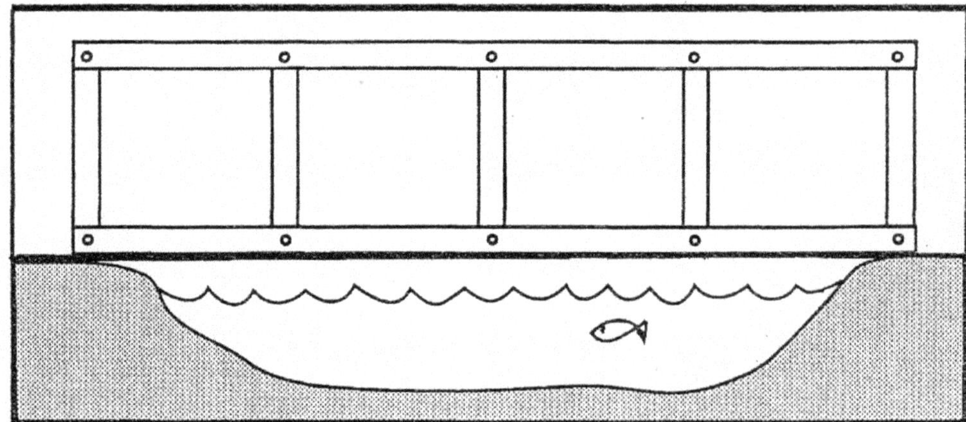

Draw in the parts that will make the bridge stable. Draw arrows to show where the load transfers from the bridge to the ground.

DESIGN A COLUMN CAPITAL

Columns

Column capitals can be ornaments for a building. The buildings made by Greek and Roman architects in ancient times had such beautiful columns that they have been copied on many buildings since they were designed. The three columns shown on the left have the names Doric, Ionic and Corinthian. These are the architectural names for ancient Greek designs called the "classical orders."

Capitals can have designs inspired by plants, geometry, animals or any interesting object, real or imaginary. Use your imagination.

Draw an original design for a column capital in the space below.

PAPER STRUCTURES FOR ARCHITECTURAL MODELS

by Stephanie Jurs

How to make geometric architectural building blocks from construction paper and other materials

MATERIALS

Strips of construction paper
Scissors
Glue
Masking tape

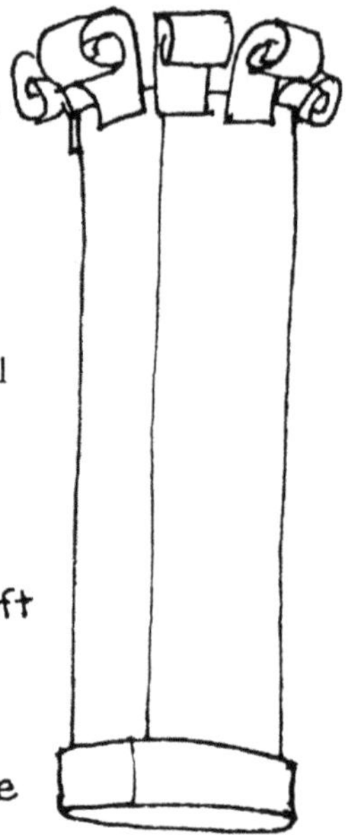

EXERCISE

Using a large piece of construction paper to which you will attach the forms, use colored paper to make the following shapes:

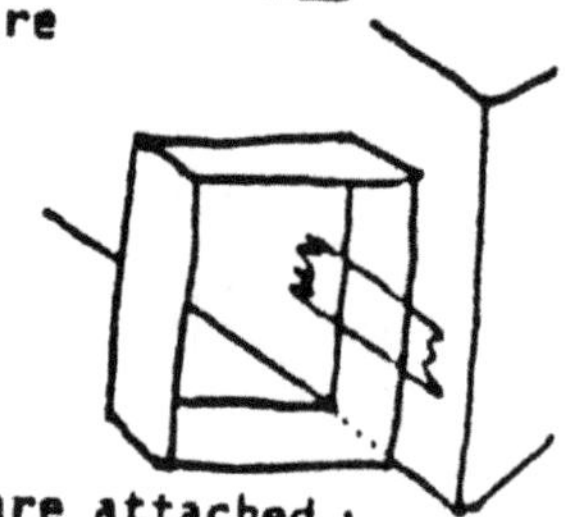

Square, circle, triangle, cylinder, cone

Cube, arch, dome, vault, double vault

Pyramid, truss system for building

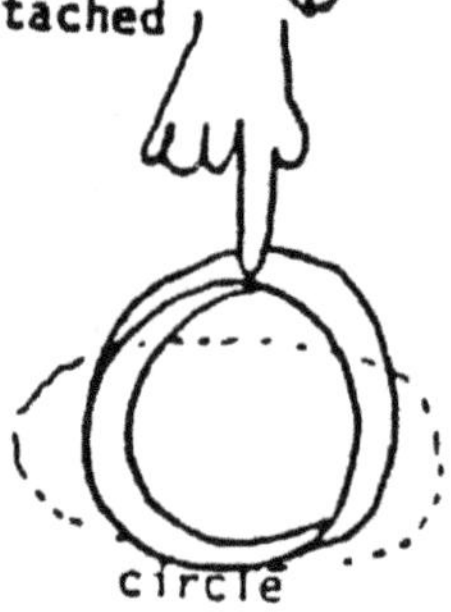

capital

Shaft

Base

Square

Square attached

circle

pyramid

vault

A fantasy castle or city

Using paper forms you now know from building them, make a fantasy castle structure or city from any of the forms you have built. Write a story about who lives in your fantasy castle and what they do there; or, with a fantasy city, try to do some original urban planning and tell about it.

Arch

Beginning of a Dome

truss system

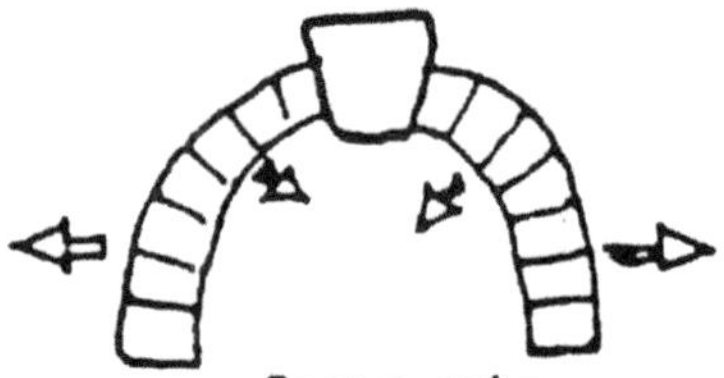

Sugar cube arch

tetrahedron

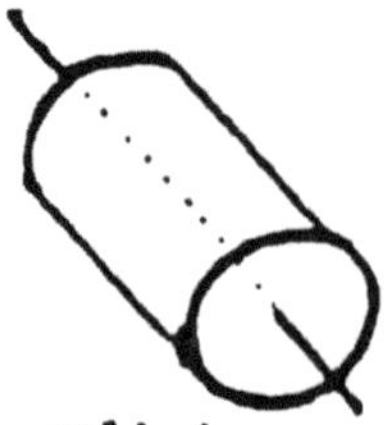

cylinder

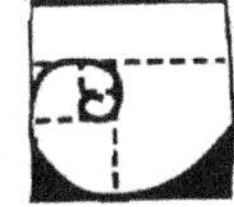

PAPER PATTERNS FOR GEOMETRIC FORMS

by John Tubbs

CONE

1. Cut out both figures along solid lines.
2. Fold "tab" along dotted line (follow arrows).
3. Glue "tab" to side "A."
4. Glue circle to bottom of cone.

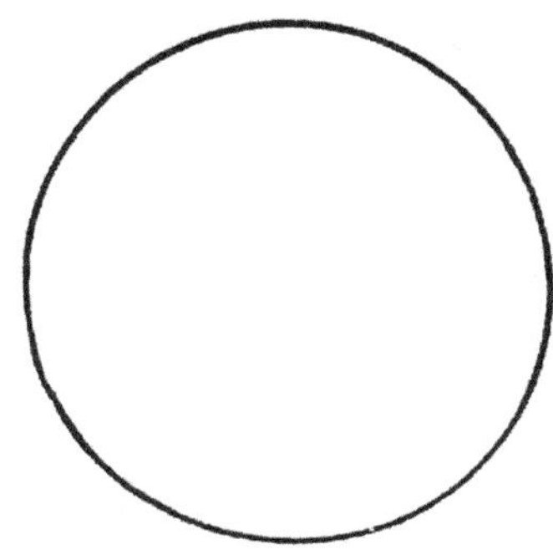

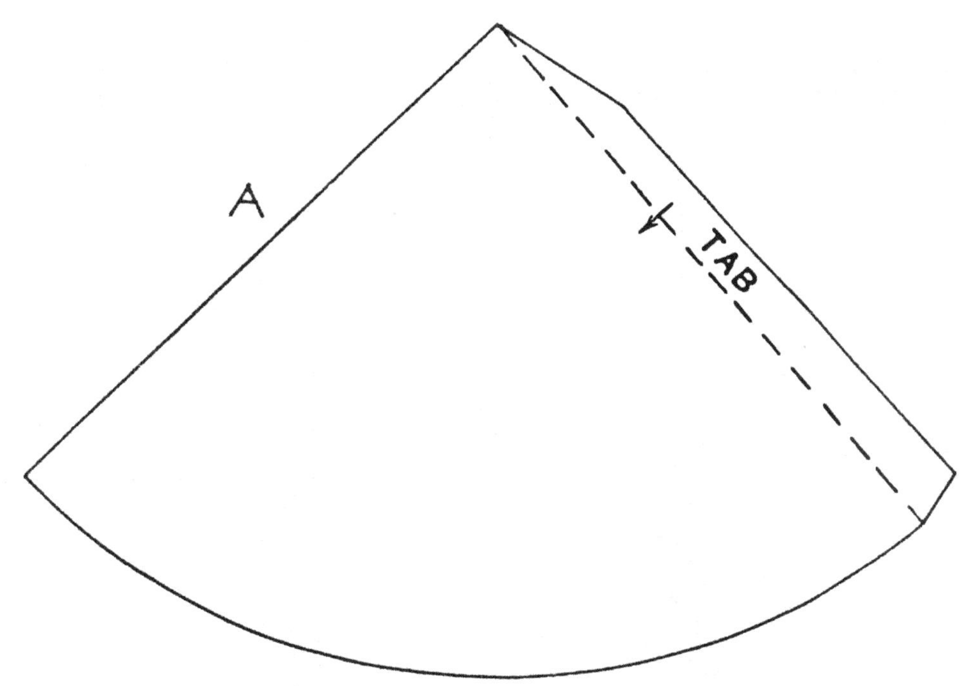

PAPER PATTERNS FOR GEOMETRIC FORMS

by John Tubbs

CUBE

1. Cut out figure along solid lines.
2. Fold "tab" along dotted lines.
3. Bring cube together,
4. Glue "tabs" to cube walls.

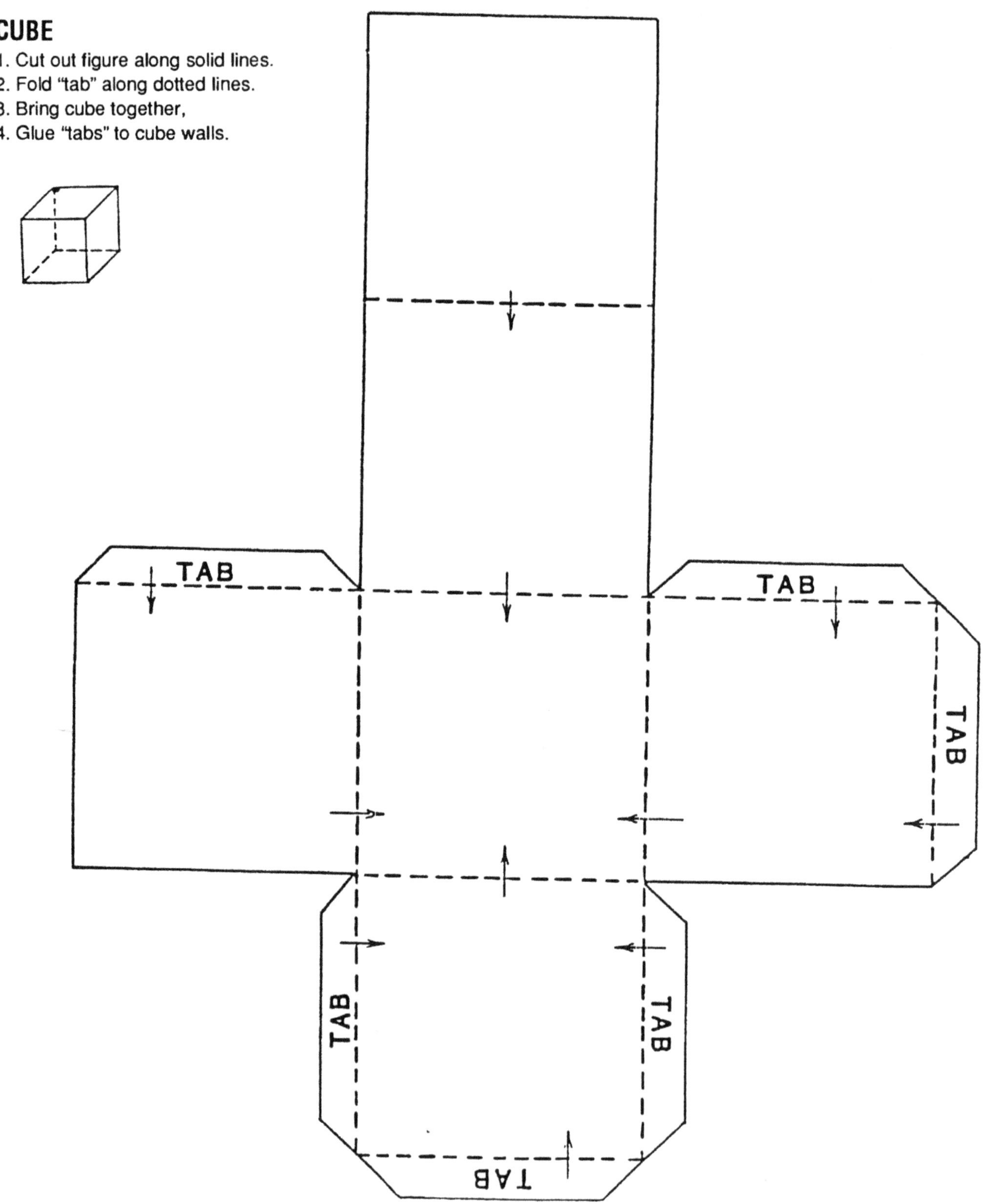

PAPER PATTERNS FOR GEOMETRIC FORMS

by John Tubbs

CYLINDER

1. Cut out figures along solid lines.
2. Fold "tab" along dotted line.
3. Glue "tab" to side "A."
4. Glue one circle each side.

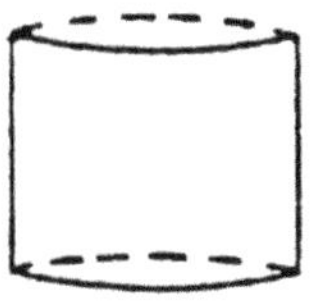

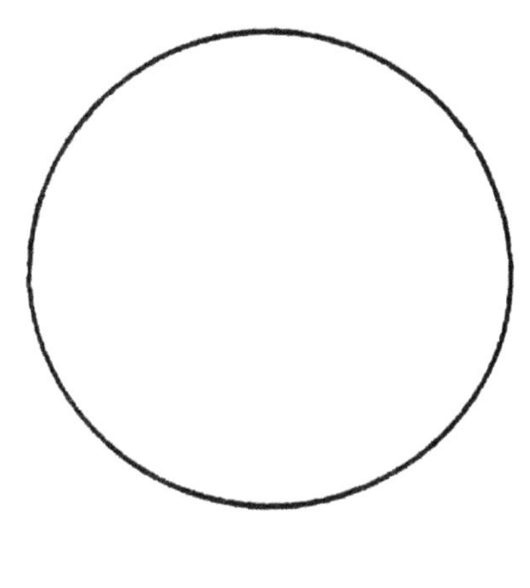

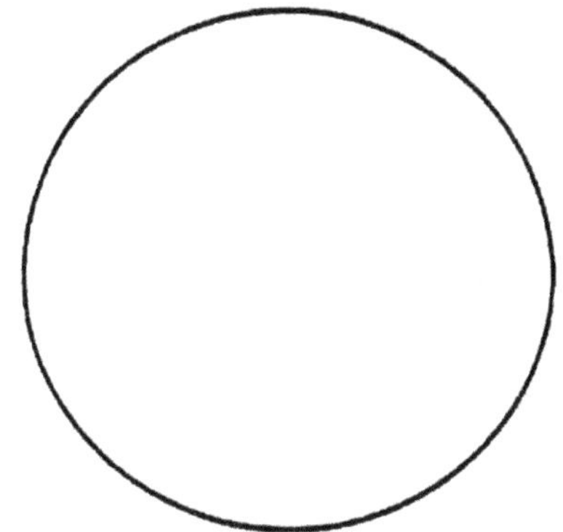

PAPER PATTERNS FOR GEOMETRIC FORMS

by John Tubbs

PYRAMID

1. Cut out figure along solid lines.
2. Fold along *all* dotted lines.
3. Bring pyramid together.
4. Glue "tabs" to pyramid walls.

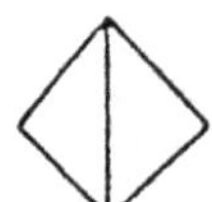

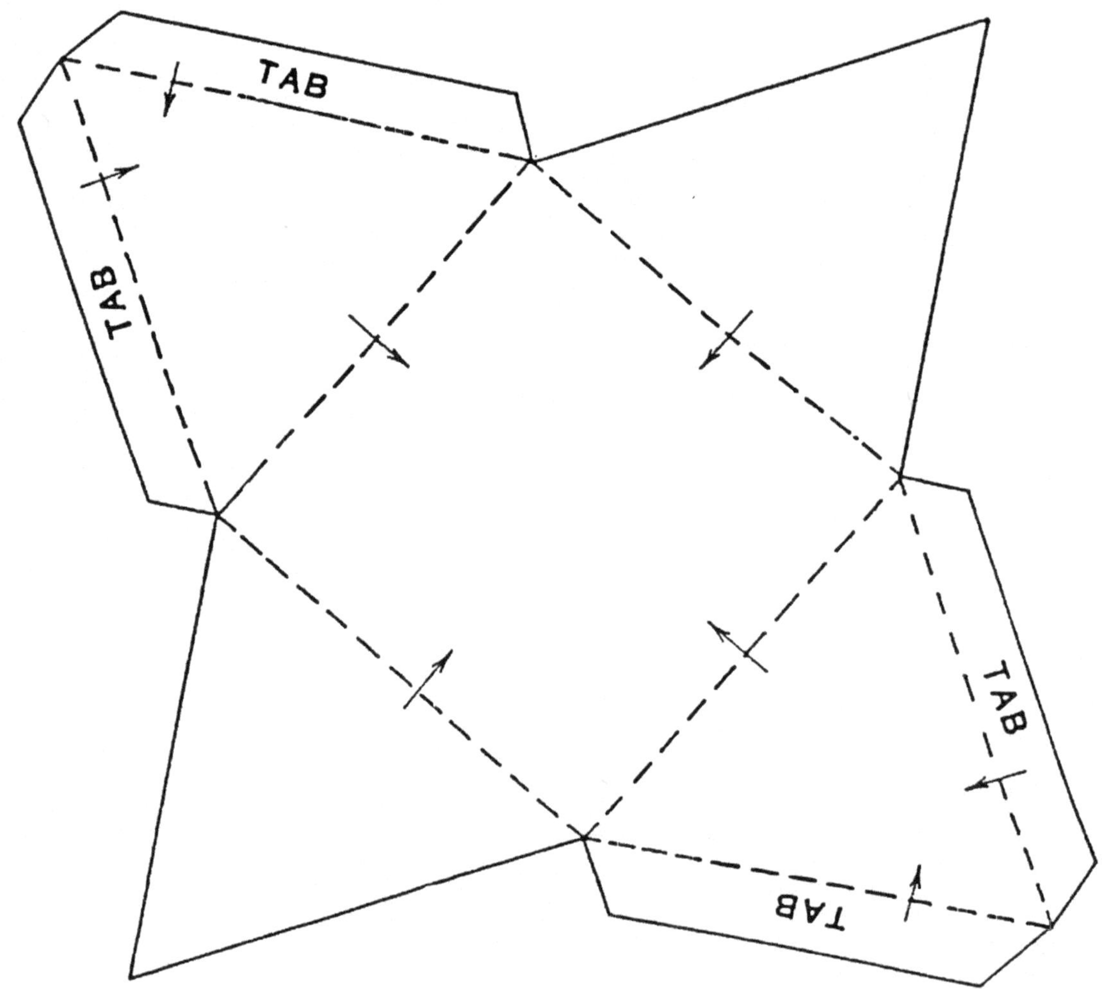

PAPER PATTERNS FOR GEOMETRIC FORMS

by John Tubbs

SPHERE

1. Cut out all six figures along solid lines.
2. Fold along dotted lines.
3. Glue all six "tabs" together.

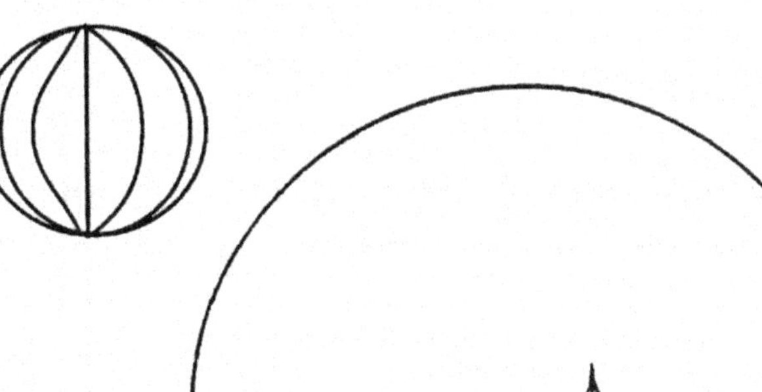

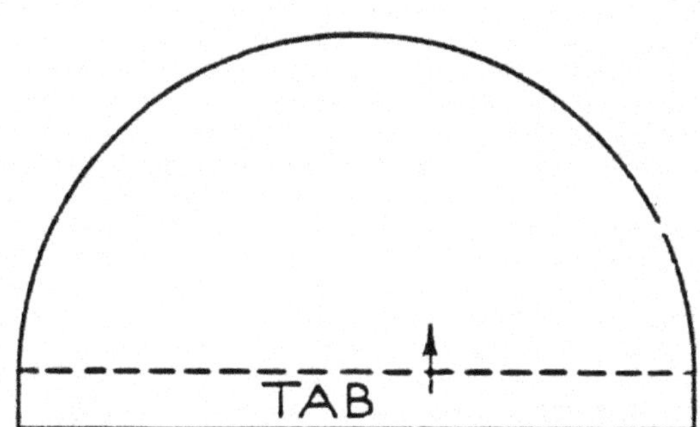

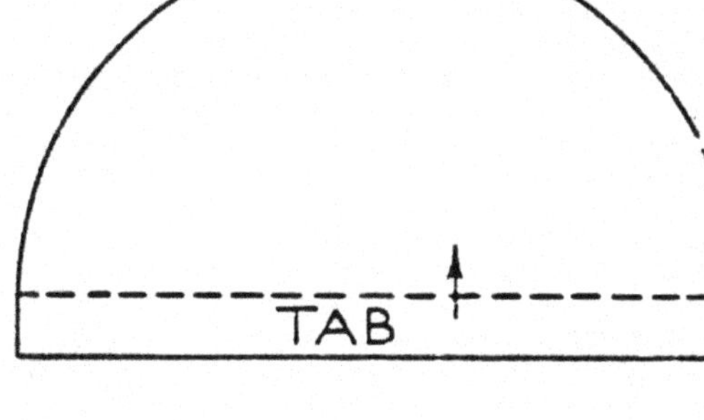

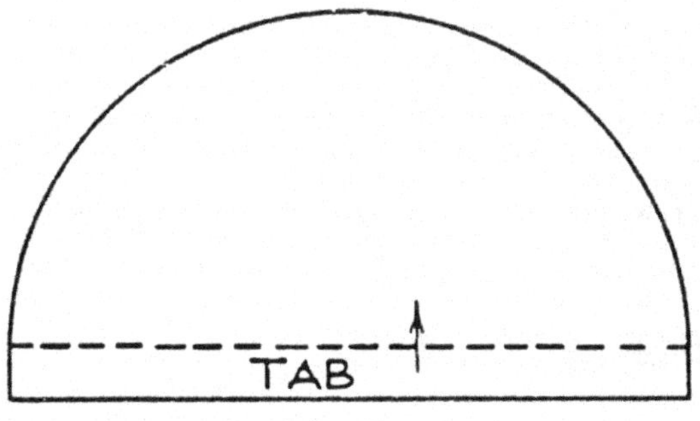

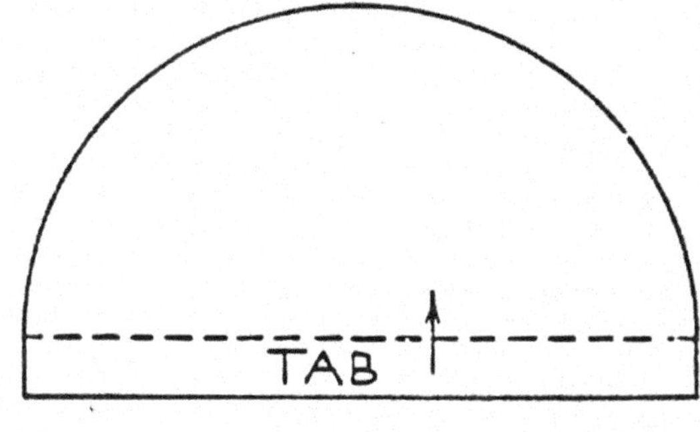

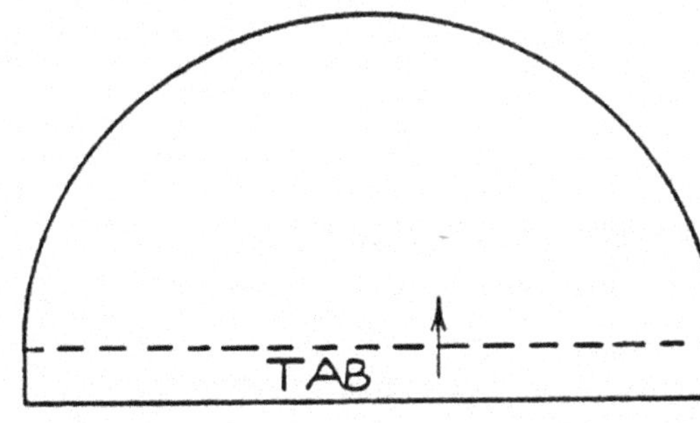

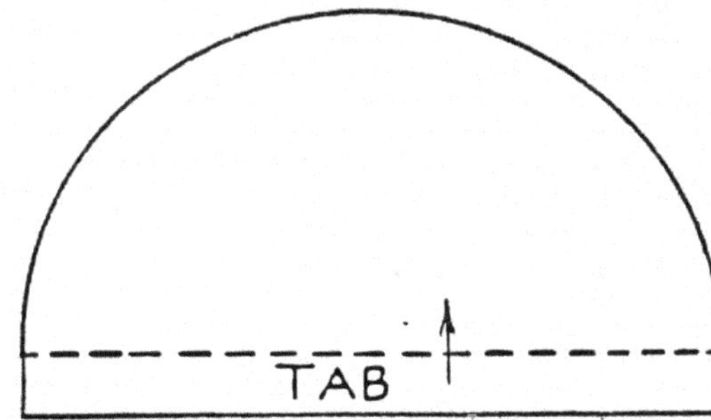

ENERGY AND PLUMBING SURVEY

ENERGY SYSTEMS

Heating, Ventilation and Cooling (HVAC) System

1. What form of energy does the heating or cooling system use?______________

2. How does the energy enter the building?____________________________

3. Draw an imaginary diagram of the heating and cooling system in the building→

From the HVAC to a room

Lighting and electrical power

1. Where is the main electrical vault for the building?___________________

2. How does the electrical power enter the building?___________________

3. Where is the electrical control panel for the building?________________

4. Draw an imaginary diagram of the electrical wiring system of the building →

From a powerline to light bulb

PLUMBING SYSTEMS

Fresh water system

1. What is the source of your area's water supply?_________________________

2. Where does the water line enter the building?__________________________

3. How is the fresh water kept separate from the waste water?________________

Waste water removal system

1. How is waste water removed from the building?________________________

2. Where does the waste go after removal from the building?________________

3. Is the waste water purified at a sewage treatment plant?________________

4. Draw an imaginary diagram of the waste water removal system →

From the drinking fountain to the sewage treatment plant

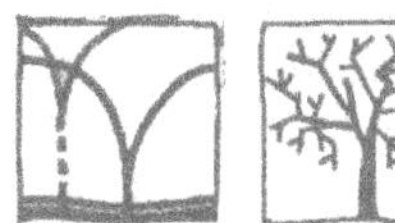

CONTOUR MAP EXERCISE

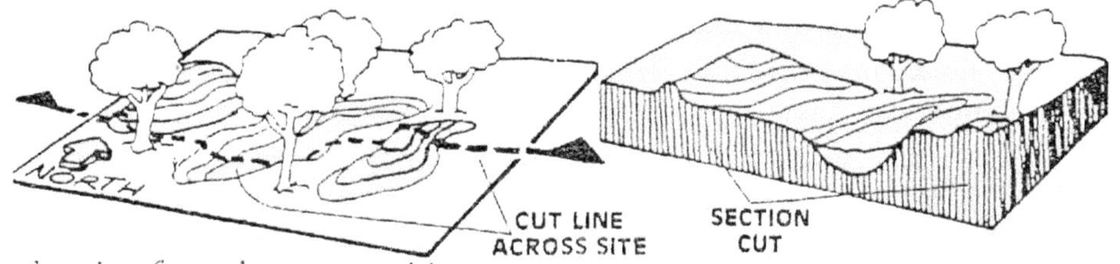

Make a section drawing from the topographic contour map.
The shoreline around the edge of the pond is at zero ground level. There are two hills shown by contour lines. The widest contour lines around the hills are ten feet above zero ground level (+10). The graph below the map shows levels from fifty feet above zero ground level to thirty feet below the surface of the pond.

1. Draw a straight line across the map.
2. Make a dotted line from each intersection of your straight line and the contour lines on the map to a point on one of the graph lines below.
3. Draw lines from point to point across the graph to show ground elevation.
4. Shade in the underground part of your section drawing.

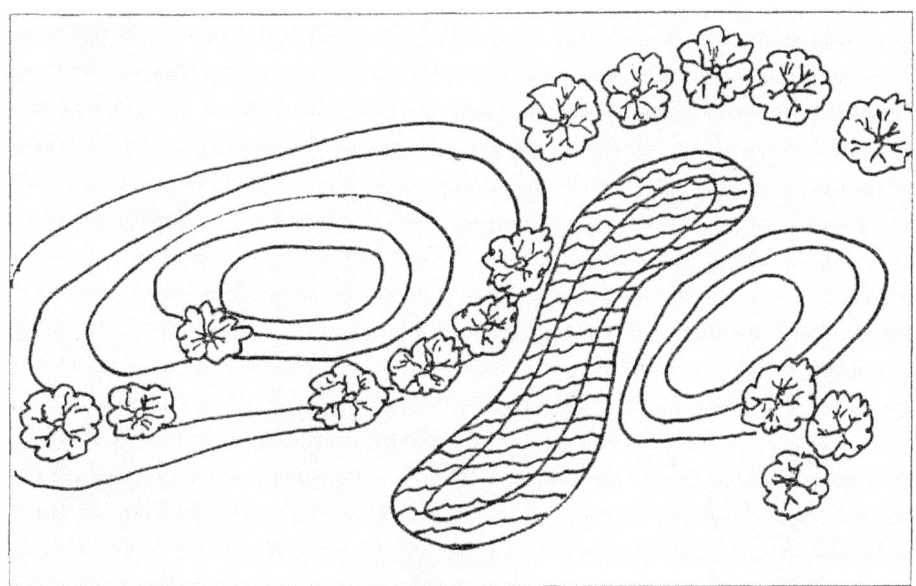

VISUAL NOTETAKING

(From Visual Notes for Architects and Designers by Norman Crowe and Paul Laseau. New York: Van Nostrand, 1984.)

Visual literacy is visual acuity and visual expression. Visual acuity is the message we receive. Visual expression is the message we send. We can observe, record, perceive, discriminate, examine, analyze and communicate. There are three levels of visual messages:

1. **Representation** Representation accurately records what we see.
2. **Abstraction** Abstraction is a simplification of what we see.
3. **Symbolism** Symbolism is a form of simplification but employs a substitute image for what is actually seen.

Representational sketches

Abstract sketches

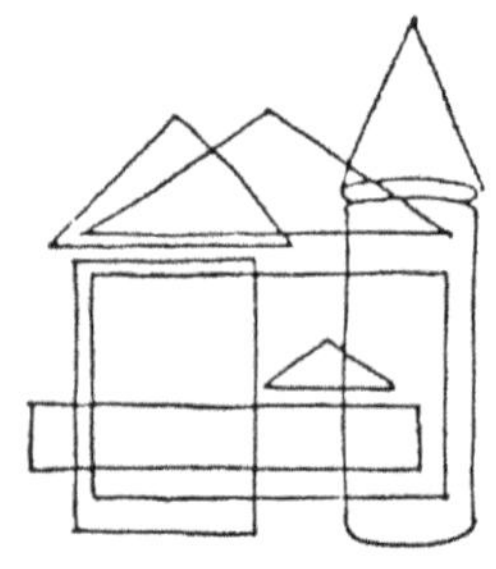

Symbolic sketches

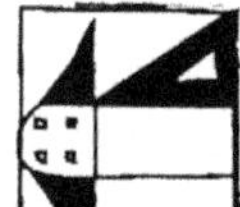   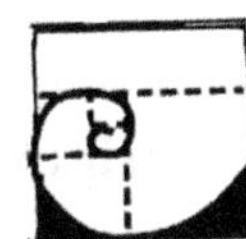 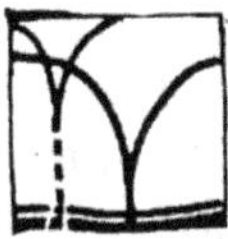   

MODEL BUILDING

by Nancy Evans

A model acts as a physical diagram of an idea, enabling the mind and senses to work together. Learning must have a firm foundation in the concrete realm (manipulating objects through action) before it can develop into the abstract and symbolic. Model building is one way to provide this experience.

TYPES OF MODELS

WORKING MODELS are experimental structures constructed quickly and free of extra details. They are used to explore and check the various stages of an idea. They enable the designer to concentrate on the space relationships of the design.

PRESENTATION MODELS represent the total composition of a design. Surfaces are painted in color and texture to represent building materials and details are rendered in various materials.
A variation of the presentation model is the schematic method which uses coded colors to represent activity zones, service systems, structural elements.

SCALE

The size of the model will be determined by the scale used. 1/4"=1'-0" is typical for smaller models. 1"=1'-0" is typical for larger models. Larger scale models (blocks, boxes, etc.) are easier for smaller hands to handle.

BASE

A site may be flat or have contoured terrain built up in sculpted dough, layers of corrugated cardboard, papier maché, etc. A flat site may have the floor plan on it as a guide for placement of the walls. The weight and scale of the model will determine the material used as a base (cardboard, plywood, foam core, masonite, etc.)

PATTERN

The floor plan and elevations form the basic pattern for a model. When thin material is used for the walls, such as posterboard, it is sometimes best to cut all the walls out of a single piece as illustrated. Then the

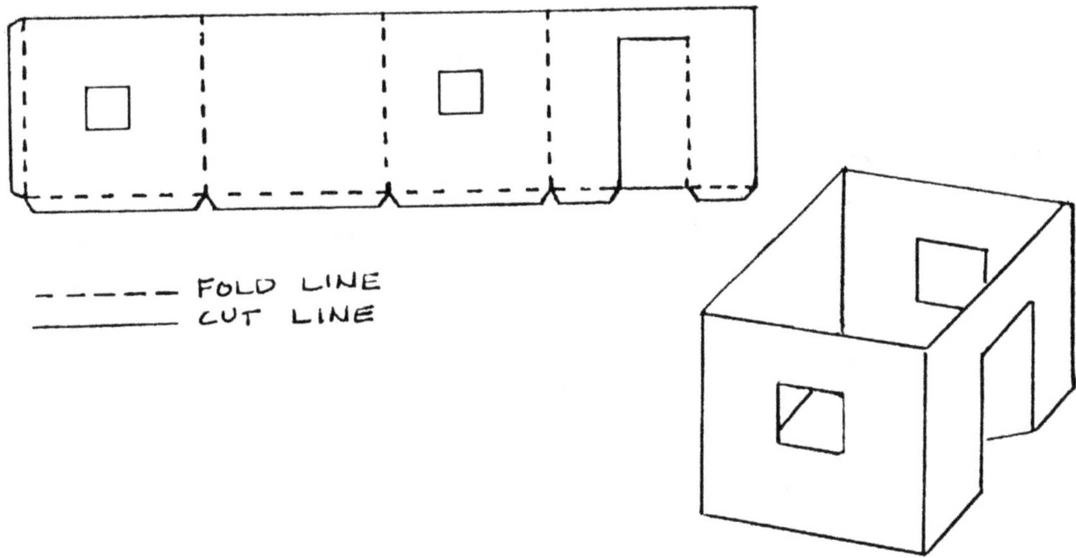

connected walls are scored and folded at exact right angles to the base to make the walls stand up straight. When thicker materials such as 1/4" foam core are used, measure their thickness to determine the amount that should be trimmed off one end of a wall, or both ends of an interior wall, if the walls are butt-jointed.

BUILDING MATERIALS

Walls can be made of paper, tagboard, posterboard, cardboard, matboard, balsa wood, etc. Scissors or an X-Acto knife (with plenty of fresh blades) used with a metal straight edge can be used for cutting materials. Glue, tape or a hot-glue gun can be used as adhesives. Additional materials (popsicle sticks, drinking straws, dowels, string, rocks, styrofoam, twigs, etc.) can be used for details.

CONSTRUCTION TECHNIQUES

Gluing tabs for walls should be included in the pre-cutting stage when drawing elevations, including doors and windows, on the wall materials. All corners and fold lines should be lightly scored along the fold lines. This can be done with a butter knife and should be done on the outside part of the fold.

When using thicker materials such as foam core, corners can be butt-jointed or beveled and glue tabs are not necessary. To assemble, glue the walls together first and then to the base or terrain.

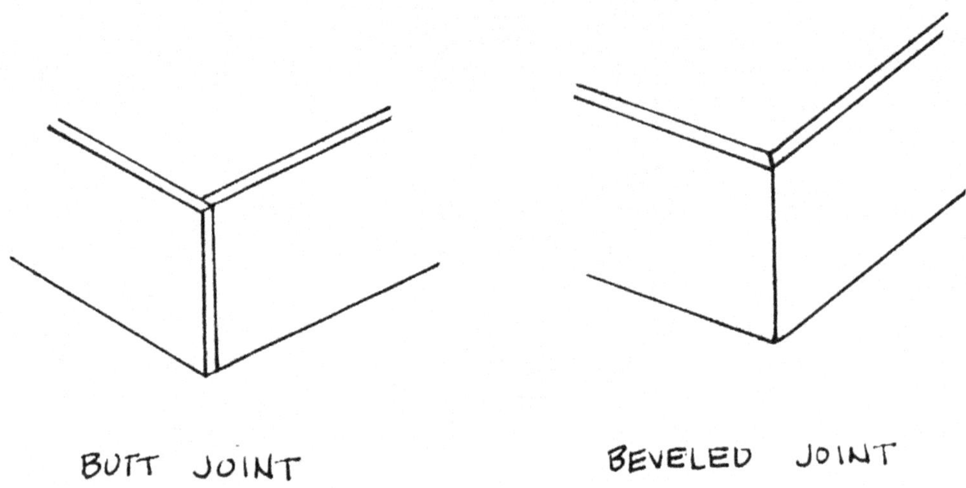

BUTT JOINT BEVELED JOINT

FINISHING TECHNIQUES

After the walls are made, add details such as roofs, balconies, canopies, etc. Finally add details such as plants, autos, people. Sandpaper, painted or unpainted, makes an interesting semblance of adobe, concrete or stucco. Color can add interest and realism or detract from the overall presentation. Paint, colored pencils, markers, etc. can be used on the site and model parts, including interiors, before construction. Touch ups can be added after construction.

READY MADE SYSTEMS

Ready-made systems can be an alternative to do-it-yourself models. Legos, Archiblocks, Lincoln Logs, etc, provide quick and familiar means of representing ideas three-dimensionally with the advantage of being easily changed.

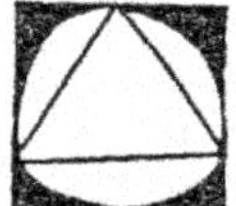 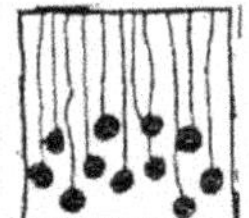 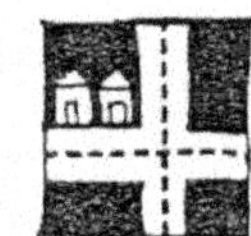

HOW TO DEVELOP A WALKING TOUR

How to develop a walking tour

A guided walk with students through a section of their city or neighborhood provides them with an opportunity to look closely at the environment, to learn about and respond to what they see, and to make critical aesthetic evaluations of the buildings around them. When teachers and students direct their attention to the familiar built environment, architecture can be defined and perceived in their own school, home, neighborhood— the stores, theaters, offices and churches.

Materials

Clipboards with drawing paper or sketchbooks; Flair pens and soft lead pencils
Optional: Cameras; kraft paper and crayons (for rubbings); map of area
Appendix pages: Visual Survey Form, Visual Notetaking, How to Develop a Slide Presentation
Poster 10 Geometric Shape and Form Chart
Teacher-designed activity sheets (e.g. scavenger hunt)

Program

Choose the area you will tour. Make sure you are very familiar with the particular buildings and sites that your class will be viewing, Your tour should have a particular theme, such as looking at terra cotta ornamentation in downtown buildings, a treasure hunt for entryway details, a survey of the architectural styles found in the school neighborhood. It is useful to begin at rhe oldest building in the tour area and walk toward the newest building. This provides a visual and historic context for the walk. In addition to the buildings themselves, remember to point out other aspects of the city including lighting standards, street furniture, drinking fountains, waiting shelters, signs, alleys, paving, and any other elements that collectively define urban streetscape.

As you design your walking tour, choose buildings that illustrate key points from the following categories:
Historical buildings and landmarks
Textures in the environment
Ornamentation
Placement and scale of a building in relationship to its neighbors.
Landscape
What happens inside the building
Building parts (roof, cornice, window, details)
Building materials (brick, stone, wood, sheet metal, terra cotta)

Things to consider in planning your walking tour

Will all the children be able to see each of the things you want to point out?
Are there places along the walk where the group can all gather closely together to hear information you want to give them?
Can the tour be completed in 30 to 40 minutes maximum?
Would you like them to complete a visual survey form as they walk the tour? (See sample survey form)
Can the children stand at different levels in order to see the buildings from more than one perspective?

Suggestions for additional field activities

Design a treasure hunt search for particular kinds of ornamentation, building materials, columns, window designs, etc.
Keep a frequency count for particular building elements you observe during your walking tour, such as rounded entryways, front porches, roof overhangs, columns, pilasters, balconies, bay windows. Graph your results.

Use binoculars to look at details on buildings that are tall.
Document the walk with photographs. Date the photographs for future historical reference.
"Pace off" the front of a building to get a rough measurement of it. Measure the length of your pace and figure out how many feet (or meters) it is. Sketch the building. Using your skills in scale drawing, paint a picture of one of the buildings you saw, drawn (approximately) to scale.

Walking tours can be simplified or expanded to fit your students. Here are some more ideas for a walking tour:

Organizing the class for a walking tour

Divide 30 people into 6 groups of 5 people each. On the day before the walking tour ask each participant to create a cognitive map of what he or she envisions the area of the walking tour to be like. A cognitive map need not be accurate, but will show how the person imagines the area that will be explored. It can be cartoonish and show features like a landmark, a skyline, busses, pigeons and the like. After the tour, have the students make a "memory map" of the area that you toured, sketching in buildings and other things that you saw.

On the tour, each group will collect data. Resources in the appendix for collecting data are the appendix pages on Visual Notetaking, the Visual Survey Form, How to Make a Slide Presentation and the Visual/Verbal Journal. Materials students need for the tour are clip boards with drawing paper or a Visual/Verbal Journal, Flair pens, soft lead pencils, a camera; optional materials: kraft paper and crayon, oil pastel or a very soft lead pencil to make rubbings. Each group should prepare for the following activities:

1. **SKETCHING** Make a variety of sketches of buildings on the tour. Use a Flair pen and a soft pencil. Sketch any part of a building. Label each sketch with notes of the name of the building, its address or location, and a few notes about it. Try the drawing techniques used in the "Light, shade and shadow" drawing described on pages 49-50. The students will need either a clip board or a sketch book like the Visual Verbal Journal for this.
2. **PHOTOGRAPHY** Color prints, Polaroid photos or 35 mm slides are useful. Entryways and ornamentation details are suggested for snapshots. Pictures of a whole bulding will turn out better using 35mm.
3. **RUBBINGS** Look around for interesting textures. Students may find manhole covers, tree grates, ornamentation on posts or planters or plaques, or even just interesting brick patterns that will make good rubbings. Brown grocery bag peper (kraft paper) and crayon, oil pastel, or very soft lead pencil will work for this. Instructions for texture rubbings are on page **42**.

A suggested focus for a walking tour: Terra Cotta Ornament in Downtown Seattle

A walking tour should have a focus. For example, a walking tour of downtown Seattle could focus on the rich diversity of late 19th C. and early 20th C. ornament made of terra cotta. Some very frequently used details are quoins, dentils, brackets, and balustrades; these should be pointed out on the Visual Survey Form. Some of the good observation points for studying terra cotta use are the Security Pacific Bank Tower plaza, the terrace on the 3rd floor of the downtown Seattle Public Library, the street level parking lot at 4th and Cherry and the plaza surrounding the Federal Office Building. The Puget Sound Bank next to the Exchange Building at 2nd and Marion has terra cotta and granite at the street level. They look very similar. Students can get up close to it and try to guess which is stone and which is terra cotta. Here are some suggested topics: what terra cotta is made of, how it is shaped, why it is a good material for use in a mild climate, what are some of the other advantages and disadvantages compared to other building materials, what the decorations are, what inspired the decoration, are the decorations regional. A good game to stimulate observation is to look for animals in the decorations. Some downtown Seattle buildings have ornamental walruses, flounders, buffalos, mountain goats, wolves, lions, dragons, flowers, fruits, and native American men in feathered headresses. Look for these; when you find them, ask students to think of a possible reason why the architects chose these images. Look for images that are described by the following words: classical, geometric, sacred, funny, realistic, abstract, historical, subtle, exagerrated. Invite students to make up spontaneous stories about these images. (See the book, Impressions of Imagination: Terra Cotta Seattle, published by Allied Arts of Seattle.)

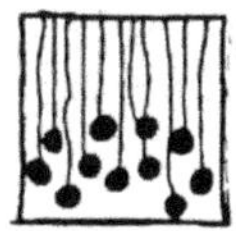

HOW TO DEVELOP A POWERPOINT PRESENTATION

Students will explore their neighborhood or downtown area on foot, taking photos of specific architectural elements using a camera or smartphone. Each student will focus on a category, such as doorways, windows, cornices, ornament and details, stairways, paving, lighting, signs, street furniture, or landscaping, and keep detailed notes on their photographs. They will then create a PowerPoint presentation, including a narrative for each slide explaining their choice, its attractiveness, and the architectural style if known. Optional music can enhance the presentation. Additionally, students can photograph negative aspects like empty lots and dilapidated buildings, as well as positive scenes like parks and outdoor cafes, to provide a balanced commentary on urban life. You may want to review and even make an appointment with a city planner to discuss your Powerpoint and see what they have to say. Be creative.

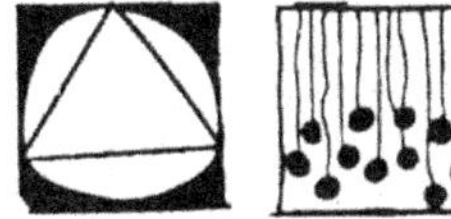

VISUAL SURVEY FORM

by Carolyn Purser

NAME AND ADDRESS OF BUILDING____

Purpose or use __House __Apartment __Hotel __Church __School __Store __Offices __Other_______
Date on building (If any) ________

SHAPE OF BUILDING

Plan__Rectangle __L-shape __T-shape __Cross shape __U-shape __H-shape __Irregular __Other
Height __1 story __1 1/2 story __2-3 story __More than 3 stories

OUTSIDE WALLS

__**Wood:** __Painted (Color(s)________________________________) __Stained __Weathered
__Shingles/shakes __Plywood __Clapboard (lapped, horizontal boards) __Flat horizontal boards
__Vertical boards __Timber or logs __Artificial boards (plastic, aluminum)

__**Brick:** __Common bricks__Clay tile (big blocks) __Adobe (unfired) __Roman (thin) __Clinker (warped)
Brick color: __Earth red __Brown __Tan __Grey __Mixed __Painted (color:______________)

__**Stone or terra cotta** Terra cotta is made of clay but looks like stone.

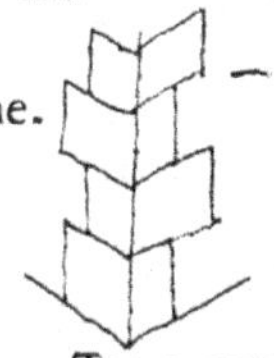

— Quoins (pronounced "coins") are corner blocks of stone or terra cotta laid in a staggered pattern on exterior wall corners.

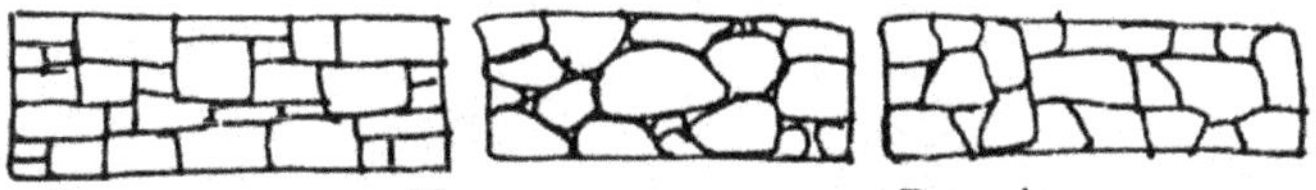

__Cut stone __Uncut stone __Rough cut stone __Terra cotta (__Glazed __Unglazed)

__**Concrete** __Poured in place __Panels __Blocks __Decorative blocks __Stucco

__**Metal** __Cast iron __Aluminum __Galvanized steel __Enameled steel __Rusty steel

__**Tile** __Glass __Ceramic or terra cotta __ Metal __Granite or marble __Plastic Color_______

ROOF

Shape of roof

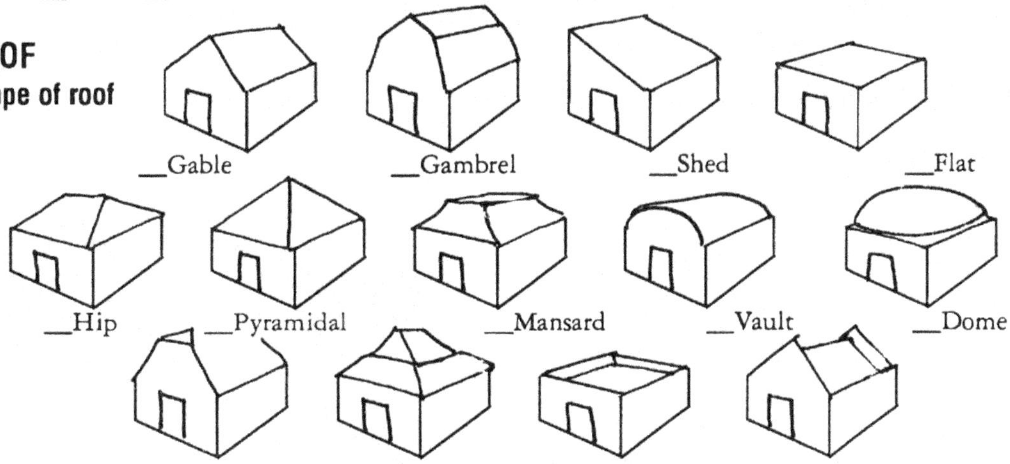

__Gable __Gambrel __Shed __Flat

__Hip __Pyramidal __Mansard __Vault __Dome

__Gable with hip __Hip with gable __Parapeted flat __Parapeted gable

Roof material: __Wood or plastic shingle or shake __Tar paper __Composition (asphalt) shingle
__Slate __Clay, plastic or concrete tile __Copper __Steel __Earth __Concrete __Glass __Thatch

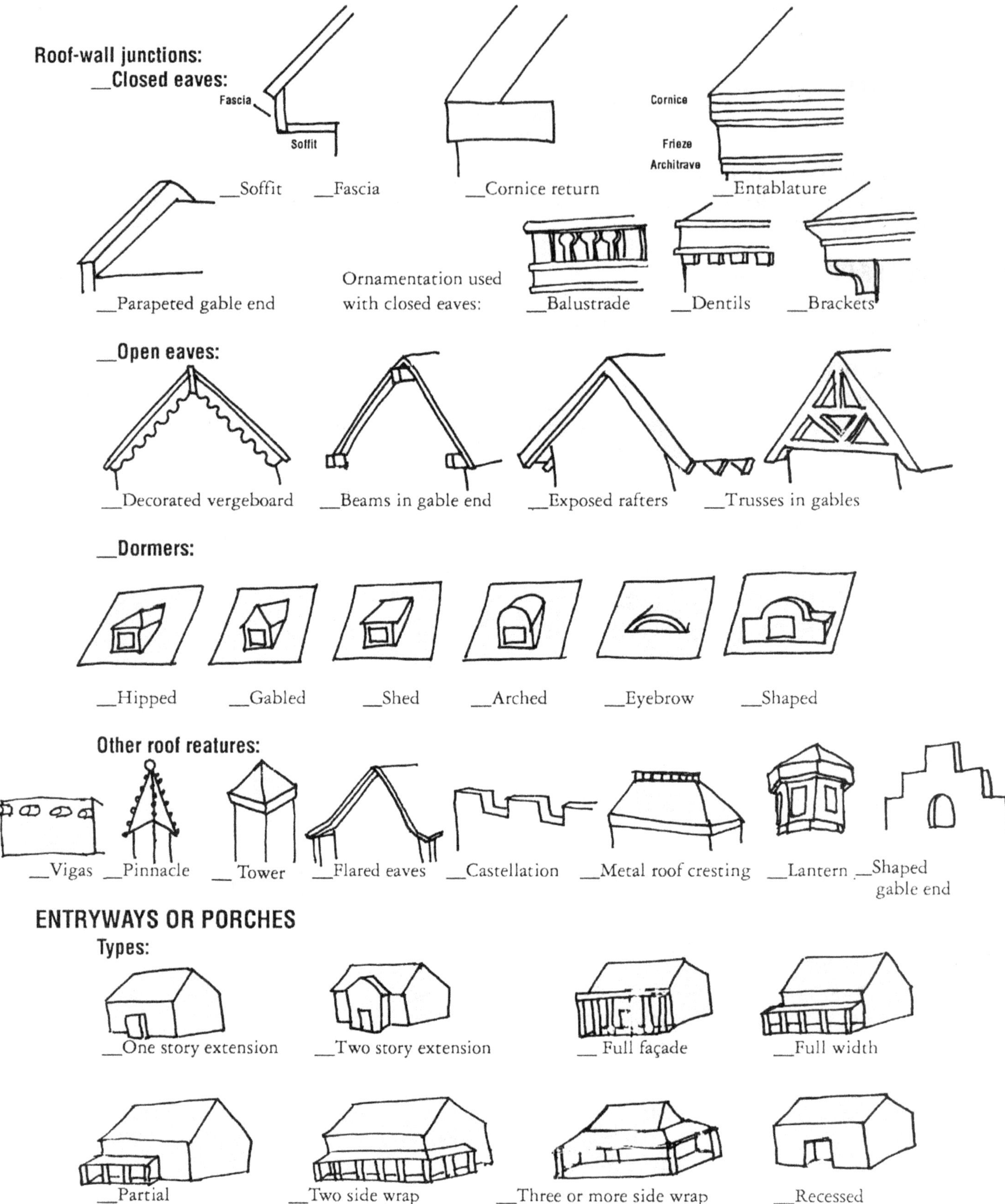
Roof-wall junctions:
__Closed eaves:
Fascia
Soffit
Cornice
Frieze
Architrave
__Soffit
__Fascia
__Cornice return
__Entablature
__Parapeted gable end
Ornamentation used with closed eaves:
__Balustrade
__Dentils
__Brackets
__Open eaves:
__Decorated vergeboard
__Beams in gable end
__Exposed rafters
__Trusses in gables
__Dormers:
__Hipped
__Gabled
__Shed
__Arched
__Eyebrow
__Shaped
Other roof reatures:
__Vigas
__Pinnacle
__ Tower
__Flared eaves
__Castellation
__Metal roof cresting
__Lantern
__Shaped gable end
ENTRYWAYS OR PORCHES
Types:
__One story extension
__Two story extension
__ Full façade
__Full width
__Partial
__Two side wrap
__Three or more side wrap
__Recessed

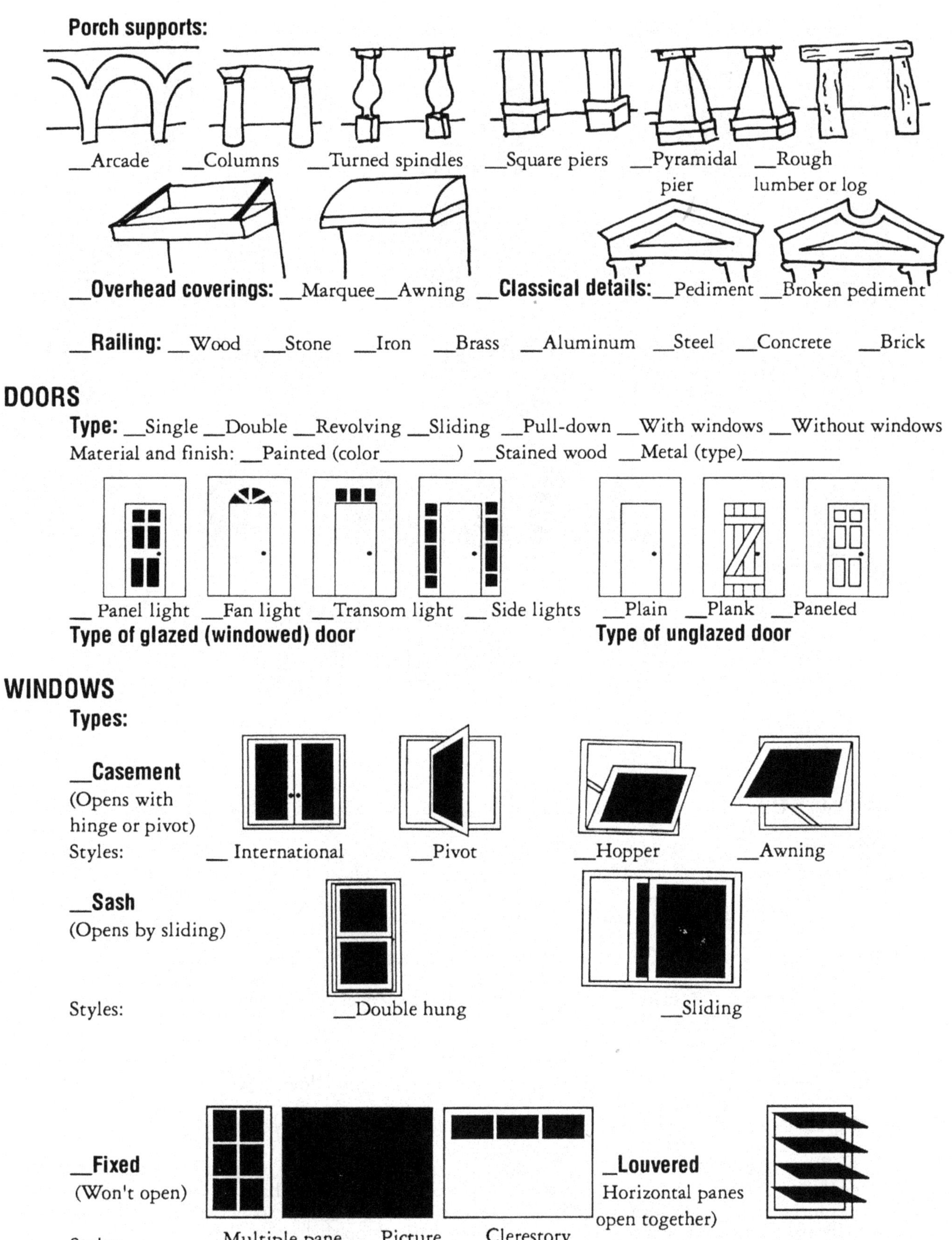

Porch supports:

__Arcade __Columns __Turned spindles __Square piers __Pyramidal pier __Rough lumber or log

__Overhead coverings: __Marquee__Awning **__Classical details:**__Pediment __Broken pediment

__Railing: __Wood __Stone __Iron __Brass __Aluminum __Steel __Concrete __Brick

DOORS

Type: __Single __Double __Revolving __Sliding __Pull-down __With windows __Without windows

Material and finish: __Painted (color________) __Stained wood __Metal (type)__________

__ Panel light __Fan light __Transom light __ Side lights

Type of glazed (windowed) door

__Plain __Plank __Paneled

Type of unglazed door

WINDOWS

Types:

__Casement
(Opens with hinge or pivot)
Styles: __ International __Pivot __Hopper __Awning

__Sash
(Opens by sliding)
Styles: __Double hung __Sliding

__Fixed
(Won't open)
Styles: __Multiple pane __Picture __Clerestory

__Louvered
Horizontal panes open together)

Window shapes and patterns (If you don't see it on this page, draw a picture of it in the margin)

__Cross __Multiple pane __Diamond pane __Lintel __Bracket mold

__Gothic __Arched __Fan light __Palladian __Circular/octagonal __Hood mold

__Paired __Ribbon __Large surrounded by small panes __Small panes over large __Keystone lintel

__Patterned upper pane __Stained glass __Bay __Ariel __Greenhouse

Details: __Pediment __Broken pediment __ Shutters __Iron bars __Awning

SITE

Location: __Urban business __Urban residential __Suburban business __Suburban residential __Rural

Landscape: __Trees __Hedge __Shrubs __Rockery __Planting containers __Garden __Natural area __Formal landscape __Informal landscape __Playground __Paving only __Weed area __ Littered area

Fence: __Wood (describe) __Iron __Chain link __Stone __Brick __Gate (material)______

Walkways: __Sidewalk __Gravel path __Stepping stones __Road shoulder __Safety barrier

Paving:__Concrete __Asphalt __Brick pavers __Cobblestones __Gravel __ Planting strip __Curb

Overhead systems: __Electrical poles __Telephone poles __Electric trolley wires

Lights:__ Street lights __Traffic lights __Ambient light from windows __Ambient light from signs

Underground utilities: __Storm sewer grates __Manhole covers __Tree grates __Fire hydrant

Sidewalk environment: __Benches __Tables and chairs __Snack bar __Trash containers __Drinking fountain __Signs __Crosswalks __Curb breaks for wheelchairs __Sounding crosswalk signals for the blind __Sculpture __Mural __Historical plaque __Newspaper stand __Pay phone __Mailbox __Play equipment __Pedestrian bridge __Bus stop shelter __Place for posters __Billboard __Graffiti Other______________________________________

PORTFOLIO ASSESSMENT

Architects keep portfolios to show their work and process to others. Students learning about design also can create visual and sometimes electronic portfolios to supplement traditional verbal or written testing found in schools. But how do educators evaluate the creative thinking process? Below are five criteria to aid in visual portfolio assessment as students present their drawings, plans, tracing, models, and more for review.

CRITERIA FOR EVALUATION

1. Fluency and Clarity of Communication

    The ability to demonstrate control in the rendering of an idea or product

    The ability to transmit an idea clearly through graphic visual means

2. Imagination, Innovation and Creativity

    The ability to demonstrate an understanding of the creative process (Evidence of the creative cycle, an impulse for creation, exploration, incubation, illumination, revision)

    Evidence of experimentation

    The ability to see things from multiple perspectives

    The ability to consider a variety of approaches

The ability to overcome resistance, to free the eyes and the mind from stereotypes and taboos, and see one's surroundings in new ways, make connections between unlikely elements, and sketch, tinker and imagine until ideas emerge

The ability to accommodate change due to the emergence of an unexpected influence (flexibility)

3. Understanding the Process

The ability to narrate or visualize the stages of development of an idea or product

Evidence of the translation of process into a product or idea (overlays of trace)

The ability to present, judge, reject, appraise, criticize, and justify

The ability to recognize patterns and the relationship between patterns

The ability to sequentially develop ideas or products

Use of principles and concepts from math, science or technology

4. Details and Overall Aesthetics

Evidence of elaboration

Evidence of understanding of functional vs decorative

Evidence of development of compositional style, design, color, rhythms, and repetition

Evidence of refined sense of expression

Evidence of high overall aesthetic quality

5. Technical Competence

The ability to identify the unique characteristics of materials, their limitations and extensions

The ability to draw schematic, plans, elevations, perspectives (shade and shadow where appropriate)

The ability to construct in 3 dimensions in either process or product

NOTE: All students use a scientific method to develop their personal ideas and solutions to problems. The process is the same for design as it is for science.

1. Student sees a need for something

2. Student makes a hypothesis about what product will be.

3. Student does research and collects data if needed.

4. Student accepts or reject or modifies the product.

5. Student presents the project.

Note: When evaluating many products at one time, the products should be numbered to protect names of subjects (privacy). Training of evaluators should occur using an inter-rater reliability index. Gestalt judgments are accepted using a rating scale of 1 as low and 5 as high. This procedure is good for doing a trend analysis of students over time where each student acts as his or her own control. Averages for a total class can be computed, but that is not the purpose of this form where it is possible to have each subject act as his own control. Scoring Matrix (may be augmented as needed.)

Student Project #	Time 1	Time 2	Time 3	Time 4	Time 5
Projects					
1. Fluency and Clarity of Communication					
2. Imagination, Innovation and Creativity					
3. Understanding the Process					
4. Details and Overall Aesthetics					
5. Technical Competence					

Rating Scale: 1 low, 2 fair, 3 good, 4 very good, 5 high

Reviewer ________________________________

RATING SCALE (LEVEL 1-5)

1

Rendering is erratic and inconsistent.
Structure and expression are not evident.

2

Control is apparent through steady or consistent repetition.
Management of material or technique is a priority.
Technical expression is demonstrated.

3
Articulation and Interpretation is understandable.
Conventional expression.
Organized.
Attempts made for structural organization.

4
Imaginative touches appear in the expression.
Deliberate use of variety and contrast to generate structural interest.
Sense of style.
Technical, expressive and structural control is demonstrated consistently.

5
Technical mastery totally serves communication.
Expression, style, and structural detail are refined.
Form and expression are fused into a coherent and personal statement.
Imaginative solutions are demonstrated.

For More Information:

Anne Taylor, PhD
Distinguished and Regents Professor Emerita
aetaylor@unm.edu

References:

Taylor, A. Vlastos, G. Marshall, A. *Architecture & Children Teacher's Guide*, Albuquerque: School Zone Institute, 1991.

Taylor A. *Linking Architecture and Education: Sustainable Design of Learning Environments*. Albuquerque: University of New Mexico Press, 2009.

RELATIONSHIP OF ARCHITECTURE AND CHILDREN THEMES TO SCIENCE, MATH AND TECHNOLOGY LEARNING GOALS

NATIONAL COUNCIL ON SCIENCE AND TECHNOLOGY EDUCATION MATRIX (American Association for the Advancement of Science)

ARCHITECTURE AND CHILDREN CURRICULA

NATIONAL COUNCIL ON SCIENCE AND TECHNOLOGY EDUCATION MATRIX		Core Curriculum 1. Phantasmagoria	2. Curriculum Model	3. Visual Vocabulary	4. Plans and Perspectives	5. Structure in Architecture	6. Entryways	7. You Are Architecture	8. Color and Texture	9. Design in Nature	10. Form in Architectural History	11. Bridges	12. Superwall Graphics	13. Preferences	14. Landscape Design	15. City Planning	Northwest Curriculum 1. Shelters	2. Cities	3. Ornament	4. Landscape	5. Asian
AIA**	Stewardship	●	●				●		●	●			●	●	●	●	●	●		●	○
	Resources	●	●			●				●				●	●		●	●	●	●	
	Change	●	●		●		●		●	●	○				●	●	●	●		●	●
MIND HABITS	Interaction	●	●	●	●	●	●	●	●	●	●	●	●		●		●	●		●	●
	Skills	●	●	●	●	●	●	●	●	●	●	●	●	●	●	●					
	Values and attitudes	●	●	●	●	●	●	●	●	●	●	●	●	●	●	●	○	●	○	●	○
THEMES	Scale			●	●	●	●	●	●	●	●	●	●	●	●	●	○	●	○	●	○
	Evolution									●	●				○					●	○
	Patterns of change					●				○	●				○	●	●	●		●	○
	Constancy					●				●	●	○									○
	Models		●	●	●	●	●	●		●	●	●		●	●	●	○				
	Systems		●		●	●		●		●		●				●	○	●			○
HISTORICAL PERSPECTIVES	Harnessing power																				
	Germs														○						
	Diversity of life				●		●				●	●		●	●	●	○			●	○
	Splitting atom									○											
	Fire																○				
	Earth's surface in motion											○			○						
	Extending time										●										
	Matter, time, energy and space					●		○			●	○									
	Uniting heavens and earth									○							●	●			○
MATHEMATICAL WORLD	Reasoning	●		●	●	●	●	●	●	●	●	●	●	●	●	●	●	●	●	●	●
	Sampling				●	●	●	●							●	●	●	●	●	●	●
	Summarizing data	●		●	●	●	●	●	●	●	●	●		●	●	●	●	●	●	●	●
	Uncertainty			●	●	○		●			○	●	○	●	○	●				●	●
	Shapes			●	●	●	●	●	●	●	○	●	●	●	●	●	○	○	●		○
	Symbolic relationships			●	●	○	●	●			○	●	●	●	●	●			●		●
	Numbers				○	○	○		○	○	○	●	●	●	●	●	●	●		●	
DESIGNED WORLD	Health technology					○		●							●	●		●			
	Information processing	●		●	●	●	●	●	●	●	●	●	●	●	●	●		●			
	Communication	●		●	●	●	○	●	●	●	●	●	●	●	●	●	○	●	●		○
	Energy use			●		●	○	●		●	●			●	●	●	○	●			
	Energy sources			●		●		●		●	●			●	●	●	○	●			
	Manufacturing			○	●	●	●	●			●	●		●	●	●	●	●			●
	Materials	●		●	●	●	○	●	●	○	●	●	●	●	●	●	●	●	●		●
	Agriculture								○	●					●	●				●	
	Human presence	●		●	○	●	●	●	○	●	●	●	○	●	●	●	●	●	●	●	●
HUMAN SOCIETY	Worldwide social systems																				
	Social conflict						●				○					○	○	●			●
	Political/economic systems										○					●	○	○			
	Social change						○				○					●		●		○	●
	Political/economic organization		○				○				●					●	●	●	○	○	●
	Group behavior		○	●	●	●	●		●		●		○	●	○	○	○	●		○	
	Cultural effects on behaviour		○	●	●		○	○			●	○			○	●		○	○		●
HUMAN ORGANISM	Mental health					●		●	○	○			○	●	●	●	○	●		○	
	Physical health					●		●						●	●	●	○	●		●	
	Learning	●	●	●	●	●	●	●	●	●	●	●	●	●	●	●	●	●	●	●	●
	Basic functions				●	●	○	○		○	●			●	●	●	○			○	
	Life cycle						○	●			●					●	●	●		○	
	Human identity		●	○		○	●	●			●		●			●	●	●	●	●	●
LIVING ENVIRONMENT	Evolution of life				○	○		○		○	●					●	●	○			
	Flow of matter and energy			○		●	●	●		●		○		●	●	●	●				
	Interdependence of life	○		○	●	●		●		●	●			●	●	●	●	●	●	●	●
	Cells					○		●		●					○		○	●		○	
	Heredity					○	○			●					○						
	Diversity of life	○			●	●	●	●	●	●	●	○		●	●	●	●	○		●	○
PHYSICAL SETTING	Forces in nature			○		●	○	○		●	○	●		●	●	●	●	○		●	
	Motion of things			○		●	○	●		●	●	●		●	●	●				○	
	Transformation of energy			○		●	○	●				●		●	●	●				○	
	Structure of matter			○		●	●	●	○	●	●	●		●	●	○	●			●	
	Forces which shape earth			○	●	●	●	●		●		●		●	●	○	●	●		●	●
	Earth				○	●	●	●	●	●	●	●		●	●	●	●			●	
	Universe				○	○			○	○							●	○			●

● Strong correlation
○ Implied

AIA** - AIA Built Environment Conceptual Framework
Compiled by School Zone Institute (7/89)

BOOKS AND OTHER RESOURCES ON ARCHITECTURE

Dillon, Patrick and Stephen Biesty. *The Story of Buildings: From the Pyramids to the Sydney Opera House and Beyond*. Massachusetts: Candlewick Press, 2014.

Hale, Christy. *Dreaming Up: A Celebration of Building*. New York: Lee & Low Books, 2012.

Macaulay, David. *Built to Last*. Boston: Clarion Books, 2010.

Nair, Prakash, AIA, and Dr. Parul Minhas. *A New Language of School Design. Evidence-Based Strategies for Student Achievement and Well Being*. Scottsdale, Arizona: Association for Learning Environments, 2023.

Pryce, Will. *World Architecture: The Masterworks*. London: Thames & Hudson, 2011.

Taylor, Anne. *Linking Architecture and Education: Sustainable Design of Learning Environments*. New Mexico, University of New Mexico Press, 2008.

Teachers' Books (Some with Lesson Plans and Activities):

Agerer, Markus S. *How to Draw Architecture: Illustrating Buildings and Cityscapes*. CreateSpace Independent Publishing Platform, 2021.

Agrest, Diana. *Architecture of Nature: Nature of Architecture*. New York: Applied Research & Design, 2019.

Beck, Barbara. *The Future Architect's Handbook*. Pennsylvania: Schiffer Kids, 2014.

Cardona, Arnaldo D. *K-12 Architecture Education: An Interdisciplinary Curriculum Guide for Art, Design, STEM and Career/Technical Teachers*. Columbus, Ohio: Gatekeeper Press, 2022.

Ching, Francis D.K. *A Visual Dictionary of Architecture*. New York: Wiley, 2011.

Ching, Francis D.K. *Architectural Graphics*. New York: Wiley, 2023.

Ching, Francis D.K. *Design Drawing*. New York: Wiley, 2018.

Ching, Francis D.K. *Drawing a Creative Process*. New York: Wiley, 2008.

Goldsworthy, Andy. *A Collaboration with Nature*. New York: Abrams; First Edition, 1990.

Gurney, Stella and Spike Lee Tailfeather. *Architecture According to Pigeons*. New York: Phaidon Press, 2013.

Koolhaas, Rem. *Elements of Architecture*. Germany: Taschen America LLC, 2018.

Laroche, Giles. *If You Lived Here: Houses of the World*. Boston: Clarion Books, 2011.

Manias, Celeste. *Julia Morgan Built a Castle*. New York: Viking Juvenile, 2006.

Paxmann, Christine. *From Mud Huts to Skyscrapers*. New York: Prestel Junior, 2012.

Salvadori, Mario. *Architecture and Engineering: An Illustrated Teachers' Manual on Why Things Stand Up*. New York: New York Academy of Sciences, 1983.

Taylor, Anne, Vlastos, George and Marshall, Allison. *Architecture and Children. A Teachers Guide*. Seattle, Washington: Architecture and Children Institute, 1991.

Trogler, George. *Beginning Experiences in Architecture: A Guide for Elementary School Teachers*. New York: Van Nostrand Reinhold Company, 1972.

Van Dusen, Chris. *If I Built a House*. New York: Rocky Pond Books, 2012.

Children's Books on Architecture:

Armstrong, Simon. *Cool Architecture: Filled with Fantastic Facts for Kids of all Ages*. New York: Portico, 2015.

Beaty, Andrea. *Iggy Peck, Architect*. New York: Harry N. Abrams, 2007.

Beaty, Andrea. *Rosie Revere, Engineer*. New York: Harry N. Abrams, 2013.

Bowkett, Steve. *Archidoodle: The Architect's Activity Book*. London: Laurence King Publishing, 2013.

Brown Glenn, Patricia. *Under Every Roof: A Kid's Style and Field Guide to the Architecture of American Homes*. New York: Wiley, 2009.

Gadzikowski, Ann. *Young Architects at Play: STEM Activities for Young Children*. Minnesota: Redleaf Press, 2020.

Guarnaccia, Steven. *Goldilocks and the Three Bears: A Tale Moderne*. New York: Harry N. Abrams, 2010.

Guarnaccia, Steven. *The Three Little Pigs: An Architectural Tale*. New York: Harry N. Abrams, 2010.

Isaacson, Philip M. *Round Buildings, Square Buildings and Buildings That Wiggle like a Fish*. New York: Knopf Books, 1988.

Johmann, Carol A. *Skyscrapers! Super Structures to Design & Build*. Tennessee: WorthyKids, 2001.

Johnson, D.B. *Henry Builds a Cabin*. Boston: Clarion Books, 2002.

Laden, Nina. *Roberto, The Insect Architect*. San Francisco: Chronicle Books, 2000.

Macauley, David. *Pyramid*. Boston: Houghton Mifflin, 1975.

———. *Cathedral: The Story of Its Construction*. Boston: Houghton Mifflin, 1973.

———. *Underground*. Boston: Houghton Mifflin, 1976.

———. *Castle*. Boston: Houghton Mifflin, 1977.·

———. *The Way Things Work*. Boston: Houghton Mifflin, 1989.

Ritchie, Scot. *Look at That Building! A First Book of Structures.* Toronto: Kids Can Press, 2011.
Viva, Frank. *Young Frank, Architect.* New York: Harry N. Abrams, 2009.

Willkens, Danielle. *Architecture for Teens: A Beginner's Book for Aspiring Architects.* California: Rockridge Press, 2021.

Wilson, Forrest. *What It Feels Like to Be a Building.* Washington, DC: Preservation Press, 1988.

Wilson, Travis Kelly. *The Aspiring Architect: An Activity Book for Kids.* Bloomington: Trafford, 2013.

Resources:

American Institute of Architects

www.aia.org

National Trust for Historical Preservation

Center for Preservation Training

https://savingplaces.org/historic-sites

American Association for State and Local History

https://www.aaslh.org/

International Interior Design Association

https://iida.org/

American Society of Interior Designers

https://www.asid.org/

American Planning Association

https://www.planning.org/

American Society of Landscape Architects

https://www.asla.org/

Association for Learning Environments

https://www.a4le.org/

Websites:

https://architectureandchildren.com/ or https://www.schoolzoneinstitute.com/

https://vimeo.com/schoolzone

https://www.next.cc/

https://www.eekwi.org/

https://www.architecture.com/education-cpd-and-careers/learning/riba-national-schools-programme/learning-resources/learning-at-home

https://www.amazon.com/

Keywords for Searching the Web:

architecture

architecture for children

environmental

sustainable

design

design education

integrated design education through architecture 'IDEA'